BENSON and HEDGES
SNOOKER YEAR

EIGHTH EDITION EDITED BY TERRY SMITH
ASSOCIATE EDITOR STEPHEN HENDRY

PELHAM BOOKS

PELHAM BOOKS

Published by the Penguin Group
27 Wrights Lane, London W8 5TZ, England
Viking Penguin, a division of Penguin Books USA Inc
375 Hudson Street, New York, NY 10014, USA
Penguin Books Australia Ltd, Ringwood, Victoria, Australia
Penguin Books Canada Ltd, 10 Alcorn Avenue, Suite 300, Toronto, Ontario, Canada, M4V 3B2
Penguin Books (NZ) Ltd, 182–190 Wairau Road, Auckland 10, New Zealand

Penguin Books Ltd, Registered Offices: Harmondsworth, Middlesex, England

First Published 1991
1 3 5 7 9 10 8 6 4 2

Typeset, printed and bound in England by
Clays Ltd, St Ives plc

A CIP catalogue record for this book is available from the British Library

ISBN 0 7207 1983 6

CONTENTS

ACKNOWLEDGEMENTS

Ever since I was entrusted with the editorship of the *Benson and Hedges Snooker Year* five years ago, there has been much talk about 'opening up' the game. Now 'open snooker' has become a reality in the 1991/92 season.

Let us hope that the greater number of professionals, including six ladies, will be a credit to the game and that snooker and, indeed, billiards, will continue to grow worldwide during the 1990s. They are wonderful sports, enjoyed and played by millions, and snooker thoroughly deserves its position as the UK's number 1 television sport.

It is always a pleasure to thank the people who have helped me compile the *Snooker Year* and my first debt of gratitude is to my Associate Editor, Stephen Hendry. Stephen is the undisputed world number 1 but no longer world champion – facts he discusses in depth in a lively chapter in which he states categorically that he sees the departure of the world trophy as no more than a temporary separation.

The snooker press room is a noisy and busy place to be, as my colleagues ensure that you, the snooker followers, hear the best reports on the radio and read the best stories in your newspapers. Many have helped me in the eighth edition of the *Snooker Year*. They are: Bob Holmes (*Daily Telegraph*), Alexander Clyde (*London Evening Standard*) and Steve Acteson (*Today*).

The WPBSA and B&SCC and their willing officials have once again contributed to the statistical content, and Roger Lee, whose look back at snooker and billiards of years gone by proved so popular last year, has this time viewed our sports through the picture postcard. My thanks go to them and to Mark Wildman, Gaye Jones, John Smyth and John Street.

No book is complete without good photographs and, while I have provided the majority of illustrations, I would like to thank the following for additional material: Frank Fennell (on page 106 below right), Trevor Jones (on pages 22, 26, 27, 29, 32, 33, 35, 39, 67, 131), John Hawken (on pages 38, 47, 54, 119), David Muscroft (on pages 109, 110, 111) and Gaye Jones (on page 139).

In previous years I have offered sincere thanks to three female colleagues who have contributed so greatly to the *Snooker Year*. Amazingly, for the fifth successive year, it is the same trio of female assistants whom I thank once more: my wife, Eileen, for gathering and checking all the facts and figures; Pat Mead, without whose shorthand and word-processing skills this book would never be written; and Ruth Baldwin who ensured that the manuscript was delivered accurately and on time. This year the *Snooker Year* was again designed by Sandie Boccacci and she has done an excellent job.

As always, I thank Benson and Hedges for allowing me the scope to produce the book, and Roger Houghton and everybody at Pelham Books for ensuring that the *Benson and Hedges Snooker Year* is now the number 1 snooker and billiards reference manual.

Lastly I must thank you, the snooker follower and fan, who guarantees that snooker, despite the critics, is still growing in stature in the UK and throughout the world.

A PERSONAL MEMO TO JOHN PARROTT: I WANT MY WORLD TITLE BACK

by Stephen Hendry

I was absolutely devastated when I lost my world title last season – it was easily the worst moment of my professional career. Twelve months earlier I had been predictably 'over the moon' as I beat Jimmy White 18–12 to claim the Embassy World Championship trophy for the first time.

When I returned to defend my title at the Crucible Theatre, I had already won seven trophies and my practice had gone so well that I didn't believe anybody could beat me. I was cueing one hundred times better and my confidence was sky-high, despite my failure to win the Tulip European Open and the Benson and Hedges Irish Masters titles.

But, as they say, 'snooker is a funny game', and I was gutted, totally gutted, when I left the Crucible arena after losing 13–11 to Steve James in the quarter-final. On reflection James deserved to win. He certainly goes for his shots and, on this occasion, they went in. I was careless and I knew I had made mistakes but, at 11–9 ahead, I just didn't believe that James could catch me. My manager, Ian Doyle, says that I became complacent and I have to give every player one hundred per cent respect. I have always been sure in my own mind that I never treat any player lightly but something must have gone wrong. Something must have snapped at the wrong time. Perhaps Ian has a point.

But the good news is that I am still number 1 by a long, long way. Despite my below-par ending to the season, I still won £694,057 and overtook Steve Davis' record earnings of £661,490. It would have been nice to finish the season with nine titles and set a new record for the most number of wins in one season. But after losing in the World Championship I was also beaten 4–0 by Davis in the final of the Continental Airlines London Masters. However, I finished the season on a winning note when I won the Trusthouse Forte Matchroom League for the first time and that meant I had equalled the Davis record of winning eight events in one season.

One of the highlights of my career was becoming the first player to win three Benson and Hedges Masters titles. The Benson and Hedges Masters is a fantastic tournament, bringing together the best

Hat-trick man: A delighted Stephen Hendry after his third successive victory in the Benson and Hedges Masters.

players in the world at the fabulous Wembley Conference Centre arena. Winning the Masters was absolutely tremendous – even though they didn't let me keep the trophy for my hat-trick of wins! To achieve the hat-trick in such a dramatic final was immensely satisfying. I must admit that when I lost all seven opening frames of the final against Mike Hallett, I thought I was a goner. When we went out for the evening's play I just wanted to win a few frames to make the scoreline respectable, but to beat Mike 9–8 was the greatest comeback of my professional life and one of the best wins of my career.

WHO SAID THAT?

'It was like undergoing a public operation under the surgeon's knife. Anyone got a rope?'

▲

– Mike Hallett after seeing leads of 7–0 and 8–2 disintegrate into a 9–8 defeat by Stephen Hendry in the final of the Benson and Hedges Masters.

Of course, I was lucky enough to achieve other landmarks as well. I won thirty-six successive ranking tournament games in a row and that shattered the record set by Steve Davis a few years ago. But record runs have to come to an end and that's exactly what happened to me in the final of the Mercantile Credit Classic when I lost 10–4 to Jimmy White. Then, when I won the Pearl Assurance British Open, I was thrilled to know that I had become the first player to win five ranking tournaments in one season.

I suppose it has been a great season for me, yet when I look back, losing that World Championship really hurt. I have to admit that John Parrott played the best snooker of the tournament and deserved his win, but I have one thing to say to my old stablemate: 'Don't have a cabinet built especially for the World Championship

trophy because I am going to get it back at the end of this season!' Parrott has always been a tough competitor but perhaps he has been underestimated in the UK because all his tournament wins had been overseas. However, I am sure this world title will have really boosted his confidence and we should be in for some tremendous battles in the next few months.

Looking down the ranking list, Gary Wilkinson – the person I beat in the final of the British Open – has done tremendously well to jump fourteen places to number 5 and it's also nice to see Neal Foulds back in the top ten at number 6. But there is very little change at the top with Davis still at number 2, White jumping one place to number 3 and Parrott at number 4.

Under attack: World number 1 Stephen Hendry is the man everyone is aiming for this season.

The new champ: John Parrott enjoys the glory a couple of days after taking Stephen Hendry's Embassy World Championship title. But Hendry insists he will win the title back this season.

Talking of Steve Davis, it was good to see him playing so much better at the end of the season. At the start of the 1990/91 season I went on record as saying that Steve was struggling and that I didn't see him as a threat for the rest of the season. But he won the Benson and Hedges Irish Masters and did well to reach the semi-final of the World Championship, and when we met in the final of the London Masters he took just fifty-five minutes to beat me 4–0. I didn't do a lot wrong but it was all over so quickly I didn't get a chance to get in the game. Let's hope that he has finally got his cueing problems sorted out because he is still the player I most like playing – and beating – in major tournaments and we can still meet in a lot of finals this season as we are ranked at numbers 1 and 2.

I suppose one thing I will really miss this season is not being introduced as 'Stephen Hendry – the world champion'. I got used to that last year and I really got a buzz every time I walked into the snooker arena. It's great to be number 1 and I am very privileged to be in that position, but take it from me that I want to be known as the world number 1 and world champion next season.

A lot of people have asked if I have changed as world champion. I can only say that I haven't and, although I am obviously recognised a lot more, I am just the same

---

WHO SAID THAT?

'Steve Davis will win titles but I don't think he is hungry enough to get to number 1 again.'

▲

– Stephen Hendry.

Ton-up duo: Stephen Hendry (right) and motorbike fan Steve James, now the world number 7, pose for pictures at Motherwell police station. And it was James who 'ran over' Hendry in their World Championship meeting.

when it comes to my family and friends. I still like going to the pictures and, like everybody else, I have to go down to the supermarket to get my groceries. People know me locally and just ignore me, and that's the way I like it. This season is going to be busier than ever with so many tourna-ments and a lot of travelling. But I came into snooker because I like the sport and enjoy playing, and even though I am number 1 nothing has changed. If I didn't enjoy snooker I would not play it – it's as simple as that. The money and the trophies are great, yet even if I wasn't a top professional I am sure I would still be playing snooker down the club with my friends.

My manager Ian Doyle has said that I will come back this season like a wounded tiger – even more dangerous. I would love to win the Benson and Hedges Masters for the fourth year in a row and I want to retain all the titles I have won, but deep down my main ambition must be to take back that World Championship trophy from John Parrott.

WHO SAID THAT?

'Stephen Hendry is a mean animal and he is wounded. Watch out next season.'

—— ▲ ——

– *Manager Ian Doyle speaking after Hendry's quarter-final defeat in the Embassy World Championship.*

SPONSOR'S INTRODUCTION

We are delighted to welcome back Stephen Hendry as our Associate Editor for this, the Eighth Edition of the *Benson and Hedges Snooker Year*.

The year 1991 saw Stephen Hendry winning the Benson and Hedges Masters in the most thrilling final against Mike Hallett, as he became the only player to take the title on three consecutive occasions. He finished the season as the world's number 1 ranked player for the second time and we feel sure that you will find his informed view of the game most interesting.

The 1990/1991 season provided all the usual shocks, upsets and excitement, and a number of new stars of the future emerged. Our Editor, Terry Smith, has captured all of these elements, and many others too, in his accurate and entertaining reflection of this snooker year.

Our snooker portfolio, which began with the Benson and Hedges Masters in 1975, continues to grow. The year 1990 saw the introduction of the Benson and Hedges Masters Satellite Tournament, open to all professionals outside the top sixteen. It proved to be a great success with ninety-nine competitors entering, and this number should be greatly increased for 1991 with the advent of open snooker.

The Benson and Hedges Snooker Challenge, for Scottish amateurs, is now entering its fourth successful year and the Benson and Hedges Welsh Senior Championship will be taking place for the second time.

We are extremely proud of our lengthy association with snooker, a game which we are confident will continue to expand and prosper.

Barry Jenner
Marketing Manager, Benson and Hedges

WHAT'S HAPPENING IN THE 1991/92 SEASON

PROPOSED SNOOKER TOURNAMENT DATES

1991

May 28–Jul 24	Qualifiers for all ranking events	Aldershot, Bolton and Sheffield
Aug 1–Sep 13	Ranking events: 32 qualifiers meet seeds 33–128	Trentham Gardens, Stoke-on-Trent
Aug 22–25	Thailand Masters Challenge	Bangkok, Thailand
Aug 28–31	555 Challenge	Hilton Hotel, Hong Kong
Sep 4–7	555 Challenge	Taj Mahal Hotel, Delhi, India
Sep 11–15	Regal Masters	Motherwell Civic Centre
Sep 16–17, 23–30	Ranking events: 32 qualifiers meet seeds 1–32	Trentham Gardens, Stoke-on-Trent
Sep 18–21	Humo Belgian Masters	Sporthal Schijnpoort, Antwerp
Oct 5–11	Dubai Duty Free Classic*	Al Nasr Stadium, Dubai
Oct 14–27	Rothmans Grand Prix*	Hexagon Theatre, Reading (0734 591591)
Nov 2–14	Benson and Hedges Championship	Masters SC, Glasgow
Nov 15–Dec 1	UK Championship*	Guild Hall, Preston (0772 58858)
Dec 5–14	World Matchplay	Brentwood Centre, Essex (0277 262616)
Dec 18–21	555 Challenge	Monte Carlo

1992

Jan 1–11	Mercantile Credit Classic*	Bournemouth International Centre (0202 297297)
Jan 21–26	Asian Open*	Bangkok, Thailand
Feb 2–9	Benson and Hedges Masters	Wembley Conference Centre, London (081 900 1234)
Feb 10–16	Regal Welsh Open*	To be confirmed
Feb 17–29	Pearl Assurance British Open*	Assembly Rooms, Derby (0332 255800)
Mar 1–7	Strachan Professional*	To be confirmed
Mar 10–14	European Open*	To be confirmed
Mar 17–30	Embassy World Championship (qualifying rounds)	Guild Hall, Preston (0772 58858)
Mar 31–Apr 5	Benson and Hedges Irish Masters	Goffs, Co. Kildare, Republic of Ireland
Apr 18–May 4	Embassy World Championship*	Crucible Theatre, Sheffield (0742 769922)

PROPOSED BILLIARDS TOURNAMENT DATES

1991

July 25–29	World Championship	Delhi, India
Nov 5–9	Radiant Grand Slam	Bombay or Bangalore

1992

Feb 4–8	Radiant Grand Slam	Delhi or Goa
Mar 4–10	Strachan UK	Sheffield

*Denotes ranking event.
All dates and venues are subject to change without prior notification.
Telephone numbers of box offices are given where applicable.

WHO SAID THIS?

'I was driving my high-powered motorbike when I spotted a bee buzzing around inside my crash helmet. I made an emergency stop, ripped off the helmet and thankfully I wasn't stung.'

– *Steve James, the world number 7, who is a motorbike fan.*

'The less said about that performance, the better – my head was in a jam jar.

– *Mike Hallett (below) after losing 9–7 to Gary Wilkinson in the first round of the Coalite World Matchplay.*

'I had never scored a 147 before – not even in practice.'

– *Ronnie O'Sullivan who, at fifteen years and ninety-seven days, became the youngest player to score a maximum break during the quarter-final of the Southern Area qualifiers of the BCE English Amateur Championship.*

'Twice before I was playing and once I was at the Cheltenham Races.'

– *Tony Meo after being present at the birth of his fourth child, Tiana, who weighed in at 7lb 12oz. He is pictured below with his wife and new daughter.*

'I have had such a bad couple of years that when I phoned my eight-year-old son and told him I had won, he whispered to his mum: "I think daddy's lying." My mum Mary was so surprised that I could have scraped her off the ceiling.'

– *Eugene Hughes after beating Nick Dyson to reach the last sixteen of the Rothmans Grand Prix.*

'I would love to own a falconry centre, learn mountaineering and climb Everest.'

– *Tony Jones, the Tulip European Open champion.*

'China is the land of bicycles and Stephen Hendry is now pedalling away with this frame.'

– *Commentator Ted Lowe during the 555 Asian Open in Guangzhou.*

'They land on the table and also the snooker balls – for some reason they seem to land on the yellow and green.'

– *Referee Alan Chamberlain talking about the problem of mosquitoes during the 555 Asian Open in Guangzhou.*

'People ask me if I would have beaten Stephen Hendry and Steve Davis in my prime. The answer is "Yes", because Steve would have been seven and Stephen would not have been born.'

– *WPBSA chairman John Spencer.*

'We deplore the inclusion of Alex Higgins.'

– *WPBSA chairman John Spencer talking about the decision to include Alex Higgins in the Mita World Masters despite the fact he was serving a season's ban for misconduct.*

'I feel that in the interests of the game it was right for me to decline the invitation, even though I was entitled to play in the event.'

– *Alex Higgins who decided to withdraw from the Mita World Masters.*

'I am very sorry to be losing Alex Higgins from the line-up but it's a tremendous gesture from him to ensure that the event goes ahead without any further problems.'

– *Promoter Barry Hearn.*

'I am a bit like Everton – I can't win at home.'

– *John Parrott talking about his failure to win a title on home soil before the World Championship.*

'I was 11–5 in front overnight but I didn't sleep a wink. It would have been easier to nail a blancmange to the ceiling.'

– *John Parrott talking of his 18–11 Embassy World Championship final victory over Jimmy White. (He is pictured below commentating during the Matchroom League.)*

'My old cue made pinging noises that you could hear three streets away. It was an old battle-axe.'

– *John Parrott talking about the new cue he had obtained just a couple of months before he won the Embassy World Championship.*

HOW THE PLAYERS ARE RANKED AND WHERE THEY STAND IN 1991/92

Members of the World Professional Billiards and Snooker Association (WPBSA) made their most momentous decision in 1990 when the two sports were thrown 'open' to any player – male or female – over the age of sixteen. That far-reaching action means that this season there are a staggering 610 players eligible to play on the £5 million-plus professional snooker circuit.

Last season there was a total of 181 playing members of the WPBSA, including thirteen billiards-only professionals. The Association has now accepted 442 new snooker players, including two who wished to play snooker and billiards and twenty-four billiards-only professionals.

Six ladies – headed by world champion Karen Corr, world number 1 Stacey Hillyard and former world champions Allison Fisher and Ann-Marie Farren – are playing on the hectic professional tour. This is not the first time that ladies have been members of the WPBSA but certainly the first time that female players will be competing on a regular day-in-day-out basis with their male counterparts.

The massive influx of new players has created an enormous administrative headache for the WPBSA at their headquarters in Bristol. The first problem was simply fitting in a huge amount of qualifying matches for the newcomers before the game's 'superstars' joined in the fray.

The early rounds of the ten ranking tournaments in the 1991/92 season were played at three clubs in England – the Royale Hampshire Snooker Lodge in Aldershot, Spencer's Snooker Club in Bolton and Radion Plaza in Sheffield. All players below the top 128 seeds plus all the new professionals took part in the early rounds, though existing professionals were exempted until a later stage of the qualifying competition.

When the field had been reduced to thirty-two qualifiers, these players then met seeds 97–128 with the thirty-two winners taking on seeds 65–96. The thirty-two successful players from these matches then met seeds 33–64. These later rounds took place at Trentham Gardens in Stoke-on-Trent, with the exception of the World Championship qualifiers which are scheduled to be held at the Guild Hall in Preston.

Happy to be playing: Cliff Thorburn who last year twice escaped death following peritonitis and a blood clot. He slipped down to number 36 in the rankings.

After this long qualification programme, thirty-two players had earned the right to meet seeds 1–32. In the World Championship the top sixteen seeds are exempt until the last thirty-two. But if a player came right through from the first qualifying round to win a ranking tournament, he or she could play up to thirteen matches.

There are ten ranking tournaments scheduled for this season. They are as follows, with the number of entries at each event in brackets: Rothmans Grand Prix (507); Dubai Duty Free Classic (430); Asian Open (431); UK Championship (509); Mercantile Credit Classic (501); Pearl Assurance British Open (503); European Open (448); Embassy World Championship (478); Strachan Professional Championship (467); Regal Welsh Championship (470).

The ranking of each player is decided by points scored in specific tournaments over a two-year period. This means that rankings for the current season have been decided on points gained in ten tournaments in 1989/90 and eight events in 1990/91. Ranking points are awarded, with the exception of the World Championship, as follows:

Winner	6 points
Runner-up	5 points
Semi-finalist loser	4 points
Quarter-finalist loser	3 points
Sixth-round proper loser	2 points
Fifth-round proper loser	1 point
Fourth-round proper loser	1 merit point
Third-round proper loser	1 'A' point
Second-round loser	Frames won in match

The World Championship carries higher points, which are awarded as follows:

Winner	10 points
Runner-up	8 points
Semi-finalist loser	6 points
Quarter-finalist loser	4 points
Second-round loser	2 points
First-round loser	1 ranking point unless member of top sixteen who receives 2 merit points
Eighth-qualifying-round loser	2 merit points
Seventh-qualifying-round loser	1 merit point
Sixth-qualifying-round loser	1 'A' point
Fifth-qualifying-round loser	Frames won in match

In the event of ties on ranking points, the player who has picked up most ranking points in the most recent season is allocated a higher placing. If there is still a tie, the player with the greatest number of merit points is given the higher placing. If scores are still equal, the number of merit points in the preceding season applies. In the unlikely event that players are still level, their positions are decided on 'A' points, followed by frames won. If, by a remote chance, the players still cannot be separated, their performances in the preceding World Championship will determine their

Colourful: Jon Birch who completed his first season at number 55 in the rankings.

Liverpool lad: Rod Lawler was delighted to start this season at number 54.

lowing criteria. All players who receive ranking points, merit points, 'A' points or frames will be ranked according to the old system, while all players who pick up none of these points will be allocated points under the new procedure for the 1991/92 season and seeded accordingly.

Star pupil: Glasgow's Alan McManus enjoyed his first season on the circuit and he comes into the rankings for the first time at number 41.

ranking order; and, if this method fails, the other ranking tournaments are worked through in reverse order until the players' positions can be established.

However, the WPBSA, at the time of writing, is in the process of changing the ranking points structure. These new points will decide the rankings of players in the 1993/94 season. Meanwhile the new professionals must be seeded for the 1992/93 season and the WPBSA will adopt the fol-

THE OFFICIAL WPBSA WORLD RANKING LIST 1991/92

(1990/91 positions in brackets)

RANKING	PLAYER	R	M	A	F
1 (1)	S Hendry (Scot)	85	1	0	0
2 (2)	S. Davis (Eng)	57	2	0	0
3 (4)	J. White (Eng)	51	2	0	0
4 (3)	J. Parrott (Eng)	48	3	0	0
5 (19)	Gary Wilkinson (Eng)	38	2	2	0
6 (13)	N. Foulds (Eng)	38	1	0	0
7 (9)	S. James (Eng)	36	5	0	0
8 (7)	M. Hallett (Eng)	33	5	0	0
9 (10)	Dennis Taylor (NI)	30	6	0	0
10 (5)	D. Mountjoy (Wales)	30	6	0	0
11 (6)	T. Griffiths (Wales)	27	5	0	0
12 (8)	D. Reynolds (Eng)	27	5	0	0
13 (16)	A. Robidoux (Can)	25	2	2	0
14 (12)	M. Clark (Eng)	25	3	0	0
15 (35)	A. Jones (Eng)	23	3	5	0
16 (21)	A. Knowles (Eng)	23	6	0	0
17 (11)	W. Thorne (Eng)	22	6	0	0
18 (23)	D. O'Kane (NZ)	21	9	0	0
19 (24)	P. Francisco (SA)	21	7	0	0
20 (32)	J. Wattana (Thai)	21	5	4	0
21 (38)	N. Bond (Eng)	20	8	4	4
22 (30)	A. Drago (Malta)	19	6	0	0
23 (20)	S. Newbury (Wales)	19	6	0	0
24 (26)	S. Francisco (SA)	18	10	0	0
25 (22)	W. Jones (Wales)	17	7	0	0
26 (17)	J. Johnson (Eng)	16	9	0	0
27 (31)	E. Charlton (Aust)	15	6	0	0
28 (29)	D. Fowler (Eng)	15	11	1	0
29 (33)	M. Bennett (Wales)	14	7	2	0
30 (25)	R. Chaperon (Can)	14	12	0	0
31 (14)	J. Virgo (Eng)	14	10	0	0
32 (28)	C. Wilson (Wales)	13	9	0	0
33 (40)	D. Morgan (Wales)	13	7	3	0
34 (15)	A. Meo (Eng)	12	8	0	0
35 (54)	B. Gollan (Can)	11	3	6	6
36 (18)	C. Thorburn (Can)	11	12	0	0
37 (43)	A. Chappel (Wales)	10	5	7	0
38 (27)	B. West (Eng)	10	12	0	0
39 (39)	W. King (Aust)	10	7	5	5
40 (45)	L. Dodd (Eng)	9	7	6	6
41 (–)	A. McManus (Scot)	9	3	0	6
42 (50)	I. Graham (Eng)	8	9	5	0
43 (47)	J. Campbell (Aust)	8	6	6	0
44 (48)	C. Roscoe (Wales)	8	4	9	0
45 (34)	E. Hughes (Rep Ire)	8	10	4	0
46 (46)	R. Marshall (Eng)	8	7	5	5
47 (42)	B. Morgan (Eng)	8	3	8	7
48 (37)	R. Williams (Eng)	7	13	1	0
49 (49)	J. McLaughlin (NI)	7	9	5	0
50 (36)	D. Roe (Eng)	7	9	4	0
51 (–)	K. Doherty (Rep Ire)	6	2	1	3
52 (59)	M. Johnston-Allen (Eng)	6	11	6	0
53 (–)	F. Chan (HK)	5	1	2	9
54 (–)	R. Lawler (Eng)	4	4	2	0
55 (–)	J. Birch (Eng)	4	2	2	3
56 (–)	J. Prince (NI)	4	2	1	5
57 (52)	J. Wych (Can)	4	11	3	0
58 (68)	K. Stevens (Can)	4	2	10	12
59 (51)	N. Gilbert (Eng)	4	6	8	0
60 (64)	N. Dyson (Eng)	4	4	7	13
61 (61)	C. Edwards (Eng)	4	2	8	11
62 (58)	J. Chambers (Eng)	4	6	9	0
63 (41)	S. Duggan (Eng)	4	6	9	0
64 (60)	M. Rowing (Eng)	3	6	7	12
65 (98)	S. Murphy (Rep Ire)	2	5	5	24
66 (109)	D. Campbell (Scot)	2	4	9	11
67 (95)	K. Owers (Eng)	2	3	6	20
68 (100)	R. Foldvari (Aust)	2	2	2	54
69 (–)	J. Whittaker (Eng)	2	1	2	13
70 (80)	A. Cairns (Eng)	2	7	6	8
71 (62)	J. O'Boye (Eng)	2	7	7	0
72 (56)	M. Macleod (Scot)	2	7	9	0
73 (82)	B. Pinches (Eng)	2	4	6	15
74 (44)	David Taylor (Eng)	2	9	7	0
75 (65)	J. Smith (Eng)	2	5	5	27
76 (67)	J. Grech (Malta)	2	4	2	7
77 (63)	B. Rowswell (Eng)	2	3	10	8
78 (66)	P. Gibson (Eng)	2	2	4	29
79 (92)	R. Harris (Eng)	1	9	6	4
80 (91)	S. Campbell (Eng)	1	7	6	15
81 (–)	G. Natale (Can)	1	1	2	11
82 (76)	M. Price (Eng)	1	10	3	13
83 (53)	P. Browne (Rep Ire)	1	7	8	0
84 (69)	R. Bales (Eng)	1	6	7	10
85 (55)	J. Spencer (Eng)	1	6	11	0
86 (70)	A. Wilson (Eng)	1	5	6	19
87 (77)	W. Oliver (Eng)	1	5	5	28
88 (81)	M. Morra (Can)	1	4	9	9

RANKING		PLAYER	R	M	A	F
89	(71)	M. Gauvreau (Can)	1	4	7	24
90	(75)	T. Murphy (NI)	1	4	11	6
91	(74)	D. Gilbert (Eng)	1	4	11	5
92	(79)	M. Smith (Eng)	1	2	6	23
93	(78)	P. Medati (Eng)	1	2	6	27
94	(83)	I. Brumby (Eng)	1	2	5	30
95	(72)	R. Edmonds (Eng)	0	8	8	9
96	(84)	J. Wright (Eng)	0	8	3	19
97	(86)	N. Terry (Eng)	0	7	7	8
98	(57)	S. Longworth (Eng)	0	6	12	0
99	(—)	C. Cookson (Eng)	0	5	1	12
100	(85)	J. Rea (Scot)	0	5	8	15
101	(94)	G. Miles (Eng)	0	5	4	24
102	(93)	E. Sinclair (Scot)	0	5	6	22
103	(87)	G. Cripsey (Eng)	0	4	8	19
104	(96)	P. Houlihan (Eng)	0	4	7	16
105	(90)	D. Martin (Eng)	0	4	6	14
106	(103)	I. Williamson (Eng)	0	3	8	21
107	(101)	S. Meakin (Eng)	0	3	5	29
108	(—)	J. Ferguson (Eng)	0	2	5	10
109	(99)	M. Fisher (Eng)	0	2	11	11
110	(102)	P. Watchorn (Rep Ire)	0	2	4	28
111	(104)	A. Kearney (Rep Ire)	0	1	8	21
112	(112)	G. Rigitano (Can)	0	1	5	34
113	(105)	E. Lawlor (Can)	0	1	5	24
114	(88)	G. Scott (Eng)	0	1	4	20
115	(110)	M. Gibson (Scot)	0	1	4	43
116	(111)	V. Harris (Eng)	0	1	4	29
117	(113)	R. Grace (SA)	0	1	3	21
118	(114)	J. Donnelly (Scot)	0	1	2	43
119	(106)	F. Ellis (SA)	0	1	1	37
120	(97)	A. Higgins (NI)	0	1	0	0
121	(107)	M. Bradley (Eng)	0	0	9	23
122	(89)	A. Harris (Eng)	0	0	7	44
123	(116)	J. Fitzmaurice (Eng)	0	0	7	27
124	(117)	J. Dunning (Eng)	0	0	6	23
125	(120)	M. Darrington (Eng)	0	0	5	33

RANKING		PLAYER	R	M	A	F
126	(73)	R. Reardon (Wales)	0	0	5	17
127	(126)	W. Kelly (Rep Ire)	0	0	5	8
128	(119)	J. Bear (Can)	0	0	4	27
129	(125)	M. Wildman (Eng)	0	0	4	20
130	(127)	J. Meadowcroft (Eng)	0	0	4	8
131	(128)	F. Davis (Eng)	0	0	3	19
132	(118)	T. Whitthread (Eng)	0	0	2	26
133	(123)	M. Watterson (Eng)	0	0	2	20
134	(121)	D. Sheehan (Rep Ire)	0	0	2	33
135	(108)	Glen Wilkinson (Aust)	0	0	2	18
136	(122)	D. Hughes (Eng)	0	0	2	15
137	(129)	G. Foulds (Eng)	0	0	2	12
138	(156)	V. Potasznyk (Aust)	0	0	1	0
139	(130)	G. Jenkins (Aust)	0	0	1	10
140	(134)	C. Everton (Wales)	0	0	1	0
141	(124)	P. Thornley (Can)	0	0	0	23
142	(141)	D. Heaton (Eng)	0	0	0	6
143	(135)	D. Mienie (SA)	0	0	0	5
144	(133)	I. Black (Scot)	0	0	0	3
145	(132)	B. Mikkelsen (Can)	0	0	0	2
146	(158)	W. Werbeniuk (Can)	0	0	0	1
147	(139)	I. Anderson (Aust)	0	0	0	0
148	(140)	B. Bennett (Eng)	0	0	0	0
149	(137)	P. Burke (Rep Ire)	0	0	0	0
150	(142)	J. Caggianello (Can)	0	0	0	0
151	(143)	L. Condo (Aust)	0	0	0	0
152	(144)	B. Demarco (Scot)	0	0	0	0
153	(145)	M. Francisco (Malta)	0	0	0	0
154	(146)	S. Frangie (Aust)	0	0	0	0
155	(147)	J. Giannaros (Aust)	0	0	0	0
156	(148)	D. Greaves (Eng)	0	0	0	0
157	(153)	S. Mizerak (USA)	0	0	0	0
158	(154)	P. Morgan (Aust)	0	0	0	0
159	(155)	M. Parkin (Eng)	0	0	0	0
160	(138)	J. Rempe (USA)	0	0	0	0
161	(157)	G. Watson (Can)	0	0	0	0

KEY TO TABLE
R – Ranking points
A – A points
M – Merit points
F – Frames won

Countries
Aust – Australia
Can – Canada
Eng – England
HK – Hong Kong
Malta – Malta
NI – Northern Ireland
NZ – New Zealand
Rep Ire – Republic of Ireland
Scot – Scotland
SA – South Africa
Thai – Thailand
Wales – Wales
USA – United States of America

	555 Challenge	Regal Masters	Humo Masters	International One-Frame Knockout	Rothmans Grand Prix	555 Asian Open	Dubai Duty Free Classic	StormSeal UK Open Championship	Benson and Hedges Satellite	Coalite World Matchplay
1 S. Hendry	7,500	35,000 3,500 (HB)	10,000		75,000	35,000 2,000 (HB)	35,000	110,000		30,000 5,000 (HB)
2 J. White	10,000	9,000	15,000		20,000 7,000 (HB)	1,500	1,500	15,000		70,000
3 S. Davis	7,500	4,500	10,000	250	2,000	750	22,000	60,000		17,500
4 J. Parrott		4,500	30,000 4,000 (HB)		10,000	6,000	1,500	30,000 9,000 (HB)		10,000
5 M. Hallett	5,000	2,000	1,500	3,000	5,000	12,000	6,000	3,000		5,000
6 Gary Wilkinson				250	5,000	750	12,000 2,000 (HB)	6,000	750	10,000
7 S. James	5,000	9,000			20,000	750	1,500	3,000		5,000
8 T. Griffiths	1,500	17,500	1,500		3,400	750	6,000	3,000		17,500
9 Dennis Taylor					3,400	22,000	750	1,500		
10 J. Wattana	20,000				250	1,500	1,500	6,000 2,000 (HB)	2,500	
11 N. Foulds				750	10,000	6,000	4,500	6,000		5,000
12 A. Drago				250	3,400	1,500	1,500	3,000	500	
13 N. Bond				500	40,000	4,500	750	15,000	100	
14 D. Morgan		4,500		5,000	3,400	1,500	4,500	3,000	1,500	
15 D. Reynolds	5,000	2,000	1,500	750	2,000	1,500	12,000	1,500		10,000
16 D. Mountjoy	5,000	4,500	1,500		2,000	4,500	6,000	3,000		5,000
17 W. Thorne				250	5,000 800 (HB)	4,500	1,500	6,000		
18 A. Jones					2,000	250	250	3,000	100	
19 A. McManus				2,000	2,000		750	30,000	3,000 700 (HB)	
20 M. Clark				250	3,400	1,500	4,500	1,500		10,000
21 A. Meo					2,000	750	750	1,500		
22 J. Johnson					2,000	750	750	6,000	250	
23 A. Robidoux					5,000	750	1,500	3,000		
24 P. Francisco				500	10,000	1,500	1,500	3,000	250	
25 K. Doherty				750			750	250	250	
26 A. Knowles				1,250 1,000 (HB)	3,400	750	1,500	15,000	100	
27 B. Gollan					2,000	1,500	250	250	50	
28 S. Francisco					3,400	4,500	4,500	6,000	750	
29 D. Fowler				250	2,000	750	750	15,000	250	
30 A. Chappel					250	12,000	250	3,000	750	
31 M. Bennett				250	2,000	6,000	750	250	250	
32 M. Johnston-Allen				250	2,000	250	750	250	50	
33 W. Jones				250	3,400	750	1,500	6,000	100	
34 C. Wilson					3,400	1,500	750	3,000	750	
35 C. Thorburn				500	2,000	750	750			
36 J. Wych					250	750	4,500 1,000 (HB)	250		
37 S. Newbury				750	3,400	750 1,000 (HB)	1,500	3,000	250	
38 D. O'Kane				250	5,000	1,500	1,500	1,500		
39 E. Charlton				500	3,400	4,500	750	1,500	100	
40 J. Virgo					2,000	1,500	750	1,500		
41 J. Birch				250	250	750	1,500	6,000	250	
42 F. Chan	1,500				250	4,500	4,500	1,500	100	
43 R. Chaperon					2,000	1,500	750	1,500	100	
44 R. Lawler				250	2,000	250	1,500	1,500	100	
45 I. Graham					5,000	250	750	1,500	500	
46 J. Prince				250	250		4,500			
47 E. Hughes					10,000	750	250	250	250	
48 S. Longworth					250	750	250	250	50	
49 B. West					3,400	750	750	3,000	100	
50 N. Dyson				750	3,400	250	250	1,500	100	
51 J. Campbell					3,400	4,500	250	1,500	500	
52 L. Dodd				250	250	6,000	250	1,500	500	
53 W. King					250	750	750	1,500		
54 K. Stevens					5,000 800 (HB)		750			
55 C. Roscoe				500	3,400	750	250	3,000	100	
56 R. Williams					2,000	750	6,000	1,500		
57 R. Marshall				250	2,000	750	250	250		
58 N. Gilbert				250	2,000	750	250	1,500	100	
59 D. Roe				1,250	250	250	750	3,000	1,500	
60 J. McLaughlin					250	4,500	750	250	250	

DURING 1990/91

Mercantile Credit Classic	Mita World Masters	Benson and Hedges Masters	Regal Welsh Championship	Pearl Assurance British Open	Tulip European Open	Benson and Hedges Irish Masters	Continental Airlines London Masters	Trusthouse Forte Matchroom League	Others*	Embassy World Championship	Total
36,000	31,500	100,000		75,000	4,500	8,056.58	12,500 / 3,500 (HB)	50,000	5,000	20,000	694,056.58
60,000	204,000	23,000		21,500	750	14,322.80	7,500	25,000	2,500	80,000 / 12,000 (HB)	599,572.80
4,500	25,000	9,000		21,500	4,500	35,807	30,000	30,000 / 5,000 (HB)	15,000	42,000	346,807.00
2,625	9,000	15,000		2,125	750	21,484.20 / 3,580.70 (HB)	7,500		25,000	135,000	327,064.90
18,000	33,250	50,000		11,000	750	5,371.05			4,500	6,000	171,371.05
9,000	9,500	6,000		44,000 / 6,000 (HB)	1,500		3,500			20,000	136,250.00
1,250	3,500	15,000		2,125	4,500	8,056.58		15,000		42,000	135,681.58
1,250	16,750	23,000	1,750	6,000	1,500	5,371.05			4,000	20,000	130,771.05
2,625	5,000	9,000 / 10,000 (HB)		11,000	6,000	14,322.80		9,000	2,500	20,000	117,097.80
4,500	32,250 / 6,000 (HB)			6,000	1,500		3,500	17,000	6,750	5,000	116,250.00
18,000	9,000	15,000		4,000	6,000			13,000	3,500	11,000	111,750.00
9,000	71,750			6,000	750				2,100	5,000	104,750.00
250	6,750			250	750	8,056.58			3,000	5,000	84,906.58
250	30,750		11,000 / 1,500 (HB)	2,125	1,500				4,000	2,750	77,275.00
1,250	3,250	9,000		6,000	4,500	5,371.05				11,000	76,621.05
2,625	5,750	9,000		4,000	6,000	5,371.05		5,000		6,000	75,246.05
1,250	11,000	9,000		2,125	4,500			20,000		6,000	71,925.00
1,250	5,750			11,000	35,000					11,000	69,600.00
4,500	3,500	9,000		2,125						11,000	68,575.00
2,625	2,750	9,000		4,000	1,500		3,500		7,000	11,000	62,525.00
1,250	9,750	15,000		6,000	1,500			11,000		11,000	60,500.00
4,500	10,250			4,000	1,500				16,500	6,000	52,500.00
2,625	6,000	6,000		11,000	750				3,150	11,000	50,775.00
1,250	16,750			4,000	4,500					5,000	48,250.00
9,000 / 5,000 (HB)	9,000			2,125	4,500	8,056.58				6,000	45,681.58
1,250	1,500			6,000	1,500					11,000	44,250.00
250	20,000			4,000	12,000					1,000	41,300.00
1,250	7,000			4,000	750					5,000	37,150.00
2,625	5,000			4,000	750					5,000	36,375.00
2,625 / 1,000 (HB)	10,500		3,750	250	750					1,000	36,125.00
2,625	5,000		7,000	4,000	750					6,000	34,875.00
250	3,500			250	22,000 / 2,000 (HB)					2,750	34,300.00
4,500	5,500		3,750	2,125	750					5,000	33,625.00
2,625	4,000		1,750	2,125	4,500				1,000	5,000	30,400.00
1,250	3,250			2,125	12,000 / 1,000 (HB)				1,500	5,000	30,125.00
1,250	13,000			2,125	1,500					5,000	29,625.00
2,625	3,500		1,750	2,125	750				1,250	6,000	28,650.00
4,500	1,250			2,125	6,000					5,000	28,625.00
4,500	1,000			4,000	1,500					6,000	27,750.00
1,250	1,000	9,000		2,125	1,500					6,000	26,625.00
2,625	8,500			2,125						1,000	23,250.00
250	5,000			4,000						500	22,100.00
4,500	3,750			2,125	750					5,000	21,975.00
9,000	3,500			250	750					2,750	21,850.00
2,625	1,500			2,125	250					6,000	20,500.00
2,625	6,500			2,125	1,500					2,750	20,500.00
250	3,500			2,125	250					2,750	20,375.00
1,250	15,500			250	250					1,000	19,800.00
2,625	1,000			2,125	750					5,000	19,500.00
1,250	5,500			250						6,000	19,250.00
2,625	1,000			2,125	250					2,750	18,900.00
1,250	3,000			250	250					5,000	18,500.00
1,250	3,000			4,000	250					6,000	17,750.00
250	3,000			4,000	250					500 / 3,000 (HB)	17,550.00
250	1,000		1,000	6,000	250					1,000	17,500.00
1,250	1,000			2,125	750					1,000	16,375.00
250	1,000			4,000	750					6,000	15,500.00
1,250	1,000			250	1,500					6,000	14,850.00
2,625	1,250			2,125	250					1,000	14,250.00
1,250	1,500			2,125	1,500					1,000	13,375.00

	555 Challenge	Regal Masters	Humo Masters	International One-Frame Knockout	Rothmans Grand Prix	555 Asian Open	Dubai Duty Free Classic	StormSeal UK Open Championship	Benson and Hedges Satellite	Coalite World Matchplay
61 K. Owers				250	5,000	250		1,500	50	
62 J. Whittaker				2,000		250	4,500			
63 C. Edwards				250	250	250	250	250	250	
64 P. Browne				500	2,000	250	250	250	500	
65 C. Cookson					2,000		250		50	
66 David Taylor					250	750	750	1,500	100	
67 A. Cairns				500	250	750	750	250	250	
68 M. Price				500		750		1,500	500	
69 R. Harris					2,000	1,500	750	1,500		
70 D. Campbell				500	250	750	1,500	1,500	100	
71 S. Murphy					2,000	250	1,500		50	
B. Pinches						250		1,500	50	
73 J. Grech					250	750		1,500	100	
74 J. Smith					2,000				50	
75 R. Edmonds				500		250	750	1,500		
76 J. O'Boye				750	2,000	1,500	750	1,500	100	
77 M. Macleod				250	2,000	1,500	250	250	50	
78 M. Rowing				500	250	250	750	1,500		
79 R. Foldvari				250					250	
80 B. Morgan					250	250	250	250	250	
81 R. Reardon										
82 J. Chambers					3,400	250	250	250		
83 S. Duggan				500	250	750	250	250	250	
84 A. Wilson				500	250		250	1,500	250	
85 S. Campbell						1,500		1,500	50	
86 G. Natale							250	3,000		
87 M. Morra					250	250		250		
88 J. Ferguson				250	2,000	250	250			
89 J. Spencer					250	250	250	250	50	
90 M. Gauvreau				750	2,000		750		500	
91 B. Rowswell				250	250	750	250	250	100	
92 W. Oliver				250	250			1,500		
93 R. Bales				250	2,000	750		250	100	
94 John Rea					250	250	750	250	50	
95 P. Gibson				750	2,000				250	
96 J. Wright					2,000					
97 S. Meakin				500	250				50	
98 M. Smith						250			500	
99 G. Cripsey				1,250		750			100	
N. Terry						250	750		100	
101 I. Williamson						250	750	250	50	
102 G. Miles					2,000			250	100	
103 J. Rempe										
104 D. Gilbert				500		250	250	250	100	
105 T. Murphy				250		250	750	250	50	
106 I. Brumby				1,250					100	
107 P. Houlihan							250	250		
P. Medati					250	250		250		
109 G. Scott					250		250		100	
110 E. Sinclair							250		100	
111 J. Fitzmaurice				250				250		
112 M. Bradley					250	250		250	100	
A. Harris						250		250	100	
114 M. Darrington						250	250		50	
M. Fisher					250		250		50	
T. Whitthread				500					50	
117 F. Davis										
118 A. Kearney						250			100	
119 J. Dunning					250		250		50	
M. Gibson								250	50	
121 V. Harris					250			250		
W. Potasznyk										
123 D. Hughes				250					100	
124 J. Donnelly				250					50	
125 J. Bear							250			
M. Watterson										
127 D. Sheehan										
P. Thornley										
P. Watchorn					250		250			
B. Werbeniuk										
131 I. Black				250					50	
P. Burke				250					50	
133 D. Greaves				250						
W. Kelly										
E. Lawlor										
G. Rigitano						250				

Mercantile Credit Classic	Mita World Masters	Benson and Hedges Masters	Regal Welsh Championship	Pearl Assurance British Open	Tulip European Open	Benson and Hedges Irish Masters	Continental Airlines London Masters	Trusthouse Forte Matchroom League	Others*	Embassy World Championship	Total
1,250	2,500				250					1,000	12,050.00
	3,000				750					1,000	11,500.00
250	1,000			250	1,500					6,000	10,500.00
1,250	1,500			250	750					2,750	10,250.00
				2,125	750					5,000	10,175.00
250	3,000			2,125	250					1,000	9,975.00
1,250				4,000	750					1,000	9,750.00
1,250				2,125	250					2,750	9,625.00
250				250						2,750	9,000.00
250				2,125	1,500					500	8,975.00
250				4,000	250					500	8,800.00
				250	750					6,000	8,800.00
1,250	1,500			2,125						1,000	8,475.00
1,250				2,125	250					2,750	8,425.00
				250	250					5,000	8,250.00
	1,000			250	250						8,100.00
250	1,500			250	750					1,000	8,050.00
250	1,000			250	250					2,750	7,750.00
				6,000	250					500	7,250.00
250	2,500			250	250					2,750	7,250.00
			1,750		250				4,500	500	7,000.00
250	1,000			250	250					1,000	6,900.00
250	1,000			250	250					2,750	6,750.00
				2,125	750					1,000	6,625.00
				2,125	250					1,000	6,425.00
				2,125	250					500	6,125.00
1,250				250	750					2,750	5,750.00
										2,750	5,500.00
250	1,000			250	250				1,500	1,000	5,300.00
					750					500	5,250.00
250	1,000			250	250					1,000	4,600.00
1,250				250						1,000	4,500.00
250										500	4,100.00
1,250					250					1,000	4,050.00
										1,000	4,000.00
					750					1,000	3,750.00
										2,750	3,550.00
1,250				250	750					500	3,500.00
					750					500	3,350.00
250				250	750					1,000	3,350.00
1,250					250					500	3,300.00
250										500	3,100.00
	3,000										3,000.00
250				250						1,000	2,850.00
250				250	250					500	2,800.00
				250						1,000	2,600.00
1,250				250						500	2,500.00
					750					1,000	2,500.00
				250						1,000	1,850.00
250				250						1,000	1,850.00
										1,000	1,500.00
										500	1,350.00
					250					500	1,350.00
					250					500	1,300.00
				250						500	1,300.00
250										500	1,300.00
250	1,000										1,250.00
250										500	1,100.00
										500	1,050.00
250										500	1,050.00
										500	1,000.00
										1,000	1,000.00
										500	850.00
										500	800.00
										500	750.00
250										500	750.00
										500	500.00
										500	500.00
											500.00
										500	500.00
											300.00
											300.00
											250.00
				250							250.00
					250						250.00
											250.00

* Norwich Union Grand Prix; European Grand Masters; Nescafé Extra Challenge; Pontin's Professional.

THE WORLD'S TOP THIRTY-TWO: A LOOK BACK AT THEIR CAREERS AND HOW THEY FARED IN 1990/91

STEPHEN HENDRY

World ranking: Number 1
Date of birth: 13 January 1969
Star sign: Capricorn
Turned professional: 1985

Country: Scotland
Prize money 1990/91: £694,056.58
Biggest pay day: £120,000 – 1990
Embassy world champion

Stephen Hendry finished the 1990/91 season without his Embassy world title but with a collection of snooker records. He equalled the Steve Davis record of eight tournament wins in one season, capturing the Regal Masters, the Rothmans Grand Prix, the 555 Asian Open, the Dubai Duty Free Classic, the StormSeal UK Championship, the Benson and Hedges Masters, the Pearl Assurance British Open and the Trusthouse Forte Matchroom League. He also achieved another milestone when he earned £694,056.58, the most prize money won in one season, beating the record of £661,490 set by Steve Davis in 1988/89. There were other landmarks as Hendry became the first player to win five ranking tournaments in one season and the first player to take the Benson and Hedges Masters title three times in a row. Just for good measure, he also established a record run of thirty-six straight victories in ranking tournament matches before he lost to Jimmy White

Way out in front: Stephen Hendry, world number 1 by 28 points.

10–4 in the final of the Mercantile Credit Classic. After such a good first half to the season, Hendry was shattered when he failed to retain his world title, losing 13–11 to Steve James in the quarter-final. However, from all sources he earned more than £1 million and has a handsome lead at the top of the world rankings.

BEST PERFORMANCES
Embassy World Championship:
Winner 1990 (beat Jimmy White 18–12)

Other Ranking Tournaments
Asian Open:
Winner 1989 (beat James Wattana 9–6)
Winner 1990 (beat Dennis Taylor 9–3)
Rothmans Grand Prix:
Winner 1987 (beat Dennis Taylor 10–7)
Winner 1990 (beat Nigel Bond 10–5)
Dubai Duty Free Classic:
Winner 1989 (beat Doug Mountjoy 9–2)
Winner 1990 (beat Steve Davis 9–1)
UK Championship:
Winner 1989 (beat Steve Davis 16–12)
Winner 1990 (beat Steve Davis 16–15)
Mercantile Credit Classic:
Runner-up 1991 (lost to Jimmy White 10–4)
Pearl Assurance British Open:
Winner 1988 (beat Mike Hallett 13–2)
Winner 1991 (beat Gary Wilkinson 10–9)
European Open:
Runner-up 1990 (lost to John Parrott 10–6)

Current Non-ranking Tournaments
Benson and Hedges Masters:
Winner 1989 (beat John Parrott 9–6)

Winner 1990 (beat John Parrott 9–4)
Winner 1991 (beat Mike Hallett 9–8)
Benson and Hedges Irish Masters:
Runner-up 1989 (lost to Alex Higgins 9–8)
World Matchplay:
Runner-up 1990 (lost to Jimmy White 18–9)
Regal Masters:
Winner 1989 (beat Terry Griffiths 10–1)
Winner 1990 (beat Terry Griffiths 10–6)

Other wins
British Isles Under-16: 1983
Scottish Amateur: 1984, 1985
Scottish Professional: 1986, 1987, 1988
Winfield Masters: 1987
Foster's World Doubles: 1987
Lion Brown New Zealand Masters: 1988
Continental Airlines London Masters: 1989, 1990
Pontin's Professional: 1990
Mita World Masters – Black and Decker Men's
Doubles: 1991
Trusthouse Forte Matchroom League: 1991

WORLD RANKING POSITIONS

| 1986/87 51 | 1988/89 4 | 1990/91 1 |
| 1987/88 23 | 1989/90 3 | 1991/92 1 |

STEVE DAVIS

World ranking: Number 2
Date of birth: 22 August 1957
Star sign: Leo
Turned professional: 1978

Country: England
Prize money 1990/91: £346,807
Biggest pay day: £105,000 – 1989
Embassy world champion

Steve Davis, who for so long dominated the world snooker stage, ended the 1990/91 season with just two titles to his name – the Benson and Hedges Irish Masters and the Continental Airlines London Masters. In the Irish Masters he beat John Parrott 9–5 and then, in just fifty-five minutes, hammered Stephen Hendry 4–0 in the London Masters. It was the first time Davis had beaten Hendry in eight meetings. Davis, still at number 2, was, however, a lot happier with his form at the end of the season and he said: 'I still feel as though I can win the world title for the seventh time.' He had been trying to sort out problems in his technique and, just before the Irish Masters, he announced that he had cured a fault in his grip and that he was looking forward to the future with optimism. During the Embassy World Championship, Davis had to rush home to his wife, Judy, who gave birth to their first son, Greg Robert. After the birth he returned to the World Championship where he reached the semi-final before going down 16–10 to John Parrott, the eventual champion.

WHO SAID THAT?

'I would like to do what golfer Nick Faldo did – completely rebuild my game.'

▲

– Steve Davis.

BEST PERFORMANCES
Embassy World Championship:
Winner 1981 (beat Doug Mountjoy 18–12)
Winner 1983 (beat Cliff Thorburn 18–6)
Winner 1984 (beat Jimmy White 18–16)
Winner 1987 (beat Joe Johnson 18–14)
Winner 1988 (beat Terry Griffiths 18–11)
Winner 1989 (beat John Parrott 18–3)

Other Ranking Tournaments
Asian Open:
Round 3 1990 (lost to Nigel Bond 5–3)
Rothmans Grand Prix:
Winner 1985 (beat Dennis Taylor 10–9)
Winner 1988 (beat Alex Higgins 10–6)
Winner 1989 (beat Dean Reynolds 10–0)
Dubai Duty Free Classic:
Runner-up 1990 (lost to Stephen Hendry 9–1)
UK Championship:
Winner 1984 (beat Alex Higgins 16–8)
Winner 1985 (beat Willie Thorne 16–14)
Winner 1986 (beat Neal Foulds 16–7)
Winner 1987 (beat Jimmy White 16–14)
Mercantile Credit Classic:
Winner 1984 (beat Tony Meo 9–8)
Winner 1987 (beat Jimmy White 13–12)
Winner 1988 (beat John Parrott 13–11)
Pearl Assurance British Open:
Winner 1986 (beat Willie Thorne 12–7)
European Open:
Semi-finalist 1990 (lost to Stephen Hendry 6–3)

Current Non-ranking Tournaments
Benson and Hedges Masters:
Winner 1982 (beat Terry Griffiths 9–5)
Winner 1988 (beat Mike Hallett 9–0)
Benson and Hedges Irish Masters:
Winner 1983 (beat Ray Reardon 9–2)
Winner 1984 (beat Terry Griffiths 9–1)
Winner 1987 (beat Willie Thorne 9–1)
Winner 1988 (beat Neal Foulds 9–4)

Winner 1990 (beat Dennis Taylor 9–4)
Winner 1991 (beat John Parrott 9–5)
World Matchplay:
Winner 1988 (beat John Parrott 9–5)
Regal Masters:
Semi-finalist 1989 (lost to Terry Griffiths 6–2)

Other Wins
Pontin's Open: 1978, 1979
Coral UK: 1980, 1981
Lada Classic: 1981 (played December 1980)
English Professional: 1981, 1985
Yamaha International Masters: 1981, 1982, 1984
Jameson International: 1981
Pot Black: 1982, 1983
Pontin's Professional: 1982
Tolly Cobbold Classic: 1982, 1983, 1984
Winfield Masters: 1982
Langs Supreme Masters: 1982, 1983, 1984
Hofmeister World Doubles: 1982, 1983, 1985, 1986
BCE International: 1983, 1984, 1987, 1988, 1989
Camus Hong Kong Masters: 1984
Riley Hong Kong Masters: 1987
Camus Singapore Masters: 1985
BCE Canadian Masters: 1986
Brazilian Masters: 1986
Camus China Masters: 1986
Matchroom League: 1987, 1988, 1989, 1990
LEP Matchroom Trophy: 1988
Fersina Windows World Cup: 1981, 1983, 1988, 1989
Norwich Union Grand Prix: 1988
Hong Kong Gold Cup: 1989
Mita World Masters – Mixed Doubles: 1991
Continental Airlines London Masters: 1991

WORLD RANKING POSITIONS

1980/81 13	1984/85 1	1988/89 1
1981/82 2	1985/86 1	1989/90 1
1982/83 4	1986/87 1	1990/91 2
1983/84 1	1987/88 1	1991/92 2

JIMMY WHITE

World ranking: Number 3
Date of birth: 2 May 1962
Star sign: Taurus
Turned professional: 1980

Country: England
Prize money 1990/91: £599,572.80
Biggest pay day: £200,000 – 1991 Mita
World Masters – Black and Decker
Men's Singles champion

Jimmy White enjoyed the best season of his career and yet still finished bitterly disappointed after losing in the final of the Embassy World Championship for the third time. White, who had been sick of being labelled 'the greatest player never to have won the world title', was beaten 18–11 by John Parrott in the final at the Crucible Theatre in Sheffield. Earlier in the season he had produced one of the most devastating spells the game had ever seen as he won three titles in the space of fifty days and a staggering £334,000. He beat Stephen Hendry in two of those finals –

18–9 in the Coalite World Matchplay and 10–4 in the Mercantile Credit Classic – and then overcame Tony Drago 10–6 in the Mita World Masters in Birmingham. That World Masters victory was worth £200,000, the highest prize ever paid in professional snooker. White's consistency earned him one move up the rankings to number 3. However, he parted company with Barry Hearn's Matchroom organisation at the end of his five-year contract.

Smiling through: Jimmy White who edged back to number 3 in the world rankings after his most successful season.

BEST PERFORMANCES
Embassy World Championship:
Runner-up 1984 (lost to Steve Davis 18–16)
Runner-up 1990 (lost to Stephen Hendry 18–12)
Runner-up 1991 (lost to John Parrott 18–11)

Other Ranking Tournaments
Asian Open:
Round 4 1990 (lost to Eddie Charlton 5–4)
Rothmans Grand Prix:
Winner 1986 (beat Rex Williams 10–6)
Dubai Duty Free Classic:
Round 4 1990 (lost to Franky Chan 5–3)
UK Championship:
Runner-up 1987 (lost to Steve Davis 16–14)
Mercantile Credit Classic:
Winner 1986 (beat Cliff Thorburn 13–12)
Winner 1991 (beat Stephen Hendry 10–4)
Pearl Assurance British Open:
Winner 1987 (beat Neal Foulds 13–9)
European Open:
Semi-finalist 1989 (lost to Terry Griffiths 5–4)

Current Non-ranking Tournaments
Benson and Hedges Masters:
Winner 1984 (beat Terry Griffiths 9–5)
Benson and Hedges Irish Masters:
Winner 1985 (beat Alex Higgins 9–5)
Winner 1986 (beat Willie Thorne 9–5)

Coalite World Matchplay:
Winner 1989 (beat John Parrott 18–9)
Winner 1990 (beat Stephen Hendry 18–9)
Regal Masters:
Semi-finalist 1990 (lost to Stephen Hendry 6–4)

Other Wins
British Isles Under-16: 1977
Pontin's Autumn Open: 1978
English Amateur: 1979
World Amateur: 1980
Indian Amateur: 1980
Langs Supreme Masters: 1981
Northern Ireland Classic: 1981
Hofmeister World Doubles: 1984
Carlsberg Challenge: 1984, 1985
Pot Black: 1986
Camus Malaysian Masters: 1986
Fersina Windows World Cup: 1988, 1989
LEP Hong Kong Masters: 1988
BCE Canadian Masters: 1988
Mita World Masters – Black and Decker Men's Singles: 1991

WORLD RANKING POSITIONS

1981/82 21	1985/86 7	1989/90 4
1982/83 10	1986/87 5	1990/91 4
1983/84 11	1987/88 2	1991/92 3
1984/85 7	1988/89 2	

JOHN PARROTT

World ranking: Number 4
Date of birth: 11 May 1964
Star sign: Taurus
Turned professional: 1983

Country: England
Prize money 1990/91: £327,064.90
Biggest pay day: £135,000 – 1991 Embassy world champion

John Parrott, who had been snooker's 'nearly man' for so many years, finally proved the doubters wrong by winning the greatest tournament of them all – the

Mersey might: World champion John Parrott who claimed snooker's ultimate prize at Sheffield.

Embassy World Championship in Sheffield. He played superbly throughout the seventeen-day marathon and took the £135,000 first prize with an 18–11 victory over Jimmy White. He had previously won four major titles but all of them were outside the UK, and the Liverpudlian, a professional since 1983, had lost a number of finals in Britain as he strove for that illusive first win. Parrott, managed by Phil Miller, at least had the satisfaction of bringing some silverware to Merseyside following the failure of Liverpool and Everton football clubs in the First Division. However, he didn't enjoy the best of form in the middle of the season and that lack of consistency saw him drop down one place in the world rankings to number 4.

BEST PERFORMANCES
Embassy World Championship:
Winner 1991 (beat Jimmy White 18–11)

Other Ranking Tournaments
Asian Open:
Quarter-finalist 1990 (lost to Tony Chappel 5–3)
Rothmans Grand Prix:
Semi-finalist 1987 (lost to Stephen Hendry 9–7)
Dubai Duty Free Classic:
Semi-finalist 1989 (lost to Doug Mountjoy 5–4)
UK Championship:
Semi-finalist 1986 (lost to Neal Foulds 9–3)
Semi-finalist 1990 (lost to Steve Davis 9–6)
Mercantile Credit Classic:
Runner-up 1988 (lost to Steve Davis 13–11)
Pearl Assurance British Open:
Semi-finalist 1988 (lost to Mike Hallett 9–8)
Semi-finalist 1989 (lost to Dean Reynolds 9–8)
European Open:
Winner 1989 (beat Terry Griffiths 9–8)
Winner 1990 (beat Stephen Hendry 10–6)

Current Non-ranking Tournaments
Benson and Hedges Masters:
Runner-up 1989 (lost to Stephen Hendry 9–6)
Runner-up 1990 (lost to Stephen Hendry 9–4)
Benson and Hedges Irish Masters:
Runner-up 1991 (lost to Steve Davis 9–5)
Coalite World Matchplay:
Runner-up 1988 (lost to Steve Davis 9–5)
Runner-up 1989 (lost to Jimmy White 18–9)
Regal Masters:
Semi-finalist 1989 (lost to Stephen Hendry 6–4)
Other Wins
Junior Pot Black: 1982, 1983
Pontin's Open: 1982, 1986
Pontin's Professional: 1988
Kent China Cup: 1988
Humo Masters: 1990
Norwich Union Grand Prix: 1990

WORLD RANKING POSITIONS

1984/85 20	1987/88 13	1990/91 3
1985/86 18	1988/89 7	1991/92 4
1986/87 17	1989/90 2	

GARY WILKINSON

World ranking: Number 5
Date of birth: 7 April 1966
Star sign: Aries
Turned professional: 1987

Country: England
Prize money 1990/91: £136,250
Biggest pay day: £50,000 – 1991 Pearl Assurance British Open runner-up plus both high-break prizes

Gary Wilkinson, from Kirkby-in-Ashfield, continued a remarkable move up the rankings with a jump of fourteen places to number 5. It has been a superb achievement by a young man who joined the professional ranks only in 1987. He reached the semi-final of the Dubai Duty Free Classic, the last eight of the Mercantile Credit Classic and the Embassy World Championship and the final of the Pearl Assurance British Open. Wilkinson, who earned £136,250, looked a likely winner of the British Open when he led Stephen Hendry 6–3 and 8–6, but inexperience proved his downfall towards the end and allowed Hendry to snatch a 10–9 win. Wilkinson still completed a remarkable rise to the top, considering he was number 39 just two years ago.

BEST PERFORMANCES
Embassy World Championship:
Quarter-finalist 1991 (lost to Jimmy White 13–3)

Other Ranking Tournaments
Asian Open:
Semi-finalist 1989 (lost to Stephen Hendry 5–4)
Rothmans Grand Prix:
Round 5 1987 (lost to Steve Newbury 5–3)
Round 5 1990 (lost to Jimmy White 5–0)
Dubai Duty Free Classic:
Semi-finalist 1990 (lost to Steve Davis 6–4)
UK Championship:
Semi-finalist 1989 (lost to Steve Davis 9–8)
Mercantile Credit Classic:
Quarter-finalist 1991 (lost to Neal Foulds 5–3)
Pearl Assurance British Open:
Runner-up 1991 (lost to Stephen Hendry 10–9)
European Open:
Round 4 1989 (lost to John Parrott 5–2)
Round 4 1991 (lost to Steve Davis 5–0)

Other Wins
No significant wins

WORLD RANKING POSITIONS

1987/88 –	1989/90 39	1991/92 5
1988/89 45	1990/91 19	

Riding high: Gary Wilkinson who leapt fourteen places to number 5 in the world rankings.

NEAL FOULDS

World ranking: Number 6
Date of birth: 13 July 1963
Star sign: Cancer
Turned professional: 1983

Country: England
Prize money 1990/91: £111,750
Biggest pay day: £42,000 – 1987 Dulux British Open runner-up plus high-break prize

Neal Foulds is one of the most popular but toughest players on the £5 million circuit and he must now surely be on the brink of becoming a regular winner. At the start of the 1987/88 season he was ranked number 3, but a loss of form and personal problems saw him slip to number 20 in 1989. Now he has reached number 6 after a solid season that produced a semi-final spot in the Mercantile Credit Classic, three major quarter-finals and a place in the last sixteen of the World Championship where he was edged out 13–12 by eventual runner-up Jimmy White. After his steady accumulation of points, Foulds is now looking for a move into the top four.

BEST PERFORMANCES
Embassy World Championship:
Semi-finalist 1987 (lost to Joe Johnson 16–9)

Other Ranking Tournaments
Asian Open:
Quarter-finalist 1990 (lost to Dennis Taylor 5–4)
Rothmans Grand Prix:
Semi-finalist 1984 (lost to Dennis Taylor 9–3)
Semi-finalist 1986 (lost to Rex Williams 9–8)
Dubai Duty Free Classic:
Round 5 1990 (lost to Stephen Hendry 5–1)
UK Championship:
Runner-up 1986 (lost to Steve Davis 16–7)
Mercantile Credit Classic:
Semi-finalist 1991 (lost to Stephen Hendry 6–4)
Pearl Assurance British Open:
Runner-up 1987 (lost to Jimmy White 13–9)
European Open:
Quarter-finalist 1990 (lost to Stephen Hendry 5–3)
Quarter-finalist 1991 (lost to Cliff Thorburn 5–2)

Current Non-ranking Tournaments
Benson and Hedges Masters:
Semi-finalist 1989 (lost to John Parrott 6–5)
Benson and Hedges Irish Masters:
Runner-up 1988 (lost to Steve Davis 9–4)

Other Wins
British Isles Under-19: 1982
Pontin's Open: 1984
BCE International: 1986
Pontin's Professional: 1987, 1991
Fersina Windows World Cup: 1988, 1989
Dubai Duty Free Masters: 1988

WORLD RANKING POSITIONS

1984/85 30	1987/88 3	1990/91 13
1985/86 23	1988/89 3	1991/92 6
1986/87 13	1989/90 20	

STEVE JAMES

World ranking: Number 7
Date of birth: 2 May 1961
Star sign: Taurus
Turned professional: 1986

Country: England
Prize money 1990/91: £135,681.58
Biggest pay day: £66,000 – 1990 Mercantile Credit Classic winner plus high-break prize

Steve James, who is one of the most exciting and most natural talents in the game, went through another 'in and out' season. James, who suffers from a mild form of diabetes, knows that more consistency could have seen him pull off a place in the top four but he was still happy to move into the top eight for the first time at number 7. He was a semi-finalist in the Rothmans Grand Prix and the Embassy World Championship. In the latter he came from 11–9 down to beat defending champion Stephen Hendry 13–11 after 'the performance of my life', but then crashed 16–9 to Jimmy White with a place in the final at stake. He has had a snooker-room extension built on his house at Cannock and even helped the builders complete their work, arriving for the World Championship with blisters on his hands. He is managed by Blackpool businessman Ramsay McLellan.

Seven up: Steve James continued his climb up the rankings to number 7.

BEST PERFORMANCES
Embassy World Championship:
Semi-finalist 1991 (lost to Jimmy White 16–9)

Other Non-ranking Tournaments
Asian Open:
Round 4 1989 (lost to Steve Duggan 5–3)
Rothmans Grand Prix:
Semi-finalist 1990 (lost to Stephen Hendry 9–5)
Dubai Duty Free Classic:
Round 5 1989 (lost to John Parrott 5–3)
UK Championship:
Round 4 1988 (lost to Cliff Thorburn 9–6)
Round 4 1990 (lost to Tony Knowles 9–7)
Mercantile Credit Classic:
Winner 1990 (beat Warren King 10–6)
Pearl Assurance British Open:
Semi-finalist 1990 (lost to Alex Higgins 9–3)

European Open:
Semi-finalist 1990 (lost to John Parrott 6–3)

Current Non-ranking Tournaments
Benson and Hedges Masters:
Quarter-finalist 1991 (lost to Jimmy White 5–4)
Benson and Hedges Irish Masters:
Quarter-finalist 1991 (lost to Steve Davis 5–3)
World Matchplay:
Round 1 1990 (lost to Terry Griffiths 9–6)

Other Wins
No significant wins

WORLD RANKING POSITIONS

| 1987/88 | 67 | 1989/90 | 16 | 1991/92 | 7 |
| 1988/89 | 32 | 1990/91 | 9 | | |

MIKE HALLETT

World ranking: Number 8
Date of birth: 6 July 1959
Star sign: Cancer
Turned professional: 1979

Country: England
Prize money 1990/91: £171,371.05
Biggest pay day: £50,000 – 1991 Benson and Hedges Masters runner-up

---

Mike Hallett, who married Janet Herring in Grimsby in June, will never forget the 1990/91 season after falling victim to one of the greatest comebacks of all time in the final of the Benson and Hedges Masters at Wembley. He looked a certainty to claim the £100,000 first prize as he led Stephen Hendry (who was going for a hat-trick of

Wedding bells: Janet and Mike Hallett who were married at the end of the 1990/91 season.

Masters titles) 7–0 and 8–2, but in the end suffered a 9–8 reversal. To make matters worse he also discovered on that same fateful day that his house had been burgled. In ranking tournaments he reached the semi-finals of the 555 Asian Open and the Mercantile Credit Classic but was not pleased with his performance in the Embassy World Championship when he was beaten 10–4 by European Open champion Tony Jones in the first round. Hallett, who dropped one place to number 8, did pick up one title as he partnered Hendry to victory in the Black and Decker Men's Doubles at the Mita World Masters in Birmingham.

BEST PERFORMANCES
Embassy World Championship:
Quarter-finalist 1987 (lost to Neal Foulds 13–9)
Quarter-finalist 1989 (lost to Steve Davis 13–3)

Other Ranking Tournaments
Asian Open:
Semi-finalist 1990 (lost to Stephen Hendry 6–1)
Rothmans Grand Prix:
Round 3 (last 16) 1983 (lost to Tony Meo 5–3)
Round 3 (last 16) 1984 (lost to Kirk Stevens 5–3)
Round 5 1986 (lost to Jimmy White 5–3)
Round 5 1988 (lost to Dennis Taylor 5–2)
Round 5 1990 (lost to Neal Foulds 5–2)
Dubai Duty Free Classic:
Quarter-finalist 1990 (lost to Stephen Hendry 5–0)
UK Championship:
Quarter-finalist 1987 (lost to Joe Johnson 9–7)
Quarter-finalist 1989 (lost to Steve Davis 9–5)
Mercantile Credit Classic:
Semi-finalist 1991 (lost to Jimmy White 6–4)
Pearl Assurance British Open:
Runner-up 1988 (lost to Stephen Hendry 13–2)
European Open:
Semi-finalist 1989 (lost to John Parrott 5–4)

Current Non-ranking Tournaments
Benson and Hedges Masters:
Runner-up 1988 (lost to Steve Davis 9–0)
Runner-up 1991 (lost to Stephen Hendry 9–8)
Benson and Hedges Irish Masters:
Quarter-finalist 1989 (lost to Steve Davis 5–4)
World Matchplay:
Quarter-finalist 1988 (lost to Steve Davis 9–2)
Regal Masters:
Quarter-finalist 1989 (lost to Stephen Hendry 6–1)

Other Wins
British Isles Under-16: 1975
Foster's World Doubles: 1987
Foster's Professional: 1988
English Professional: 1989
Hong Kong Open: 1989
Mita World Masters – Black and Decker Men's
Doubles: 1991
Pontin's Open: 1991

WORLD RANKING POSITIONS

1980/81 –	1984/85 25	1988/89 9
1981/82 29	1985/86 28	1989/90 6
1982/83 31	1986/87 27	1990/91 7
1983/84 32	1987/88 16	1991/92 8

DENNIS TAYLOR

World ranking: Number 9
Date of birth: 19 January 1949
Star sign: Capricorn
Turned professional: 1971

Country: Northern Ireland
Prize money 1990/91: £117,097.80
Biggest pay day: £60,000 – 1985 Embassy
world champion

Dennis Taylor, a professional for twenty years, decided to join the Cuemasters stable of Ian Doyle last season and team up with world number 1 Stephen Hendry. Taylor, who has never been lower than number 13 in the rankings, moved up one place to number 9 following yet another consistent season. His best performance was in reaching the final of the 555 Asian Open where he lost 9–3 to Stephen Hendry, and the popular Irishman also made it to the quarter-finals of the Embassy World Championship before losing 13–7 to Steve Davis. Of course, Taylor's most momentous moment came in 1985 when he won the World Championship but there has been a string of other fine victories over the years.

In the soup: Dennis Taylor tries the local food in China. Taylor moved one place up the rankings to number 9.

BEST PERFORMANCES
Embassy World Championship:
Winner 1985 (beat Steve Davis 18–17)

Other Ranking Tournaments
Asian Open:
Runner-up 1990 (lost to Stephen Hendry 9–3)
Rothmans Grand Prix:
Winner 1984 (beat Cliff Thorburn 10–2)
Dubai Duty Free Classic:
Round 3 1990 (lost to Steve Murphy 5–4)
UK Championship:
Semi-finalist 1985 (lost to Willie Thorne 9–7)
Mercantile Credit Classic:
Quarter-finalist 1988 (lost to John Parrott 5–1)
Pearl Assurance British Open:
Quarter-finalist 1985 (lost to Kirk Stevens 5–2)
Quarter-finalist 1987 (lost to Tony Knowles 5–4)
Quarter-finalist 1991 (lost to Stephen Hendry 5–1)
European Open:
Quarter-finalist 1991 (lost to Tony Jones 5–3)

Current Non-ranking Tournaments
Benson and Hedges Masters:
Winner 1987 (beat Alex Higgins 9–8)
Benson and Hedges Irish Masters:
Runner-up 1990 (lost to Steve Davis 9–4)
World Matchplay:
Quarter-finalist 1988 (lost to Stephen Hendry 9–7)
Quarter-finalist 1989 (lost to John Parrott 9–6)
Regal Masters:
Round 1 1989 (lost to John Rea 6–5)

Other Wins
Irish Professional: 1982, 1985, 1986, 1987
Costa del Sol Classic: 1984
Guinness World Cup: 1985
BCE Canadian Masters: 1985
Camus Thailand Masters: 1985
Kit-Kat Break for World Champions: 1985
Winfield Masters: 1986
Car Care Plan World Cup: 1986
Tuborg World Cup: 1987
Carling Challenge: 1987
Labatt Canadian Masters: 1987
Matchroom Trophy: 1987
British Caledonian Tokyo Masters: 1987

WORLD RANKING POSITIONS

1976/77 9	1982/83 13	1987/88 8
1977/78 4	1983/84 13	1988/89 10
1978/79 8	1984/85 11	1989/90 8
1979/80 2	1985/86 4	1990/91 10
1980/81 6	1986/87 3	1991/92 9
1981/82 5		

DOUG MOUNTJOY

World ranking: Number 10
Date of birth: 8 June 1942
Star sign: Gemini
Turned professional: 1976

Country: Wales
Prize money 1990/91: £75,246.05
Biggest pay day: £88,000 – 1988
Tennents UK Open winner plus high-break prize

Doug Mountjoy, who had been a model of consistency in the previous couple of seasons, was not at his best during the 1990/91 campaign and dropped to number 10 in the world rankings. Mountjoy was a disappointed 10–2 first-round loser to Gary Wilkinson in the World Championship though he did manage quarter-final placings in the Dubai Duty Free Classic and the Tulip European Open.

Dropping down: Doug Mountjoy who slipped five places to number 10.

BEST PERFORMANCES
Embassy World Championship:
Runner-up 1981 (lost to Steve Davis 18–12)

Other Ranking Tournaments
Asian Open:
Round 5 1989 (lost to James Wattana 5–2)
Round 5 1990 (lost to Neal Foulds 5–3)
Rothmans Grand Prix:
Quarter-finalist 1984 (lost to Cliff Thorburn 5–3)
Quarter-finalist 1989 (lost to James Wattana 5–2)
Dubai Duty Free Classic:
Runner-up 1989 (lost to Stephen Hendry 9–2)
UK Championship:
Winner 1988 (beat Stephen Hendry 16–12)
Mercantile Credit Classic:
Winner 1989 (beat Wayne Jones 13–11)
Pearl Assurance British Open:
Round 5 1987 (lost to Cliff Thorburn 5–4)
Round 5 1989 (lost to John Parrott 5–2)
Round 5 1990 (lost to Alex Higgins 5–3)
European Open:
Quarter-finalist 1990 (lost to Steve Davis 5–0)
Quarter-finalist 1991 (lost to Brady Gollan 5–2)

Current Non-ranking Tournaments
Benson and Hedges Masters:
Winner 1977 (beat Ray Reardon 7–6)
Benson and Hedges Irish Masters:
Winner 1979 (beat Ray Reardon 6–5)
World Matchplay:
Quarter-finalist 1989 (lost to Jimmy White 9–5)
Regal Masters:
Quarter-finalist 1990 (lost to Jimmy White 6–5)

Other Wins
Welsh Amateur: 1968, 1976
World Amateur: 1976
Pontin's Open: 1974, 1976
Pot Black: 1978, 1985
Coral UK: 1978
Pontin's Professional: 1979, 1983
State Express World Cup: 1979, 1980
Champion of Champions: 1980
Welsh Professional: 1980, 1982, 1984, 1987, 1989
Camus Hong Kong Masters: 1983

WORLD RANKING POSITIONS

1977/78	14	1982/83	7	1987/88	14
1978/79	14	1983/84	12	1988/89	24
1979/80	13	1984/85	15	1989/90	10
1980/81	14	1985/86	15	1990/91	5
1981/82	6	1986/87	14	1991/92	10

TERRY GRIFFITHS

World ranking: Number 11
Date of birth: 16 October 1947
Star sign: Libra
Turned professional: 1978

Country: Wales
Prize money 1990/91: £130,771.05
Biggest pay day: £57,000 – 1988 Embassy
World Championship runner-up

Terry Griffiths enjoyed his best moments of the 1990/91 season away from the ranking tournament circuit, which explains his slip of five places to number 11. He finished runner-up to Stephen Hendry in the Regal Masters in Glasgow for the second successive year and earned semi-final places in the Coalite World Matchplay and the Benson and Hedges Masters. The accumulation of points didn't come easy to Griffiths, though he finished the season in better form with a quarter-final placing in the World Championship before suffering a 13–10 defeat by John Parrott, the eventual champion. Griffiths also reached the last eight of the Mita World Masters where, after a controversial match, he lost 9–8 to Tony Drago.

Going down: Terry Griffiths who has slipped five places to number 11.

BEST PERFORMANCES
Embassy World Championship:
Winner 1979 (beat Dennis Taylor 24–16)

Other Ranking Tournaments
Asian Open:
Semi-finalist 1989 (lost to James Wattana 5–0)
Rothmans Grand Prix:
Quarter-finalist 1982 (lost to Jimmy White 5–2)
Quarter-finalist 1985 (lost to Cliff Thorburn 5–1)
Dubai Duty Free Classic:
Quarter-finalist 1990 (lost to Steve Davis 5–2)
UK Championship:
Semi-finalist 1988 (lost to Doug Mountjoy 9–4)
Semi-finalist 1989 (lost to Stephen Hendry 9–7)
Mercantile Credit Classic:
Quarter-finalist 1984 (lost to Steve Davis 5–4)
Quarter-finalist 1985 (lost to Cliff Thorburn 5–4)
Quarter-finalist 1987 (lost to Jimmy White 5–3)
Quarter-finalist 1988 (lost to Steve Newbury 5–4)
Pearl Assurance British Open:
Quarter-finalist 1986 (lost to Willie Thorne 5–4)
European Open:
Runner-up 1989 (lost to John Parrott 9–8)

Current Non-ranking Tournaments
Benson and Hedges Masters:
Winner 1980 (beat Alex Higgins 9–5)

Benson and Hedges Irish Masters:
Winner 1980 (beat Doug Mountjoy 9–8)
Winner 1981 (beat Ray Reardon 9–7)
Winner 1982 (beat Steve Davis 9–5)
Coalite World Matchplay:
Semi-finalist 1990 (lost to Jimmy White 9–2)
Regal Masters:
Runner-up 1989 (lost to Stephen Hendry 10–1)
Runner-up 1990 (lost to Stephen Hendry 10–6)

Other Wins
Welsh Amateur: 1975
English Amateur: 1977, 1978
State Express World Cup: 1979, 1980
Pontin's Professional: 1981, 1985, 1986
Coral UK: 1982
Lada Classic: 1982
Pontin's Open: 1983
Pot Black: 1984
Welsh Professional: 1985, 1986, 1988
Camus Hong Kong Masters: 1985
BCE Belgian Classic: 1986

WORLD RANKING POSITIONS

1979/80	8	1984/85	8	1988/89	5
1980/81	5	1985/86	8	1989/90	5
1981/82	3	1986/87	10	1990/91	6
1982/83	14	1987/88	6	1991/92	11
1983/84	9				

DEAN REYNOLDS

World ranking: Number 12
Date of birth: 11 January 1963
Star sign: Capricorn
Turned professional: 1981

Country: England
Prize money 1990/91: £76,621.05
Biggest pay day: £42,000 – 1989 Anglian Windows British Open runner-up; 1989 Rothmans Grand Prix runner-up

The highlight of a disappointing season for Dean Reynolds came in the Dubai Duty Free Classic when he reached the semi-final before going down 6–1 to Stephen Hendry. Otherwise Reynolds could not regularly repeat the performances that made him such a dangerous competitor twelve months earlier and he dropped four places to number 12. He was desperately unlucky in the Coalite World Matchplay when he lost 9–8 to Hendry in the quarter-final, but there was controversy in the Benson and Hedges Irish Masters when he was docked one frame for arriving late and later admitted that he had a 'drink problem'. Reynolds' World Championship hopes were ended 13–12 by Steve James in the second round. Reynolds became a father for the first time last season when his wife Joanne presented him with a son, Dean Jnr.

Troubled season: Dean Reynolds who dropped four places to number 12.

BEST PERFORMANCES
Embassy World Championship:
Quarter-finalist 1989 (lost to Tony Meo 13–9)

Other Ranking Tournaments
Asian Open:
Round 4 1989 (lost to Wayne Jones 5–2)
Round 4 1990 (lost to Tony Chappel 5–3)
Rothmans Grand Prix:
Runner-up 1989 (lost to Steve Davis 10–0)
Dubai Duty Free Classic:
Semi-finalist 1990 (lost to Stephen Hendry 6–1)
UK Championship:
Round 5 1986 (lost to Steve Davis 9–5)
Round 5 1988 (lost to Terry Griffiths 9–6)
Round 5 1989 (lost to Stephen Hendry 9–8)
Mercantile Credit Classic:
Semi-finalist 1987 (lost to Jimmy White 9–8)
Pearl Assurance British Open:
Runner-up 1989 (lost to Tony Meo 13–6)
European Open:
Round 5 1991 (lost to Dene O'Kane 5–4)

Current Non-ranking Tournaments
Benson and Hedges Masters:
Round 1 (last 16) 1983 (lost to Ray Reardon 5–1)
Round 1 (last 16) 1988 (lost to Steve Davis 5–2)
Round 2 1991 (lost to Tony Meo 5–2)
Benson and Hedges Irish Masters:
Round 1 1991 (lost to Steve James 5–2)
World Matchplay:
Semi-finalist 1989 (lost to Jimmy White 9–8)

Other Wins
British Isles Under-19: 1981
Junior Pot Black: 1981
English Professional: 1988

WORLD RANKING POSITIONS

1982/83 22	1986/87 29	1989/90 15
1983/84 19	1987/88 15	1990/91 8
1984/85 22	1988/89 22	1991/92 12
1985/86 24		

ALAIN ROBIDOUX

World ranking: Number 13
Date of birth: 25 July 1960
Star sign: Leo
Turned professional: 1986 (earned full status 1988)

Country: Canada
Prize money 1990/91: £50,775
Biggest pay day: £19,500 – 1988
Rothmans Grand Prix semi-finalist

Alain Robidoux, a French-speaking Canadian from Montreal, has now taken over the mantle of Canada's top player and is comfortably established in the top sixteen at number 13. A former Canadian champion, he is slowly but surely gaining a reputation as one of snooker's hardest men to beat. Even so, Robidoux knows he could have done better on the ranking tournament circuit last season, and in the World Championship he lost 13–8 to Stephen Hendry in the second round. In the Pearl Assurance British Open, he came through to the quarter-final but suffered a 5–3 defeat at the hands of Jimmy White.

BEST PERFORMANCES
Embassy World Championship:
Round 2 1991 (lost to Stephen Hendry 13–8)

Other Ranking Tournaments
Asian Open:
Round 3 1990 (lost to Joe O'Boye 5–4)
Rothmans Grand Prix:
Semi-finalist 1988 (lost to Alex Higgins 9–7)
Dubai Duty Free Classic:
Round 4 1989 (lost to Nigel Bond 5–4)
Round 4 1990 (lost to Stephen Hendry 5–1)
UK Championship:
Quarter-finalist 1989 (lost to Terry Griffiths 9–2)

Mercantile Credit Classic:
Round 4 1991 (lost to Alan McManus 5–3)
Pearl Assurance British Open:
Quarter-finalist 1991 (lost to Jimmy White 5–3)
European Open:
Round 5 1989 (lost to Terry Griffiths 5–3)

Other Wins
Canadian Amateur: 1983, 1985, 1987
Canadian Professional: 1988
British Car Rental World Cup: 1990

WORLD RANKING POSITIONS
1988/89	102	1990/91	16
1989/90	35	1991/92	13

Canadian cracker: Alain Robidoux who moved three places up the rankings to number 13.

MARTIN CLARK

World ranking: Number 14
Date of birth: 27 October 1968
Star sign: Scorpio
Turned professional: 1987

Country: England
Prize money 1990/91: £62,525
Biggest pay day: £11,250 – 1990 Pearl
Assurance British Open quarter-finalist

Martin Clark, a professional since 1987, failed to maintain his steady move up the snooker rankings and slipped down two places to number 14. He regularly picked up a point in the ranking tournaments but reached the last sixteen on only two occasions – in the Dubai Duty Free Classic and the Embassy World Championship. He was disappointed with his debut in the Benson and Hedges Masters when he lost 5–1 to Jimmy White in the second round, but he did reach the quarter-final of the Coalite World Matchplay before losing 9–5 to Steve Davis.

Trophy time: Martin Clark, who dropped to number 14, enjoyed his first professional tournament win in the European Grand Masters.

BEST PERFORMANCES
Embassy World Championship:
Round 2 1991 (lost to Gary Wilkinson 13–9)

Other Ranking Tournaments
Asian Open:
Quarter-finalist 1989 (lost to Gary Wilkinson 5–0)
Rothmans Grand Prix:
Round 4 1987 (lost to Mick Fisher 5–4)
Round 4 1989 (lost to Tony Knowles 5–2)
Round 4 1990 (lost to Alain Robidoux 5–3)
Dubai Duty Free Classic:
Round 5 1989 (lost to Danny Fowler 5–3)
Round 5 1990 (lost to Doug Mountjoy 5–0)
UK Championship:
Round 4 1988 (lost to Danny Fowler 9–6)
Round 4 1989 (lost to Joe Johnson 9–6)
Mercantile Credit Classic:
Quarter-finalist 1989 (lost to Willie Thorne 5–4)
Pearl Assurance British Open:
Quarter-finalist 1989 (lost to Mike Hallett 5–3)
Quarter-finalist 1990 (lost to Alex Higgins 5–3)
European Open:
Quarter-finalist 1989 (lost to Terry Griffiths 5–1)

Current Non-ranking Tournaments
Benson and Hedges Masters:
Round 2 1991 (lost to Jimmy White 5–1)
World Matchplay:
Quarter-finalist 1990 (lost to Steve Davis 9–5)

Other Wins
British Isles Under-19: 1984
European Grand Masters: 1990

WORLD RANKING POSITIONS

| 1988/89 | 41 | 1990/91 | 12 |
| 1989/90 | 17 | 1991/92 | 14 |

TONY JONES

World ranking: Number 15
Date of birth: 15 April 1960
Star sign: Aries
Turned professional: 1983

Country: England
Prize money 1990/91: £69,600
Biggest pay day: £35,000 – 1991 Tulip
European Open champion

Tony Jones produced one of the best performances of the 1990/91 season when, against all the odds, he captured the Tulip European Open title in Rotterdam with a 9–7 final defeat of Mark Johnston-Allen. The European Open produced a series of shock results as Jones beat Alain Robidoux, Darren Morgan, Steve James, Dennis Taylor and Brady Gollan on his way to the final. That victory earned him 6 points and completed a remarkable end of season run that saw him jump twenty places to number 15. Jones was a quarter-finalist in the Pearl Assurance British Open, while he reached the last sixteen of the Embassy World Championship. In the first round of the World Championship, he had enjoyed an excellent 10–4 victory over Mike Hallett. He is a member of Mark McCormack's International Management Group stable and last season earned the most money of his career.

Jones the cue: Tony Jones who won the Tulip European Open and moved into the top sixteen at number 15.

BEST PERFORMANCES
Embassy World Championship:
Round 2 1991 (lost to Dennis Taylor 13–8)

Other Ranking Tournaments
Asian Open:
Quarter-finalist 1989 (lost to Terry Griffiths 5–3)
Rothmans Grand Prix:
Round 5 1989 (lost to Tony Knowles 5–4)
Dubai Duty Free Classic:
Round 4 1989 (lost to Danny Fowler 5–4)
UK Championship:
Round 1 (last 32) 1984 (lost to Alex Higgins 9–7)
Round 4 1986 (lost to Tony Knowles 9–2)
Round 4 1989 (lost to Terry Griffiths 9–8)
Round 4 1990 (lost to John Parrott 9–3)

Mercantile Credit Classic:
Fourth qualifying round 1985 (lost to Silvino Francisco 5–1)
Round 4 1986 (lost to Bill Werbeniuk 5–3)
Pearl Assurance British Open:
Quarter-finalist 1991 (lost to Gary Wilkinson 5–3)
European Open:
Winner 1991 (beat Mark Johnston-Allen 9–7)

Other Wins
English Amateur: 1983

WORLD RANKING POSITIONS

1983/84 –	1986/87 55	1989/90 62
1984/85 –	1987/88 46	1990/91 35
1985/86 50	1988/89 49	1991/92 16

TONY KNOWLES

World ranking: Number 16
Date of birth: 13 June 1955
Star sign: Gemini
Turned professional: 1980

Country: England
Prize money 1990/91: £44,250
Biggest pay day: £18,000 – 1987 Dulux
British Open semi-finalist

Tony Knowles slipped down to number 21 in the world rankings at the start of the 1990/91 season and there were many people in the game who thought he might never regain his place in the top sixteen. Knowles, who was number 2 in 1984, proved the doubters wrong and this fluent potter climbed five places to number 16. He has always had extraordinary belief in his own ability and showed it by being a quarter-finalist in the UK Championship and then securing the points he needed for that top-sixteen place by going through to the second round of the Embassy World Championship. Unfortunately, he could not maintain his form and suffered a 13–1 defeat at the hands of the eventual world champion, John Parrott. Knowles has never shied away from commenting on what he considers to be inadequacies in the game and now, at the age of thirty-six, will be looking for a move back into the top ten.

Back in the limelight: Tony Knowles returns to the top sixteen at number 16.

BEST PERFORMANCES
Embassy World Championship:
Semi-finalist 1983 (lost to Cliff Thorburn 16–15)
Semi-finalist 1985 (lost to Dennis Taylor 16–5)
Semi-finalist 1986 (lost to Joe Johnson 16–8)

Other Ranking Tournaments
Asian Open:
Round 5 1989 (lost to Silvino Francisco 5–2)
Rothmans Grand Prix:
Winner 1983 (beat Joe Johnson 9–8)
Dubai Duty Free Classic:
Round 4 1990 (lost to Doug Mountjoy 5–3)
UK Championship:
Quarter-finalist 1984 (lost to Kirk Stevens 9–7)
Quarter-finalist 1985 (lost to Jimmy White 9–4)
Quarter-finalist 1990 (lost to John Parrott 9–7)
Mercantile Credit Classic:
Semi-finalist 1988 (lost to John Parrott 9–4)
Pearl Assurance British Open:
Semi-finalist 1987 (lost to Neal Foulds 9–2)
European Open:
Round 4 1991 (lost to Willie Thorne 5–2)

Current Non-ranking Tournaments
Benson and Hedges Masters:
Semi-finalist 1984 (lost to Terry Griffiths 6–4)
Semi-finalist 1986 (lost to Cliff Thorburn 6–4)
Benson and Hedges Irish Masters:
Semi-finalist 1985 (lost to Jimmy White 6–4)
World Matchplay:
Round 1 1988 (lost to Dennis Taylor 9–7)

Other Wins
British Isles Under-19: 1972, 1974
Pontin's Autumn Open: 1979
BCE International: 1982
State Express World Team Classic: 1983
Winfield Masters: 1984

WORLD RANKING POSITIONS

1981/82	20	1985/86	3	1989/90	12
1982/83	15	1986/87	4	1990/91	21
1983/84	4	1987/88	7	1991/92	16
1984/85	2	1988/89	8		

WILLIE THORNE

World ranking: Number 17
Date of birth: 4 March 1954
Star sign: Pisces
Turned professional: 1975

Country: England
Prize money 1990/91: £71,925
Biggest pay day: £50,000 – 1986
Matchroom Trophy champion

Willie Thorne was understandably upset after he lost his place in the top sixteen following his 10–8 first-round defeat by Alan McManus in the Embassy World Championship. Thorne had been an ever-present in the top sixteen since 1984, but his failure to get past the last sixteen of any ranking tournament lost him his place. He has also had problems off the table with self-admitted financial worries and the breakdown of his marriage. Gary Lineker, the England soccer captain, is one of Thorne's great pals and there is often a group of top footballers present when Thorne is in action.

Out of form: World number 17 Willie Thorne who dropped out of the top sixteen for the first time since 1984.

BEST PERFORMANCES
Embassy World Championship:
Quarter-finalist 1982 (lost to Alex Higgins 13–10)
Quarter-finalist 1986 (lost to Cliff Thorburn 13–6)

Other Ranking Tournaments
Asian Open:
Quarter-finalist 1989 (lost to Stephen Hendry 5–2)
Rothmans Grand Prix:
Semi-finalist 1983 (lost to Tony Knowles 9–7)
Dubai Duty Free Classic:
Round 4 1990 (lost to Darren Morgan 5–2)
UK Championship:
Runner-up 1985 (lost to Steve Davis 16–14)
Mercantile Credit Classic:
Winner 1985 (beat Cliff Thorburn 13–8)
Pearl Assurance British Open:
Runner-up 1986 (lost to Steve Davis 12–7)
European Open:
Round 5 1989 (lost to Jimmy White 5–3)
Round 5 1991 (lost to Doug Mountjoy 5–4)

Current Non-ranking Tournaments
Benson and Hedges Masters:
Quarter-finalist 1986 (lost to Steve Davis 5–4)
Quarter-finalist 1987 (lost to Cliff Thorburn 5–3)
Quarter-finalist 1990 (lost to Stephen Hendry 5–1)
Benson and Hedges Irish Masters:
Runner-up 1986 (lost to Jimmy White 9–5)
Runner-up 1987 (lost to Steve Davis 9–1)
World Matchplay:
Round 1 1988 (lost to Mike Hallett 9–8)
Round 1 1989 (lost to Doug Mountjoy 9–2)

Other Wins
British Isles Under-16: 1970
British Isles Under-19: 1973
Pontin's Open: 1980
Pontin's Professional: 1984
Camus Hong Kong Masters: 1986
Matchroom Trophy: 1986
Kent China Cup: 1987
Lion Brown Masters: 1989

WORLD RANKING POSITIONS

1976/77 –	1982/83 16	1987/88 11
1977/78 20	1983/84 18	1988/89 13
1978/79 15	1984/85 12	1989/90 9
1979/80 17	1985/86 11	1990/91 11
1980/81 19	1986/87 7	1991/92 17
1981/82 22		

DENE O'KANE

World ranking: Number 18
Date of birth: 24 February 1963
Star sign: Pisces
Turned professional: 1984

Country: New Zealand
Prize money 1990/91: £28,625
Biggest pay day: £25,000 – 1989 Hong Kong
Open runner-up plus high-break prize

Dene O'Kane, New Zealand's only snooker professional, has now achieved his highest placing in the world rankings at number 18 following another solid season. He reached the last sixteen of the Rothmans Grand Prix and the Mercantile Credit Classic and went one stage further in the Tulip Euro-pean Open where he was beaten 5–2 by Mark Johnston-Allen, the eventual runner-up. However, O'Kane's hopes of moving into the top sixteen ended when he failed to qualify for the World Championship after a 10–7 defeat by Ian Graham in the fifth and final qualifying round.

BEST PERFORMANCES
Embassy World Championship:
Quarter-finalist 1987 (lost to Jimmy White 13–6)

Other Ranking Tournaments
Asian Open:
Round 4 1989 (lost to John Virgo 5–3)
Round 4 1990 (lost to Neal Foulds 5–0)
Rothmans Grand Prix:
Round 5 1990 (lost to John Parrott 5–2)
Dubai Duty Free Classic:
Round 4 1989 (lost to Alex Higgins 5–3)
Round 4 1990 (lost to Martin Clark 5–1)
UK Championship:
Round 5 1987 (lost to Willie Thorne 9–7)
Mercantile Credit Classic:
Quarter-finalist 1990 (lost to Silvino Francisco 5–4)
Pearl Assurance British Open:
Quarter-finalist 1985 (lost to Steve Davis 5–1)
Quarter-finalist 1988 (lost to John Parrott 5–2)
European Open:
Quarter-finalist 1991 (lost to Mark Johnston-Allen 5–2)

Other Wins
New Zealand Amateur: 1980

WORLD RANKING POSITIONS

1985/86 32	1988/89 24	1990/91 23
1986/87 39	1989/90 28	1991/92 18
1987/88 35		

Tucking in: Dene O'Kane who comes into the top twenty for the first time at number 18.

PETER FRANCISCO

World ranking: Number 19
Date of birth: 14 February 1962
Star sign: Aquarius
Turned professional: 1984

Country: South Africa
Prize money 1990/91: £48,250
Biggest pay day: £18,000 – 1987
Rothmans Grand Prix semi-finalist

Peter Francisco continued to enjoy better fortunes on the pro tour and is now nicely poised for a return to the top sixteen – a position he occupied in 1988/89. A steady flow of points earned him a five-place jump to number 19, with his best performance coming in the Rothmans Grand Prix where he reached the last eight before losing 5–0 to Stephen Hendry, the eventual winner. Francisco was disappointed in the World Championship when he failed to qualify for the final stages. In the final qualifying round he led Robert Marshall 8–4 after scoring two centuries but lost 10–9. Francisco also revealed during the season that he had felt like quitting snooker when injury and illness affected his career a couple of years ago but was persuaded to keep going following a phone call to his father, Mannie, in South Africa.

On the move: South African Peter Francisco continued his upward climb to number 19.

BEST PERFORMANCES
Embassy World Championship:
Round 1 1988 (lost to Willie Thorne 10–6)
Round 1 1989 (lost to Dean Reynolds 10–7)
Round 1 1990 (lost to Dean Reynolds 10–7)

Other Ranking Tournaments
Asian Open:
Round 5 1989 (lost to Gary Wilkinson 5–4)
Rothmans Grand Prix:
Semi-finalist 1987 (lost to Dennis Taylor 9–4)
Dubai Duty Free Classic:
Quarter-finalist 1989 (lost to John Parrott 5–1)
UK Championship:
Round 5 1989 (lost to Mark Bennett 9–3)
Mercantile Credit Classic:
Round 5 1986 (lost to Steve Davis 5–0)
Round 5 1987 (lost to Silvino Francisco 5–1)
Round 5 1988 (lost to Dennis Taylor 5–3)

Round 5 1990 (lost to Steve Newbury 5–3)
Pearl Assurance British Open:
Quarter-finalist 1989 (lost to Tony Meo 5–3)
European Open:
Round 5 1991 (lost to Brady Gollan 5–2)

Current Non-ranking Tournaments
Benson and Hedges Masters:
Round 1 1989 (lost to Neal Foulds 5–2)
World Matchplay:
Round 1 1988 (lost to Terry Griffiths 9–7)

Other Wins
South African Amateur: 1981, 1982, 1983

WORLD RANKING POSITIONS

1985/86 59	1988/89 14	1990/91 24
1986/87 26	1989/90 25	1991/92 19
1987/88 18		

JAMES WATTANA

World ranking: Number 20
Date of birth: 17 January 1970
Star sign: Capricorn
Turned professional: 1989

Country: Thailand
Prize money 1990/91: £116,250
Biggest pay day: £30,000 – 1991 Mita
World Masters – Black and Decker
Men's Singles semi-finalist

Most players would be happy with reaching number 20 in the world rankings after just two seasons on the cut-throat professional circuit, but James Wattana was disappointed with his failure to go even higher. This former world amateur champion, one of the greatest natural talents in the game, was prepared for a big push towards the top sixteen after rising to number 32 in his first season. In that season he reached the final of the 555 Asian Open and the semifinal of the Rothmans Grand Prix, but last season he failed to progress past the last sixteen of any ranking tournament. He was particularly disappointed in the Embassy World Championship when he failed to qualify after a 10–8 defeat by outsider Craig Edwards. Wattana's best moment of the season – indeed of his professional career so far – came in the non-ranking 555 World Series Challenge in Hong Kong, when he beat Jimmy White 9–3 in the final to take the £20,000 first prize. Many observers felt it was one of the most complete performances of the season.

Maximum man: James Wattana who scored a maximum 147 during the Mita World Masters and finished the season at number 20.

BEST PERFORMANCES
Embassy World Championship:
Fifth qualifying round 1990 (lost to Alex Higgins 10–6)
Fifth qualifying round 1991 (lost to Craig Edwards 10–8)

Other Ranking Tournaments
Asian Open:
Runner-up 1989 (lost to Stephen Hendry 9–6)
Rothmans Grand Prix:
Semi-finalist 1989 (lost to Dean Reynolds 9–8)
Dubai Duty Free Classic:
Round 4 1989 (lost to John Parrott 5–3)
Round 4 1990 (lost to Dean Reynolds 5–3)
UK Championship:
Round 5 1990 (lost to Jimmy White 9–7)
Mercantile Credit Classic:
Round 5 1991 (lost to Gary Wilkinson 5–2)

Pearl Assurance British Open:
Round 5 1991 (lost to Gary Wilkinson 5–2)
European Open:
Round 4 1991 (lost to Brady Gollan 5–3)

Current Non-ranking Tournaments
Benson and Hedges Masters:
Round 1 1990 (lost to Steve Davis 5–2)

Other Wins
Camus Masters: 1986
Asian Amateur: 1986, 1988
World Amateur: 1988
555 World Series Challenge: 1990

WORLD RANKING POSITIONS

1989/90	1990/91	1991/92
–	32	20

NIGEL BOND

World ranking: Number 21
Date of birth: 15 November 1965
Star sign: Scorpio
Turned professional: 1989

Country: England
Prize money 1990/91: £84,906.58
Biggest pay day: £40,000 – 1990
Rothmans Grand Prix runner-up

Nigel Bond, a former English amateur champion from Darley Dale in Derbyshire, has reached number 21 in the world rankings after just two seasons. Even so, after a brilliant start to the 1990/91 season, he finished with a disappointing run and lost his chance of going into the top sixteen. The highlight of his season was a final place in the Rothmans Grand Prix where he led stablemate Stephen Hendry 5–3 only to lose 10–5. A quarter-final place in the StormSeal UK Championship gave him 10 points from four tournaments, but then he failed to score a single point in the second half of the season and didn't qualify for the first round of the World Championship after a 10–8 defeat by Joe Johnson.

BEST PERFORMANCES
Embassy World Championship:
Fifth qualifying round 1990 (lost to Steve Newbury 10–6)
Fifth qualifying round 1991 (lost to Joe Johnson 10–8)

Other Ranking Tournaments
Asian Open:
Round 5 1990 (lost to Dennis Taylor 5–1)
Rothmans Grand Prix:
Runner-up 1990 (lost to Stephen Hendry 10–5)
Dubai Duty Free Classic:
Round 5 1989 (lost to Peter Francisco 5–4)
UK Championship:
Quarter-finalist 1990 (lost to Steve Davis 9–7)

Mercantile Credit Classic:
Round 2 1990 (lost to Colin Roscoe 5–4)
Round 2 1991 (lost to Alan McManus 5–2)
Pearl Assurance British Open:
Round 2 1990 (lost to Tony Chappel 5–4)
Round 2 1991 (lost to Ken Doherty 5–4)
European Open:
Quarter-finalist 1990 (lost to John Parrott 5–3)

Current Non-ranking Tournaments
Benson and Hedges Irish Masters:
Quarter-finalist 1991 (lost to John Parrott 5–3)

Other Wins
English Amateur: 1989

WORLD RANKING POSITIONS

1989/90	–	1990/91	38	1991/92	21

TONY DRAGO

World ranking: Number 22
Date of birth: 22 September 1965
Star sign: Virgo
Turned professional: 1985

Country: Malta
Prize money 1990/91: £104,750
Biggest pay day: £70,000 – 1991 Mita World Masters – Black and Decker Men's Singles runner-up

Tony Drago, the world number 20 three years ago, has now started to climb back to snooker's higher echelons after being in the doldrums at number 30 for two successive seasons. He scored in six of the world ranking tournaments and reached the quarter-final of the Mercantile Credit Classic before losing a superb match 5–4 to Stephen Hendry. However, the highlight of Drago's season came in the £1 million Mita

'Thanks, pals': Tony Drago and his friends who flew over from Malta to support him in the final of the Mita World Masters.

BEST PERFORMANCES
Embassy World Championship:
Quarter-finalist 1988 (lost to Steve Davis 13–4)

Other Ranking Tournaments
Asian Open:
Round 5 1989 (lost to Terry Griffiths 5–3)
Rothmans Grand Prix:
Round 5 1985 (lost to Cliff Wilson 5–2)
Round 5 1987 (lost to Willie Thorne 5–2)
Dubai Duty Free Classic:
Round 5 1989 (lost to Stephen Hendry 5–3)
UK Championship:
Quarter-finalist 1986 (lost to Steve Davis 9–8)
Mercantile Credit Classic:
Quarter-finalist 1991 (lost to Stephen Hendry 5–4)
Pearl Assurance British Open:
Round 5 1991 (lost to Alain Robidoux 5–0)
European Open:
Round 3 1989 (lost to Mark Bennett 5–1)
Round 3 1990 (lost to Nigel Bond 5–2)
Round 3 1991 (lost to Nigel Gilbert 5–2)

Other Wins
Malta Amateur: 1984

WORLD RANKING POSITIONS

1986/87 37	1988/89 20	1990/91 30
1987/88 32	1989/90 30	1991/92 22

World Masters where he beat John Campbell, Tony Jones, John Parrott, Gary Wilkinson, Terry Griffiths and Darren Morgan on his way to the final. Unfortunately he lost 10–6 to Jimmy White but still collected £70,000 on the biggest pay day of his career since he joined the paid ranks in 1985. Already a world record holder for the fastest frame victory of three minutes, Drago became the fastest match winner when he needed just eighty-one minutes – an average of nine minutes per frame – to beat Joe O'Boye 9–0 in the third round of the UK Championship.

STEVE NEWBURY

World ranking: Number 23
Date of birth: 21 April 1956
Star sign: Taurus
Turned professional: 1984

Country: Wales
Prize money 1990/91: £28,650
Biggest pay day: £15,000 – 1988
Mercantile Credit Classic semi-finalist

Steve Newbury was certainly disappointed with his 1990/91 season after collecting only 5 ranking points and failing to progress past the last thirty-two of any ranking tournament. That meagre collection of points meant a drop of three places for the Welshman, though he did qualify for the first round proper of the Embassy World Championship only to lose 10–5 to Canadian Alain Robidoux. Newbury, who hails from Neath, is a talented performer and will be keen to reverse his slide in fortunes this season.

Slipping back: Steve Newbury of Wales dropped three places to number 23.

BEST PERFORMANCES
Embassy World Championship:
Round 1 1989 (lost to Steve Davis 10–5)
Round 1 1990 (lost to Mike Hallett 10–9)
Round 1 1991 (lost to Alain Robidoux 10–5)

Other Ranking Tournaments
Asian Open:
Round 3 1989 (lost to Steve Duggan 5–3)
Round 3 1990 (lost to Murdo Macleod 5–4)
Rothmans Grand Prix:
Quarter-finalist 1987 (lost to Dennis Taylor 5–2)
Dubai Duty Free Classic:
Round 4 1990 (lost to Neal Foulds 5–2)
UK Championship:
Round 4 1990 (lost to Alan McManus 9–3)

Mercantile Credit Classic:
Semi-finalist 1988 (lost to Steve Davis 9–2)
Pearl Assurance British Open:
Quarter-finalist 1990 (lost to Robert Marshall 5–4)
European Open:
Round 4 1990 (lost to Stephen Hendry 5–1)

Other Wins
Welsh Amateur: 1980

WORLD RANKING POSITIONS

1985/86 34	1988/89 25	1990/91 20
1986/87 40	1989/90 19	1991/92 23
1987/88 45		

SILVINO FRANCISCO

World ranking: Number 24
Date of birth: 3 May 1946
Star sign: Taurus
Turned professional: 1978

Country: South Africa
Prize money 1990/91: £37,150
Biggest pay day: £50,000 – 1985 Dulux
British Open champion

Silvino Francisco enjoyed a solid season as he collected 8 ranking points and moved two places up the rankings to number 24. He was, however, disappointed at not being permitted to play in the fifth round of the 555 Asian Open in Guangzhou because the Chinese authorities would not allow him to enter the country as a result of his South African passport. In the World Championship, Francisco failed to negotiate the fifth and final qualifying round when he lost 10–6 to Tony Jones, the European Open champion.

BEST PERFORMANCES
Embassy World Championship:
Quarter-finalist 1982 (lost to Ray Reardon 13–8)

Other Ranking Tournaments
Asian Open:
Quarter-finalist 1989 (lost to James Wattana 5–2)
Rothmans Grand Prix:
Semi-finalist 1986 (lost to Jimmy White 9–6)
Dubai Duty Free Classic:
Round 5 1990 (lost to Gary Wilkinson 5–2)
UK Championship:
Round 5 1985 (lost to Terry Griffiths 9–5)
Round 5 1987 (lost to Terry Griffiths 9–3)
Round 5 1990 (lost to Alan McManus 9–4)
Mercantile Credit Classic:
Semi-finalist 1990 (lost to Warren King 6–5)
Pearl Assurance British Open:
Winner 1985 (beat Kirk Stevens 12–9)

European Open:
Round 4 1990 (lost to Mark Bennett 5–3)

Current Non-ranking Tournaments
Benson and Hedges Masters:
Quarter-finalist 1987 (lost to Dennis Taylor 5–3)

Other Wins
South African Amateur: 1968, 1969, 1974, 1977
South African Professional: 1985, 1986

WORLD RANKING POSITIONS

1979/80 –	1984/85 17	1988/89 12
1980/81 –	1985/86 13	1989/90 23
1981/82 –	1986/87 12	1990/91 26
1982/83 17	1987/88 10	1991/92 24
1983/84 21		

WAYNE JONES

World ranking: Number 25
Date of birth: 24 December 1959
Star sign: Capricorn
Turned professional: 1984

Country: Wales
Prize money 1990/91: £33,625
Biggest pay day: £38,000 – 1989
Mercantile Credit Classic runner-up plus
high-break prize

Wayne Jones didn't progress past the last sixteen of any tournament last season and that meant a drop of three places to number 25. The unassuming Welshman also failed in his bid to reach the first round proper of the Embassy World Championship when he was beaten 10–8 by fellow countryman Mark Bennett. Jones knows that he must improve if he is to achieve his aim of reaching the top sixteen.

BEST PERFORMANCES
Embassy World Championship:
Round 2 1989 ?(lost to Dean Reynolds 13–9)

Other Ranking Tournaments
Asian Open:
Round 5 1989 (lost to Stephen Hendry 5–0)
Rothmans Grand Prix:
Round 4 1985 (lost to Peter Francisco 5–3)
Round 4 1986 (lost to Silvino Francisco 5–4)
Round 4 1988 (lost to Jimmy White 5–1)
Round 4 1990 (lost to Mike Hallett 5–2)
Dubai Duty Free Classic:
Round 4 1989 (lost to Barry West 5–2)
Round 4 1990 (lost to Mike Hallett 5–2)
UK Championship:
Quarter-finalist 1986 (lost to Alex Higgins 9–5)

Mercantile Credit Classic:
Runner-up 1989 (lost to Doug Mountjoy 13–11)
Pearl Assurance British Open:
Round 2 (last 32) 1985 (lost to Bob Chaperon 5–2)
European Open:
Round 5 1990 (lost to John Parrott 5–0)

Other Wins
British Isles Under-16: 1976
Welsh Amateur: 1983

WORLD RANKING POSITIONS

1985/86 49	1988/89 34	1990/91 22
1986/87 56	1989/90 31	1991/92 25
1987/88 34		

JOE JOHNSON

World ranking: Number 26
Date of birth: 29 July 1952
Star sign: Leo
Turned professional: 1979

Country: England
Prize money 1990/91: £52,500
Biggest pay day: £70,000 – 1986 Embassy world champion

Happier days: Joe Johnson before he suffered a heart attack.

BEST PERFORMANCES
Embassy World Championship:
Winner 1986 (beat Steve Davis 18–12)

Other Ranking Tournaments
Asian Open:
Round 4 1989 (lost to Tony Drago 5–2)
Rothmans Grand Prix:
Runner-up 1983 (lost to Tony Knowles 9–8)
Dubai Duty Free Classic:
Round 3 1989 (lost to Nigel Bond 5–3)
Round 3 1990 (lost to Jim Wych 5–1)
UK Championship:
Semi-finalist 1987 (lost to Jimmy White 9–4)
Mercantile Credit Classic:
Semi-finalist 1985 (lost to Cliff Thorburn 9–2)
Pearl Assurance British Open:
Quarter-finalist 1989 (lost to Dean Reynolds 5–4)
European Open:
Round 5 1989 (lost to Martin Clark 5–4)
Round 5 1990 (lost to John Parrott 5–2)

Current Non-ranking Tournaments
Benson and Hedges Masters:
Semi-finalist 1988 (lost to Steve Davis 6–3)
Benson and Hedges Irish Masters:
Quarter-finalist 1987 (lost to Terry Griffiths 5–0)
Quarter-finalist 1988 (lost to Steve Davis 5–0)
World Matchplay:
Quarter-finalist 1988 (lost to John Parrott 9–7)

Other Wins
British Isles Under-19: 1971
Langs Supreme Scottish Masters: 1987
Norwich Union Grand Prix: 1989
Nescafe Extra: 1991

WORLD RANKING POSITIONS

1980/81 –	1984/85 19	1988/89 11
1981/82 –	1985/86 16	1989/90 11
1982/83 –	1986/87 8	1990/91 17
1983/84 23	1987/88 5	1991/92 26

Joe Johnson's poor start to the 1990/91 season meant that, despite a better second half to the campaign, he dropped nine places to number 26. Johnson picked up 7 late points, including 1 point in the Embassy World Championship where he reached the first round before losing 10–6 to Dennis Taylor. However, Johnson, one of the game's most popular players, tragically suffered a heart attack at the end of the season and, at the time of writing, his career was in the balance. The highlight of Johnson's career came in 1986 when he beat Steve Davis 18–12 in the World Championship final.

EDDIE CHARLTON

World ranking: Number 27
Date of birth: 31 October 1929
Star sign: Scorpio
Turned professional: 1960

Country: Australia
Prize money 1990/91: £27,750
Biggest pay day: £8,333.33 – 1988 Fersina Windows World Team Cup runner-up

---

Eddie Charlton, sixty-two, is a snooker phenomenon and has once again kept his place in the world's top thirty-two with a jump of four places to number 27. He reached the last sixteen of the 555 Asian Open and the Mercantile Credit Classic and once again qualified for the first round of the Embassy World Championship where he lost 10–7 to Neal Foulds. A professional since 1960, he has enjoyed a glittering career but has never captured a major snooker title, though he has twice featured in World Championship finals only to lose on both occasions – in 1973 and 1975. Last season Charlton, a cue sports all-rounder, joined the professional pool-playing ranks and he is also a very accomplished billiards player.

Travelling man: Globe-trotting Eddie Charlton meets up with a local official during the 555 Asian Open in Guangzhou.

BEST PERFORMANCES
Embassy World Championship:
Runner-up 1973 (lost to Ray Reardon 38–32)
Runner-up 1975 (lost to Ray Reardon 31–30)

Other Ranking Tournaments
Asian Open:
Round 5 1990 (lost to Les Dodd 5–2)
Rothmans Grand Prix:
Semi-finalist 1982 (lost to Ray Reardon 10–7)
Dubai Duty Free Classic:
Round 4 1989 (lost to David Roe 5–3)
UK Championship:
Round 2 (last 16) 1984 (lost to Willie Thorne 9–7)
Mercantile Credit Classic:
Quarter-finalist 1984 (lost to Mark Wildman 5–4)
Pearl Assurance British Open:
Round 5 1986 (lost to John Virgo 5–4)
European Open:
Quarter-finalist 1989 (lost to John Parrott 5–1)

Current Non-ranking Tournaments
Benson and Hedges Masters:
Semi-finalist 1975 (lost to John Spencer 5–2)
Semi-finalist 1976 (lost to Ray Reardon 5–4)
Semi-finalist 1983 (lost to Cliff Thorburn 6–5)
Benson and Hedges Irish Masters:
Quarter-finalist 1983 (lost to Steve Davis 5–1)
Quarter-finalist 1985 (lost to Tony Knowles 5–3)

Other Wins
Pot Black: 1972, 1973, 1980
World Matchplay: 1976
Limosin International: 1979
Kronenbrau 1308 Classic: 1979
Australian Professional: 1964–67, 1969–84

WORLD RANKING POSITIONS

1976/77	3	1982/83	5	1987/88	26
1977/78	3	1983/84	6	1988/89	19
1978/79	3	1984/85	6	1989/90	22
1979/80	3	1985/86	12	1990/91	31
1980/81	3	1986/87	25	1991/92	27
1981/82	8				

DANNY FOWLER

World ranking: Number 28
Date of birth: 30 July 1956
Star sign: Leo
Turned professional: 1984

Country: England
Prize money 1990/91: £36,375
Biggest pay day: £21,000 – 1989
Rothmans Grand Prix semi-finalist

Danny Fowler, the former dustman from Worksop known affectionately as 'Dustbin Danny', began the 1990/91 season hoping for a major move towards the top thirty-two. Unfortunately, that breakthrough did not materialise and Fowler, by virtue of a quarter-final placing in the UK Championship, could manage only a one-place jump to number 28. At the UK event in Preston he enjoyed an excellent 9–8 fifth-round win over Gary Wilkinson but then came unstuck 9–3 against Stephen Hendry who went on to claim the title.

Here's hoping. Danny Fowler will be looking to improve his world ranking of 28 this season.

BEST PERFORMANCES
Embassy World Championship:
Round 1 1986 (lost to Terry Griffiths 10–2)
Round 1 1988 (lost to Tony Knowles 10–8)
Round 1 1990 (lost to Jimmy White 10–4)

Other Ranking Tournaments
Asian Open:
Round 3 1989 (lost to Joe Johnson 5–4)
Round 3 1990 (lost to Jack McLaughlin 5–3)
Rothmans Grand Prix:
Semi-finalist 1989 (lost to Steve Davis 9–2)
Dubai Duty Free Classic:
Semi-finalist 1989 (lost to Stephen Hendry 5–4)
UK Championship:
Quarter-finalist 1990 (lost to Stephen Hendry 9–3)

Mercantile Credit Classic:
Round 5 1987 (lost to Stephen Hendry 5–4)
Pearl Assurance British Open:
Round 2 (last 32) 1985 (lost to Malcolm Bradley 5–4)
Round 4 1991 (lost to Jimmy White 5–3)
European Open:
Round 5 1989 (lost to Jim Wych 5–4)

Other Wins
No significant wins

WORLD RANKING POSITIONS

1984/85 –	1987/88 40	1990/91 29
1985/86 55	1988/89 43	1991/92 28
1986/87 33	1989/90 36	

MARK BENNETT

World ranking: Number 29
Date of birth: 23 September 1963
Star sign: Libra
Turned professional: 1986

Country: Wales
Prize money 1990/91: £34,875
Biggest pay day: £12,000 – 1989
StormSeal UK Open quarter-finalist

Mark Bennett, who originally came from Blackwood in Gwent, has reached the top thirty-two for the first time at number 29. An aggressive and entertaining potter, he was a quarter-finalist in the 555 Asian Open and then endured an average season before he clinched his top thirty-two place by qualifying for the first round of the Embassy World Championship with a 10–8 victory over fellow Welshman Wayne Jones in Sheffield. Unfortunately, Bennett then went down 10–6 to Martin Clark. Away from the ranking tournament circuit, he was a finalist in the Regal Welsh Professional Championship but had to settle for the runner-up position after losing 9–3 to title holder Darren Morgan.

Debut boy: Welshman Mark Bennett is in the top thirty-two for the first time at number 29.

BEST PERFORMANCES
Embassy World Championship:
Round 1 1987 (lost to Dennis Taylor 10–4)
Round 1 1990 (lost to John Parrott 10–9)
Round 1 1991 (lost to Martin Clark 10–6)

Other Ranking Tournaments
Asian Open:
Quarter-finalist 1990 (lost to Stephen Hendry 5–3)
Rothmans Grand Prix:
Round 4 1986 (lost to Paddy Browne 5–0)
Dubai Duty Free Classic:
Round 3 1989 (lost to Dene O'Kane 5–2)
Round 3 1990 (lost to Peter Francisco 5–1)
UK Championship:
Quarter-finalist 1989 (lost to Stephen Hendry 9–2)

Mercantile Credit Classic:
Round 4 1988 (lost to Martin Clark 5–2)
Round 4 1991 (lost to Bob Chaperon 5–3)
Pearl Assurance British Open:
Round 4 1990 (lost to Alex Higgins 5–2)
Round 4 1991 (lost to Tony Knowles 5–1)
European Open:
Round 5 1990 (lost to Neal Foulds 5–2)

Other Wins
Welsh Amateur: 1985

WORLD RANKING POSITIONS

1986/87 –	1988/89 52	1990/91 33
1987/88 54	1989/90 47	1991/92 29

BOB CHAPERON

World ranking: Number 30
Date of birth: 18 May 1958
Star sign: Taurus
Turned professional: 1983

Country: Canada
Prize money 1990/91: £21,975
Biggest pay day: £75,000 – 1990 Pearl
Assurance British Open champion

Bob Chaperon was happy to keep his place in the top thirty-two after a disappointing season in which he lost his Pearl Assurance British Open title and gained just 3 ranking points. His only performance of note was in reaching the last sixteen of the Mercantile Credit Classic in Bournemouth where he was beaten 5–3 by Malta's Tony Drago.

There was further disappointment when the World Cup, won so well by Canada in 1990, failed to take place. In the Embassy World Championship, Chaperon did not survive the fifth and final qualifying round when he lost 10–8 to Nigel Gilbert. Altogether a season to forget for this popular Canadian.

'Hi, Mum': Bob Chaperon greets his mother Yvette who flew over from her Canadian home for a holiday in England.

BEST PERFORMANCES
Embassy World Championship:
Round 1 1988 (lost to Mike Hallett 10–2)
Round 1 1989 (lost to Terry Griffiths 10–6)

Other Ranking Tournaments
Asian Open:
Round 4 1990 (lost to Mark Bennett 5–4)
Rothmans Grand Prix:
Quarter-finalist 1987 (lost to John Parrott 5–2)
Dubai Duty Free Classic:
Round 3 1989 (lost to Brian Rowswell 5–4)
Round 3 1990 (lost to Jon Birch 5–0)
UK Championship:
Round 4 1989 (lost to John Parrott 9–8)

Mercantile Credit Classic:
Round 5 1991 (lost to Tony Drago 5–3)
Pearl Assurance British Open:
Winner 1990 (beat Alex Higgins 10–8)
European Open:
Round 4 1990 (lost to Steve Davis 5–0)

Other Wins
Canadian Amateur: 1981

WORLD RANKING POSITIONS

1984/85 –	1987/88 41	1990/91 25
1985/86 44	1988/89 29	1991/92 30
1986/87 53	1989/90 29	

JOHN VIRGO

World ranking: Number 31
Date of birth: 4 March 1946
Star sign: Pisces
Turned professional: 1976

Country: England
Prize money 1990/91: £26,625
Biggest pay day: £12,000 – 1988 Tennents
UK Open quarter-finalist

John Virgo endured a terrible 1990/91 season as he accumulated just 2 ranking tournament points and only just maintained his place in the top thirty-two at number 31. It is the first time he has been outside snooker's top twenty since he turned professional in 1976, and has ended a three-year run in the top sixteen. Away from the table Virgo continued to enjoy popularity with his excellent exhibition act and was invited to join top comedian Jim Davidson in hosting the BBC TV quiz programme *Big Break*, based on a snooker-playing format and general-knowledge questions.

BEST PERFORMANCES
Embassy World Championship:
Semi-finalist 1979 (lost to Dennis Taylor 19–12)

Other Ranking Tournaments
Asian Open:
Round 5 1989 (lost to Willie Thorne 5–2)
Rothmans Grand Prix:
Semi-finalist 1982 (lost to Jimmy White 10–4)
Dubai Duty Free Classic:
Round 5 1989 (lost to Jack McLaughlin 5–4)
UK Championship:
Quarter-finalist 1988 (lost to Doug Mountjoy 9–8)
Mercantile Credit Classic:
Quarter-finalist 1985 (lost to Willie Thorne 5–1)
Pearl Assurance British Open:
Semi-finalist 1986 (lost to Willie Thorne 9–4)
European Open:
Round 5 1989 (lost to Eddie Charlton 5–4)

Current Non-ranking Tournaments
Benson and Hedges Masters:
Round 1 1980 (lost to Cliff Thorburn 5–3)

Round 1 1983 (lost to Doug Mountjoy 5–1)
Round 1 1984 (lost to Ray Reardon 5–3)
Round 1 1989 (lost to Jimmy White 5–2)
Round 1 1990 (lost to Jimmy White 5–3)
Round 2 (last 16) 1991 (lost to Stephen Hendry 5–1)

Other Wins
British Isles Under-16: 1962
British Isles Under-19: 1965
Coral UK: 1979
Pontin's Professional: 1980
Bombay International: 1980
Professional Snooker League: 1984

WORLD RANKING POSITIONS

1977/78 18	1982/83 19	1987/88 19
1978/79 19	1983/84 14	1988/89 15
1979/80 10	1984/85 18	1989/90 13
1980/81 12	1985/86 19	1990/91 14
1981/82 13	1986/87 19	1991/92 31

CLIFF WILSON

World ranking: Number 32
Date of birth: 10 May 1934
Star sign: Taurus
Turned professional: 1979

Country: Wales
Prize money 1990/91: £30,400
Biggest pay day: £7,500 – 1987
Mercantile Credit Classic quarter-finalist

Cliff Wilson clung on to his place in the top thirty-two by virtue of obtaining 2 more merit points than Darren Morgan, the Welsh champion. It was hardly a spectacular season for the jovial Welshman, though he did obtain points in five ranking tournaments, with his best performance coming in the Tulip European Open where he qualified for the last sixteen in Rotterdam. But Wilson's trip to Holland was short-lived as he was beaten 5–3 by Dennis Taylor. In the Mita World Masters, Wilson and Tony Chappel reached the last eight of the men's doubles. Wilson, a former world amateur champion, will be hoping for a better 1991/92 season.

BEST PERFORMANCES
Embassy World Championship:
Round 1 1980 (lost to Doug Mountjoy 10–6)
Round 1 1981 (lost to David Taylor 10–6)
Round 1 1982 (lost to Eddie Charlton 10–5)
Round 1 1983 (lost to Doug Mountjoy 10–2)
Round 1 1986 (lost to Eddie Charlton 10–6)
Round 1 1988 (lost to Joe Johnson 10–7)
Round 1 1989 (lost to Steve Duggan 10–1)
Round 1 1990 (lost to Cliff Thorburn 10–6)

Other Ranking Tournaments
Asian Open:
Round 4 1990 (lost to Dennis Taylor 5–4)
Rothmans Grand Prix:
Quarter-finalist 1985 (lost to Dennis Taylor 5–2)
Dubai Duty Free Classic:
Round 4 1989 (lost to Tony Drago 5–0)
UK Championship:
Round 2 (last 16) 1984 (lost to Cliff Thorburn 9–3)
Mercantile Credit Classic:
Quarter-finalist 1987 (lost to Dean Reynolds 5–1)
Pearl Assurance British Open:
Round 5 1987 (lost to John Virgo 5–2)
Round 5 1989 (lost to Dean Reynolds 5–0)
European Open:
Round 5 1991 (lost to Dennis Taylor 5–3)

Current Non-ranking Tournaments
Benson and Hedges Masters:
Round 1 1989 (lost to Steve Davis 5–2)

Other Wins
British Isles Under-19: 1952, 1953
Welsh Amateur: 1956, 1977, 1979
World Amateur: 1978
Pontin's Autumn Open: 1976

WORLD RANKING POSITIONS

1980/81 –	1984/85 23	1988/89 16
1981/82 23	1985/86 22	1989/90 18
1982/83 26	1986/87 23	1990/91 28
1983/84 20	1987/88 17	1991/92 32

Golden oldie: Cliff Wilson who hung on to his place in the top thirty-two at number 32.

A YEAR ON THE PROFESSIONAL CIRCUIT

555 WORLD SERIES CHALLENGE

James Wattana, the man they call the 'Thai-phoon', required just 138 minutes to win the 555 World Series Challenge – the first tournament of the 1990/91 season – at the Hilton Hotel in Hong Kong. He became the first Asian player to collect a major professional trophy when he beat four players in the top six to win the £20,000 first prize.

The young Thai, who was to experience disappointment during the rest of the season, thrashed Terry Griffiths (5–0), Doug Mountjoy (5–1), Steve Davis (5–2) and then Jimmy White (9–3). More than twenty million snooker fans in Thailand watched the final live and, after the first session, Wattana led White 5–3. Wattana had been superb in the first session but was even better at night when, in just forty-six minutes, he fired in breaks of 61, 62, 56 and 74. White, the world number 4, failed to pot a ball in two of those frames.

White said: 'James is a great kid and a great player and plays the game like I do.

Thai take-away: James Wattana is a happy man after winning the 555 World Series Challenge in Hong Kong. It was his first professional title.

---

555 World Series Challenge Results

FIRST ROUND:	J. Wattana (Thai) bt T. Griffiths (Wales) 5–0; D. Reynolds (Eng) bt K. Kwok (HK) 5–0; M. Hallett (Eng) bt F. Chan (HK) 5–1; S. James (Eng) bt U. Khaimuk (Thai) 5–2 Losers: £1,500
QUARTER-FINALS:	S. Davis (Eng) bt Reynolds 5–2; J. White (Eng) bt Hallett 5–3; S. Hendry (Scot) bt James 5–4; Wattana bt D. Mountjoy (Wales) 5–1 Losers: £5,000
SEMI-FINALS:	White bt Hendry 5–2; Wattana bt S. Davis 5–2 Losers: £7,500
FINAL:	Wattana bt White 9–3 Loser: £10,000 Winner: £20,000

High break: 127 – J. Wattana

One day he will get into the top four.' White must have thought he was on his way to the title when he thrashed Stephen Hendry 5–2 in a semi-final that lasted just seventy-nine minutes. He had arrived in Hong Kong nursing a shoulder injury that he had collected while playing cricket, but he recovered after receiving treatment from a local Chinese herbalist.

Wattana's 'idol' as an up-and-coming player had been Davis and he was delighted with his semi-final victory over the six-times world champion that also included a tournament high break of 127 in the first frame.

The World Series events feature the top eight players in the world plus invited professionals and local amateurs.

REGAL MASTERS

Stephen Hendry collected the first of his eight titles of the season when he captured the £96,000 Regal Masters with a 10–6 beating of Welshman Terry Griffiths at the Civic Centre in Motherwell. In 1989 Griffiths and Hendry had also fought out the Regal final but that match was one-sided as Hendry raced to a 10–1 victory.

Griffiths put up a much better fight this time, and by the end of the first session it was anybody's game at 4–4. But then Hendry, in front of his own devoted Scottish fans, collected four of the first five frames of the evening, though Griffiths pulled back to 8–6 with a break of 55 after trailing 50–0. Hendry made it 9–6 and finished the match off in style with a 138 total clearance that took just eight minutes and clinched the £3,500 high-break prize to go with the main cheque of £35,000. The young Scot said: 'I am determined this season to prove I am here to stay as number 1. That's even more important than winning the world title.'

Ten players took part in the Masters, which had been switched from the Scottish Exhibition Centre in Glasgow to improve attendances. The plan worked and there were some good crowds, especially in the semi-final when Hendry came back from 4–3 down to beat Jimmy White 6–4.

There was controversy after Steve James had hammered Steve Davis 6–1 in the

quarter-final with the former world champion attending press and television interviews but then heading home without signing autographs. Promoter Ian Doyle said: 'I wish to express my displeasure at the

The first of eight: Stephen Hendry with the Regal Masters trophy and a bottle of champagne for the high break of 138.

behaviour of Steve Davis. I can only apologise to the fans, some of whom bought pictures and posters, and, of course, were left with them unsigned. Steve chose to leave by a side entrance. That was bad enough, but he didn't even have the courtesy of visiting my sponsor's lounge.'

Doyle threatened to withhold Davis's cheque for £4,500 but paid the money when Barry Hearn, the manager of Davis, issued a statement. It said: 'At no time was Davis specifically invited to attend the sponsor's hospitality room. As the game's number 1 ambassador, Steve is fully aware of the importance of sponsors and fans and obviously is very sorry if he has unintentionally upset anyone.'

WHO SAID THAT?

'Steve was great – I was rubbish. He was potting them off the lampshades, but I enjoyed every minute of it.'

▲

– *Steve Davis talking about his 6–1 defeat by Steve James in the quarter-final of the Regal Masters.*

Regal Masters Results

FIRST ROUND:	D. Morgan (Wales) bt D. Reynolds (Eng) 6–3; S. James (Eng) bt M. Hallett (Eng) 6–5 Losers: £2,000
QUARTER-FINALS:	S. Hendry (Scot) bt D. Morgan 6–4; J. White (Eng) bt D. Mountjoy (Wales) 6–5; T. Griffiths (Wales) bt J. Parrott (Eng) 6–3; James bt S. Davis (Eng) 6–1 Losers: £4,500
SEMI-FINALS:	Hendry bt White 6–4; Griffiths bt James 6–3 Losers: £9,000
FINAL:	Hendry bt Griffiths 10–6 Loser: £17,500 Winner: £35,000

High break: 138 – S. Hendry £3,500

Previous Year's Results

YEAR	WINNER	RUNNER-UP	SCORE
1989	S. Hendry (Scot)	T. Griffiths (Wales)	10–1

HUMO BELGIAN MASTERS

There are some sportsmen who seem to have lucky venues. John Parrott is such a player – he is just happy to play anywhere in Europe.

Parrott twice won the European Open in France in 1989 and 1990, while success in the UK eluded this young Liverpudlian. He was a winner in Europe again in the second leg of the World Series – the Humo Belgian Masters – at the Sporthal Schijnpoort in Antwerp.

As well as the snooker, Antwerp was also hosting a two-day visit from Italian tenor Luciano Pavarotti, who was reputedly being paid a fee of £800,000. The snooker was sold out but could not compete with the 60,000 who packed the local Sports Palace to listen to Pavarotti.

Parrott earned £30,000 for his 9–6 final victory over White in a high-scoring affair that saw White kick off with a break of 104. As the match was shown live on

Belgian TV, Parrott knocked in a 120 that earned the £4,000 high-break prize and also put him 8–5 ahead. White took the fourteenth frame but Parrott's 76 gave him yet another overseas title.

WHO SAID THAT?

'John Parrott to serve.'

▲

– A local referee who got his sports muddled up during the Humo Belgian Masters in Antwerp.

Parrott had been delighted with his 5–3 victory over world champion Stephen Hendry in the semi-final. The latter, who forfeited a 2–0 lead, commented: 'I went to sleep. My concentration went out of the window.' In the other semi-final, White beat Steve Davis 5–4 with a break of 88 in the decider after Davis led 2–0. Then, at 4–2 down, Davis knocked in breaks of 106 and 88. Hendry had produced some excellent snooker in his 5–2 quarter-final defeat of Doug Mountjoy when he included breaks of 92, 44, 60, 103 and 97. Mountjoy said: 'Hendry is a class above everybody at the moment.' Four Belgian amateurs took part in the first round in which Mike Hallett and Dean Reynolds were both happy to squeeze home 3–2.

Humo Belgian Masters Results

FIRST ROUND:	D. Mountjoy (Wales) bt P. Delsemme (Bel) 3–1; T. Griffiths (Wales) bt D. Lathouwers (Bel) 3–0; M. Hallett (Eng) bt M. Lannoye (Bel) 3–2; D. Reynolds (Eng) bt S. Lemmens (Bel) 3–2
QUARTER-FINALS:	S. Hendry (Scot) bt Mountjoy 5–2; J. Parrott (Eng) bt Griffiths 5–1; S. Davis (Eng) bt Hallett 5–1; J. White (Eng) bt Reynolds 5–0 Losers: £1,500
SEMI-FINALS:	Parrott bt Hendry 5–3; White bt Davis 5–4 Losers: £10,000
FINAL:	Parrott bt White 9–6 Loser: £15,000 Winner: £30,000

High break: 120 – J. Parrott £4,000

INTERNATIONAL ONE-FRAME KNOCK-OUT

Darren Morgan returned home to Cwmfelinfach £5,000 richer after winning the revolutionary International One-Frame Knock-Out at Trentham Gardens, Stoke-on-Trent. The International was funded by the WPBSA to the tune of £40,000 and, although voted a hit by the players and spectators, it seems there is no gap left in the calendar for the event to be repeated.

An excellent turn-out of 116 players took part and by the time the field had been reduced to sixteen, only Dean Reynolds, Neal Foulds and Mike Hallett were carrying the flag of the top sixteen. In the end it was Morgan, the Welsh champion, who came home a winner with a 2–1 victory over stablemate Mike Hallett in a final that was increased to a 'marathon' distance of three frames! Morgan commented: 'It's been tremendous fun and we were able to have a laugh and a joke with the officials during the tournament. Most of the other players I spoke to said it was a great event.'

Tony Knowles, who scored the tournament best break of 120, also backed the format. 'It's absolutely tailor-made for TV,' he said. 'Every match is sudden-death, and when you think of some of the boring matches shown in main tournaments, this would be great for ITV, BBC or the satellite companies. It's an ideal opportunity for TV to show new faces.'

Runner-up Hallett was lucky to escape injury during the event when he was involved in a car crash with Bill Oliver, who suffered a serious head wound that needed fifteen stitches and a broken bone in his neck.

Instant success: Welshman Darren Morgan after his triumph in the novel International One-frame Knock-out in Stoke-on-Trent.

International One-frame Knock-out Results

THIRD ROUND:	M. Gauvreau (Can) bt C. Roscoe (Wales) 77–16; A. McManus (Scot) bt A. Wilson (Eng) 71–69; K. Doherty (Rep Ire) bt R. Edmonds (Eng) 66–32; I. Brumby (Eng) bt S. Meakin (Eng) 60–9; J. Whittaker (Eng) bt D. Gilbert (Eng) 63–25; M. Hallett (Eng) bt T. Whitthread (Eng) 79–34; D. Morgan (Wales) bt A. Cairns (Eng) 74–38; G. Cripsey (Eng) bt P. Francisco (SA) 64–30; P. Gibson (Eng) bt P. Browne (Rep Ire) 62–50; A. Knowles (Eng) bt C. Thorburn (Can) 76–64; N. Foulds (Eng) bt M. Rowing (Eng) 74–27; N. Dyson (Eng) bt D. Campbell (Scot) 86–11; D. Reynolds (Eng) bt M. Price (Eng) 69–42; D. Roe (Eng) bt S. Duggan (Eng) 62–52; S. Newbury (Wales) bt N. Bond (Eng) 67–36; J. O'Boye (Eng) bt E. Charlton (Aust) 79–4 Losers: £500
FOURTH ROUND:	Brumby bt N. Foulds 72–17; D. Morgan bt Newbury 68–9; Cripsey bt Gauvreau 68–47; Whittaker bt P. Gibson 56–14; Roe bt Dyson 77–43; McManus bt O'Boye 62–36; Hallett bt Doherty 68–46; Knowles bt Reynolds 66–16 Losers: £750
QUARTER-FINALS:	Whittaker bt Brumby 69–29; D. Morgan bt Roe 78–2; Hallett bt Knowles 50–37; McManus bt Cripsey 66–62 Losers: £1,250
SEMI-FINALS:	D. Morgan bt Whittaker 77–14; Hallett bt McManus 66–21 Losers: £2,000
FINAL:	D. Morgan bt Hallett (frames) 2–1 Loser: £3,000 Winner: £5,000

High break: 120 – A. Knowles £1,000

ROTHMANS GRAND PRIX

Stephen Hendry was celebrating two successes at the Rothmans Grand Prix at the Hexagon Theatre in Reading – his title victory and the return of his priceless cue.

Hendry, who eventually beat stablemate Nigel Bond 10–5 in the final, will never

WHO SAID THAT?

'I thought I would never see the cue again. I will be taking it to bed with me tonight.'

▲

– Stephen Hendry after his stolen cue was returned safely during the Rothmans Grand Prix in Reading.

forget a night at the Ramada Hotel when his cue was stolen from a practice room. The young Scot, who was absolutely shattered by the incident, said: 'I was just practising and nipped out for a couple of minutes to get a drink. When I returned the cue was gone.' The police were called in, a reward, originally offered at £1,000, was increased to £10,000 by manager Ian Doyle, and then the following lunchtime the cue was spotted by a youth who saw it being tossed away from a car. Hendry,

convinced that he would never see the cue again, has not let the prized implement out of his sight since.

Even so, Hendry was twice on the brink of defeat against South African Silvino Francisco in the fourth round and then against Canadian Alain Robidoux in the last sixteen, but he recovered and booked his final place only to find himself in trouble again against Bond.

Bond, from the tiny Derbyshire village of Darley Dale, gave notice of his intentions with a 5–2 victory over Steve Davis in the third round and then worked his way through the field, finally scoring a brilliant 9–8 victory over Jimmy White in the semi-final by winning the final two frames.

Bond looked in trouble when he trailed Hendry 3–0 in the final but then produced a quite remarkable forty-minute spell when he scored two centuries, including a 139 total clearance, and breaks of 65 and 85 to take a 4–3 lead. He added the eighth frame

Great final: Stephen Hendry (left) and Nigel Bond after the Rothmans Grand Prix final which Hendry won 10–5.

Rothmans Grand Prix Results

FOURTH ROUND		FIFTH ROUND		QUARTER-FINALS		SEMI-FINALS		FINAL	
N. Bond (Eng)	5								
v		Bond	5						
E. Charlton (Aust)	3			Bond	5				
W. Thorne (Eng)	5	v							
v		Thorne	1						
T. Drago (Malta)	3			v		Bond	9		
N. Foulds (Eng)	5								
v		N. Foulds	5						
C. Roscoe (Wales)	2	v		Foulds	2				
M. Hallett (Eng)	5								
v		Hallett	2			v		Bond	5
W. Jones (Wales)	2								
I. Graham (Eng)	5								
v		Graham	2						
C. Wilson (Wales)	3	v		E. Hughes	2				
N. Dyson (Eng)	3								
v		E. Hughes	5			v		White	8
E. Hughes (Rep Ire)	5								
Dennis Taylor (NI)	3								
v		Gary Wilkinson	0						
Gary Wilkinson (Eng)	5	v		White	5				
J. White (Eng)	5								
v		White	5					v	
S. Newbury (Wales)	2								
J. Parrott (Eng)	5								
v		Parrott	5						
B. West (Eng)	1	v		Parrott	3				
J. Campbell (Aust)	3								
v		O'Kane	2			v		James	5
D. O'Kane (NZ)	5								
S. James (Eng)	5								
v		James	5						
J. Chambers (Eng)	2	v		James	5				
T. Griffiths (Wales)	2								
v		Stevens	2			v		Hendry	10
K. Stevens (Can)	5								
D. Morgan (Wales)	1								
v		P. Francisco	5						
P. Francisco (SA)	5	v		P. Francisco	0				
K. Owers (Eng)	5								
v		Owers	1			v		Hendry	9
A. Knowles (Eng)	4								
M. Clark (Eng)	3								
v		Robidoux	3						
A. Robidoux (Can)	5	v		Hendry	5				
S. Hendry (Scot)	5								
v		Hendry	5						
S. Francisco (SA)	4								
Losers: £3,400		Losers: £5,000		Losers: £10,000		Losers: £20,000		Loser: £40,000	
								Winner: £75,000	

High break: 140 – J. White £7,000

Previous Years' Results

YEAR	WINNER	RUNNER-UP	SCORE
1982	(Professional Players Tournament)		
	R. Reardon (Wales)	J. White (Eng)	10–5
1983	(PPT)		
	A. Knowles (Eng)	J. Johnson (Eng)	9–8
1984	Dennis Taylor (NI)	C. Thorburn (Can)	10–2
1985	S. Davis (Eng)	Dennis Taylor (NI)	10–9
1986	J. White (Eng)	R. Williams (Eng)	10–6
1987	S. Hendry (Scot)	Dennis Taylor (NI)	10–7
1988	S. Davis (Eng)	A. Higgins (NI)	10–6
1989	S. Davis (Eng)	D. Reynolds (Eng)	10–0

as well to make it 5–3 at the interval and a major upset seemed on the cards. Hendry returned in a different frame of mind and Bond's giant-killing dream came to an end as the Scot won seven frames in a row for his 10–5 success. Hendry said: 'If Nigel had won the opening frame at night, I could well have lost 10–3. In that afternoon session not even Steve Davis has performed against me like that.' Bond was far from down-hearted and went home with his parents – £40,000 richer.

NORWICH UNION GRAND PRIX

John Parrott continued his remarkable run of success in Europe when he beat Steve Davis 4–2 to take the £25,000 first prize in the Norwich Union Grand Prix in Monte Carlo. Parrott, following successes in France (twice) and Belgium, enjoyed his fourth overseas success when he came back from 2–1 down to take the trophy with breaks of 30, 64 and 52. He was in a similar position in the semi-final and again won three frames in a row to beat Stephen Hendry 4–2, while Davis accounted for defending champion Joe Johnson by the same score.

Norwich Union Grand Prix Results

QUARTER-FINALS: J. Parrott (Eng) bt J. White (Eng) 4–1; S. Hendry (Scot) bt Dennis Taylor (NI) 4–1; J. Johnson (Eng) bt T. Griffiths (Wales) 4–2; S. Davis (Eng) bt M. Hallett (Eng) 4–1
Losers: £2,500

SEMI-FINALS: Parrott bt Hendry 4–2; S. Davis bt Johnson 4–2
Losers: £5,000

FINAL: Parrott bt S. Davis 4–2
Loser: £15,000
Winner: £25,000

High break: 138 – J. Parrott

Previous Years' Results

YEAR	WINNER	RUNNER-UP	SCORE
1988	S. Davis (Eng)	J. White (Eng)	5–4
1989	J. Johnson (Eng)	S. Hendry (Scot)	5–3

555 ASIAN OPEN

Many people think that snooker stars live in the world of first-class travel and five-star hotels but there was nothing glamorous about the four-hour jet-foil trip from Hong Kong to Guangzhou in China for the 555 Asian Open. Getting on and off the jet-foil involved a pushing and shoving match with the local Chinese before the snooker party eventually arrived at the China Hotel in readiness for the final stages of this £200,000 tournament at the Guangdong TV studios.

Only fifteen players made the journey to China because South African Silvino Francisco was refused an entry visa. In the end Stephen Hendry chalked up his twenty-first successive victory in ranking tournament matches when he beat Irishman Dennis Taylor 9–3 in the final. A live TV audience in excess of one hundred million witnessed the final outcome, and Taylor commented: 'I know that Stephen Hendry has a long way to go to equal Steve Davis in terms of titles, but on pure ability he could be the best player this game has seen. It was certainly no disgrace losing to the world number 1.'

WHO SAID THAT?

'Stephen Hendry is certainly the best long potter in the game and certainly better than Alex Higgins at his best.'

▲

– Irishman Dennis Taylor talking after the final of the 555 Asian Open which Hendry won 9–3.

In the money: Stephen Hendry collects £35,000 after retaining the 555 Asian Open title in Guangzhou, China.

Davis and Jimmy White failed to make the trip to China, but that left the way open for some of the 'lesser' pros to shine. Tony Chappel, the world number 43 from Swansea, certainly enjoyed his visit as he reached the semi-final with victories over John Parrott and Franky Chan before losing 6–5 to Taylor after the Irishman had trailed 3–0 and 4–1. In the second semi-final Hendry flattened Mike Hallett 6–1 in just ninety-seven minutes, with Hallett saying: 'I threw it away – I was diabolical.'

The Asian Open, the first ranking tournament in China, was an overall success, especially when Taylor delighted the packed crowd and the large TV audience by performing his exhibition routine. Comedy was proved once again to be universal by the fact that the Chinese laughed at Taylor's 'Irish' jokes when told to them through an interpreter.

555 Asian Open Results

FOURTH ROUND		FIFTH ROUND		QUARTER-FINALS		SEMI-FINALS		FINAL	
S. Hendry (Scot)	5								
v		Hendry	5						
J. O'Boye (Eng)	3			Hendry	5				
W. Thorne (Eng)	5	v							
v		Thorne	4						
J. Wattana (Thai)	2					Hendry	6		
M. Bennett (Wales)	5			v					
v		M. Bennett	5						
R. Chaperon (Can)	4	v		M. Bennett	3				
J. Campbell (Aust)	5	J. Campbell	4						
v						v		Hendry	9
M. Macleod (Scot)	4								
M. Hallett (Eng)	5	Hallett	w/o						
v		v		Hallett	5				
S. Campbell (Eng)	1	S. Francisco							
R. Harris (Eng)	3					Hallett	1		
v				v					
S. Francisco (SA)	5								
J. Virgo (Eng)	1	Dodd	5						
v		v		Dodd	4				
L. Dodd (Eng)	5	Charlton	2						
J. White (Eng)	4								
v								v	
E. Charlton (Aust)	5								
J. Parrott (Eng)	5	Parrott	5						
v		v		Parrott	3				
P. Francisco (SA)	0	McLaughlin	2						
M. Clark (Eng)	4					Chappel	5		
v				v					
J. McLaughlin (NI)	5								
D. Morgan (Wales)	2	Chan	1						
v		v		Chappel	5				
F. Chan (HK)	5	Chappel	5						
D. Reynolds (Eng)	2							Dennis Taylor	3
v				v					
A. Chappel (Wales)	5								
D. Mountjoy (Wales)	5	Mountjoy	3						
v		v		Foulds	4				
B. Gollan (Can)	4	Foulds	5						
N. Foulds (Eng)	5					Dennis Taylor	6		
v				v					
D. O'Kane (NZ)	0								
Dennis Taylor (NI)	5	Dennis Taylor	5						
v		v		Dennis Taylor	5				
C. Wilson (Wales)	4	Bond	1						
N. Bond (Eng)	5								
v									
A. Drago (Malta)	1								

Losers: £1,500	Losers: £4,500	Losers: £6,000	Losers: £12,000	Loser: £22,000
				Winner: £35,000

High break: 110 – S. Hendry £2,000

Previous Year's Results			
YEAR	WINNER	RUNNER-UP	SCORE
1989	S. Hendry (Scot)	J. Wattana (Thai)	9–6

DUBAI DUTY FREE CLASSIC

The Dubai Duty Free Classic, which went ahead as the storm clouds gathered before the Gulf War, was another personal triumph for Stephen Hendry who retained the title. A crowd approaching 2,000 – a mixture of local Arabs, ex-patriots and troops and sailors on leave – packed into the Al Nasr Stadium to watch him demolish Steve Davis 9–1 in a one-sided final.

Davis had never been beaten by such a margin in a major final, while Hendry took his winning streak in ranking tournament matches to twenty-five. Afterwards Davis said: 'Stephen is the best I have played against. Ray Reardon was a brilliant tactician, Alex Higgins and Terry Griffiths could do tremendous things, but Stephen has a good all-round game.'

As the temperatures soared to 100° Fahrenheit, Hendry was as cool as ever. 'I never dreamt I would beat Steve as easily as that,' he said. 'He's dished out a lot of punishment to me in the past and it's nice to give him some back. I would love to play Steve with both of us at our best because he is certainly the greatest player I have ever faced, and for him to pay me the compliment of saying I'm the best he's played could not come from anyone better.'

Sixteen players qualified for the final stages of the Dubai Classic, and although there were precious ranking points at stake, the players, their families and friends could relax around the pool of the Dubai International Hotel and play some golf at the fabulous Emirates Golf Club which must rank as one of the wonders of the modern world.

Throughout the stay Hendry dropped just three frames, while Davis had to battle all the way, especially when he edged past Gary Wilkinson 6–4 in the semi-final. In the opening matches Rex Williams produced some excellent tactical play to beat Hong Kong's Franky Chan 5–2, but there was heartache for new professional Jason Whittaker who had to pull out when he lost the first four frames to Terry Griffiths after suffering a severe stomach upset. In the quarter-finals Hendry demolished Hallett 5–0, at which the latter promptly broke his cue into six pieces. However, Hallett said: 'It wasn't in temper – I needed to change my cue and didn't want the temptation of going back to my old one again.'

Perhaps the most telling remark came from John Spencer, the chairman of the WPBSA, who said after the final: 'We have just seen the two greatest players of our time.' The sailors from the warships stationed in the seas around Dubai surely agreed.

WHO SAID THAT?

'I want to become a legend. Joe Davis was a legend, Steve Davis is a legend and even Alex Higgins is a legend. That's hopefully what I can become in the next few years.'

— ▲ —

– Stephen Hendry after winning the Dubai Duty Free Classic for the second successive year.

Dubai Duty Free Classic Results

FOURTH ROUND		FIFTH ROUND		QUARTER-FINALS		SEMI-FINALS		FINAL	
S. Hendry (Scot)	5								
v		Hendry	5						
A. Robidoux (Can)	1			Hendry	5				
N. Foulds (Eng)	5	v							
v		N. Foulds	1						
S. Newbury (Wales)	2					Hendry	6		
W. Thorne (Eng)	2			v					
v		D. Morgan	2						
D. Morgan (Wales)	5	v		Hallett	0				
M. Hallett (Eng)	5	Hallett	5						
v						Hendry	9		
W. Jones (Wales)	2					v			
D. Reynolds (Eng)	5	Reynolds	5						
v		v		Reynolds	5				
J. Wattana (Thai)	3	Prince	4						
J. Prince (NI)	5			v		Reynolds	1		
v									
A. Drago (Malta)	4								
R. Williams (Eng)	5	Williams	5	Williams	2				
v		v							
R. Lawler (Eng)	2	Chan	2						
J. White (Eng)	3								
v								v	
F. Chan (HK)	5								
J. Parrott (Eng)	3	Gary Wilkinson	5						
v		v		Gary Wilkinson	5				
Gary Wilkinson (Eng)	5	S. Francisco	2						
S. James (Eng)	3			v		Gary Wilkinson	4		
v									
S. Francisco (SA)	5								
M. Clark (Eng)	5	Clark	0	Mountjoy	4				
v		v							
D. O'Kane (NZ)	1	Mountjoy	5						
D. Mountjoy (Wales)	5							S. Davis	1
v						v			
A. Knowles (Eng)	3								
T. Griffiths (Wales)	5	Griffiths	5						
v		v		Griffiths	2				
J. Birch (Eng)	2	Whittaker	0						
D. Campbell (Scot)	3			v		S. Davis	6		
v									
J. Whittaker (Eng)	5								
S. Murphy (Rep Ire)	3	Wych	2	S. Davis	5				
v		v							
J. Wych (Can)	5	S. Davis	5						
S. Davis (Eng)	5								
v									
P. Francisco (SA)	1								

Losers: £1,500   Losers: £4,500   Losers: £6,000   Losers: £12,000   Loser: £22,000
Winner: £35,000

High break: 105 – Gary Wilkinson £2,000

Previous Year's Results

YEAR	WINNER	RUNNER-UP	SCORE
1989	S. Hendry (Scot)	D. Mountjoy (Wales)	9–2

STORMSEAL UK CHAMPIONSHIP

Over the years there have been many snooker matches that can rightly be hailed as 'classics' and Stephen Hendry's 16–15 final defeat of Steve Davis in the StormSeal UK Championship easily fell into that category. The Guild Hall at Preston has seen many memorable matches, yet there was that special buzz as Hendry and Davis came out to do battle with a £110,000 first prize at stake.

Hendry had certainly had the upper hand in recent matches, but Davis had shown renewed endeavour as he fought his way through to yet another UK final. However, Hendry raced into a 6–1 lead and there was little evidence of the brilliant match-play snooker that was to follow from the two greatest players in the game. By the end of the first day, Davis had dragged himself back to 8–6 to prove the point of his pre-match comment: 'They will have to scrape me off the table.' Day 2 will long live in the memory of those privileged to watch it live at the Guild Hall and also for the millions who witnessed this epic battle on TV. Hendry began brilliantly with a 122 and eventually took four of the first seven frames to lead 12–9, while Davis responded with an excellent century and then cut the deficit to 12–11. Amazingly, Davis went on to lead 15–14 and opened a 49-point lead in frame 30 as Hendry's unbeaten record, which stretched back to the previous March, looked to have come to

an end. Hendry eventually levelled at 15–15 after a break that included a quite remarkable blue along the rail and then clinched the title by winning frame 31 with a break of 98 after Davis missed a red that could have set him up for his own match-winning break.

Davis said: 'It's difficult to recall just how good the great matches are, but I'd have to say that's one of the best five games I've ever been involved in.'

Debut hero: Alan McManus who competed in the UK Championship for the first time and played brilliantly to reach the semi-final before losing to the eventual winner Stephen Hendry.

StormSeal UK Open Results

FOURTH ROUND		FIFTH ROUND		QUARTER-FINALS		SEMI-FINALS		FINAL	
S. Hendry (Scot)	9								
v		Hendry	9						
A. Chappel (Wales)	3			Hendry	9				
N. Foulds (Eng)	9								
v		N. Foulds	2						
C. Wilson (Wales)	4			v		Hendry	9		
D. Roe (Eng)	5								
v		Fowler	9						
D. Fowler (Eng)	9			Fowler	3				
D. Mountjoy (Wales)	6								
v		Gary Wilkinson	8						
Gary Wilkinson (Eng)	9					v		Hendry	16
T. Griffiths (Wales)	5								
v		S. Francisco	4						
S. Francisco (SA)	9			McManus	9				
A. McManus (Scot)	9								
v		McManus	9						
S. Newbury (Wales)	3			v		McManus	5		
J. Wattana (Thai)	9								
v		Wattana	7						
D. Morgan (Wales)	2			White	6				
J. White (Eng)	9								
v		White	9					v	
P. Francisco (SA)	7								
J. Parrott (Eng)	9								
v		Parrott	9						
A. Jones (Eng)	3			Parrott	9				
G. Natale (Can)	5								
v		Johnson	8						
J. Johnson (Eng)	9			v		Parrott	6		
S. James (Eng)	7								
v		Knowles	9						
A. Knowles (Eng)	9			Knowles	7				
M. Hallett (Eng)	7								
v		W. Jones	8						
W. Jones (Wales)	9					v		S. Davis	15
J. Birch (Eng)	9								
v		Birch	6						
A. Drago (Malta)	6			Bond	7				
N. Bond (Eng)	9								
v		Bond	9						
A. Robidoux (Can)	5			v		S. Davis	9		
W. Thorne (Eng)	9								
v		Thorne	5						
C. Roscoe (Wales)	1			S. Davis	9				
S. Davis (Eng)	9								
v		S. Davis	9						
B. West (Eng)	5								

Losers: £3,000	Losers: £6,000	Losers: £15,000	Losers: £30,000	Loser: £60,000
				Winner: £110,000

High break: 140 – J. Parrott £9,000

Previous Years' Results

YEAR	WINNER	RUNNER-UP	SCORE
1977	(Super Crystalate) P. Fagan (Rep Ire)	D. Mountjoy (Wales)	12–9
1978	(Coral) D. Mountjoy (Wales)	David Taylor (Eng)	15–9
1979	(Coral) J. Virgo (Eng)	T. Griffiths (Wales)	14–13
1980	(Coral) S. Davis (Eng)	A. Higgins (NI)	16–6
1981	(Coral) S. Davis (Eng)	T. Griffiths (Wales)	16–3
1982	(Coral) T. Griffiths (Wales)	A. Higgins (NI)	16–15
1983	(Coral) A. Higgins (NI)	S. Davis (Eng)	16–15
1984	(Coral) S. Davis (Eng)	A. Higgins (NI)	16–8
1985	(Coral) S. Davis (Eng)	W. Thorne (Eng)	16–14
1986	(Tennents) S. Davis (Eng)	N. Foulds (Eng)	16–7
1987	(Tennents) S. Davis (Eng)	J. White (Eng)	16–14
1988	(Tennents) D. Mountjoy (Wales)	S. Hendry (Scot)	16–12
1989	(StormSeal) S. Hendry (Scot)	S. Davis (Eng)	16–12

Hendry, meanwhile, was even more ecstatic: 'It's the greatest match I have played in – a mega match in every way.'

The final overshadowed other great games like the 9–6 victory by Glasgow rookie Alan McManus over Jimmy White in the quarter-final. McManus also beat Dennis Taylor, Steve Newbury and Silvino Francisco on his way to a £30,000 pay day. In the semi-finals, McManus led Hendry 3–1 and can be rightly proud of his performance, even though he eventually lost 9–5. In the other semi-final Davis and Parrott slugged it out yet again, Davis winning 9–6.

BENSON AND HEDGES SATELLITE TOURNAMENT

When he turned professional last season, Alan McManus could not have believed that he would earn a 'wild card' call-up to the Benson and Hedges Masters, snooker's longest-running and best-known invitation tournament. But that's exactly what happened to the young Glaswegian, who won the Benson and Hedges Satellite Tournament at the Masters Club in his home town – the sponsors guaranteed the winner a 'wild card' Masters place.

After his 9–5 victory over James Wattana in the Satellite final, McManus said: 'I went to Wembley a couple of years ago as a spectator to watch Stephen Hendry and Steve Davis play. To be going back as a player is quite unbelievable. Wembley is the best venue I have seen.'

It had been an incredible month for McManus as he had also reached the semifinal of the StormSeal UK Championship. He collected a £700 high-break prize bonus at the Satellite Tournament for a run of 142 as well.

There had nearly been a 147 when Wattana potted fifteen reds, fifteen blacks and all the colours up to black in his fourth-round meeting with Mark Bennett but then failed on a hard cut on the last ball.

The Benson and Hedges Satellite event was an innovative addition to the professional circuit and was open to all players outside the world's top sixteen who were already guaranteed a place at the Masters.

Benson and Hedges Satellite Tournament Results

FOURTH ROUND:	I. Graham (Eng) bt J. Johnson (Eng) 5–1; J. Wattana (Thai) bt M. Bennett (Wales) 5–3; M. Smith (Eng) bt B. Morgan (Eng) 5–4; A. Chappel (Wales) bt P. Francisco (SA) 5–4; M. Price (Eng) bt P. Gibson (Eng) 5–4; C. Wilson (Wales) bt A. Wilson (Eng) 5–1; D. Roe (Eng) bt D. Fowler (Eng) 5–4; J. Campbell (Aust) bt S. Newbury (Wales) 5–2; Gary Wilkinson (Eng) bt C. Edwards (Eng) 5–4; A. Drago (Malta) bt R. Foldvari (Aust) 5–2; D. Morgan (Wales) bt K. Doherty (Rep Ire) 5–2; L. Dodd (Eng) bt J. Birch (Eng) 5–4; M. Gauvreau (Can) bt A. Cairns (Eng) 5–3; S. Francisco (SA) bt S. Duggan (Eng) 5–2; A. McManus (Scot) bt E. Hughes (Rep Ire) 5–1; P. Browne (Rep Ire) bt J. McLaughlin (NI) 5–4 Losers: £250
FIFTH ROUND:	Wattana bt Graham 5–2; Chappel bt M. Smith 5–1; C. Wilson bt Price 5–4; Roe bt J. Campbell 5–3; Gary Wilkinson bt Drago 5–3; D. Morgan bt Dodd 5–2; S. Francisco bt Gauvreau 5–4; McManus bt Browne 5–3 Losers: £500
QUARTER-FINALS:	Wattana bt Chappel 5–0; Roe bt C. Wilson 5–4; D. Morgan bt Gary Wilkinson 5–2; McManus bt S. Francisco 5–2 Losers: £750
SEMI-FINALS:	Wattana bt Roe 5–3; McManus bt D. Morgan 5–4 Losers: £1,500
FINAL:	McManus bt Wattana 9–5 Loser: £2,500 Winner: £3,000

High break: 142 – A. McManus £700

COALITE WORLD MATCHPLAY

Our Jimmy: Jimmy White with proud mum Lil and wife Maureen after retaining the Coalite World Matchplay trophy.

When Jimmy White retained the Coalite World Matchplay title at the Brentwood Centre in Essex, little did he know that he was about to embark on one of the most lucrative winning runs in snooker history. Following his 18–9 final defeat of Stephen Hendry, the 'Whirlwind' went on to claim the top prizes in the Mercantile Credit Classic and the Mita World Masters to earn a quite remarkable £334,000 in just fifty days.

White, who collected £70,000 for his Matchplay triumph, had handed Hendry his first defeat on British soil so far that season and it was a victory that was thoroughly deserved. Hendry was suffering from a cold but he said: 'It would have been a better match if I had been 100 per cent fit, but Jimmy played the better snooker and deserved his victory!'

At one stage Hendry trailed 7–2, but then compiled breaks of 93, 142, 35, 38 and 80 to win four frames in a row with that 142 earning him the £5,000 high-break prize and setting a new record for the World Matchplay. However, White won the last three frames of the session to go into day 2 10–6 ahead. By the end of the third session, White was virtually home and dry at 17–7 and, although Hendry compiled two half-century breaks, White grabbed frame 27 for his emphatic victory. He remarked: 'I'm not being disrespectful to my fellow professionals, but it's a joke how I kept getting beaten by so many mugs. That's probably because I played like a mug myself.'

In the semi-finals White thrashed Terry Griffiths 9–2, the last three frames taking just twenty-eight minutes as he knocked in breaks of 92, 85 and 102. In the other semi-final Hendry beat Davis 9–6. In the quarter-finals Hendry looked on his way out against Dean Reynolds as the world

number 8 from Grimsby compiled three centuries. Hendry eventually won 9–8 when, in the deciding frame, he trailed 56–17 but fluked a red and finished perfectly on a colour to win the frame with a 52.

The Matchplay features the top twelve players in the world based on the results of the previous season.

Coalite World Matchplay Results

FIRST ROUND		QUARTER-FINALS		SEMI-FINALS		FINAL	
		J. White (Eng)	9				
Gary Wilkinson (Eng)	9	v		White	9		
v		Gary Wilkinson	6				
M. Hallett (Eng)	7			v		White	18
S. James (Eng)	6						
v		Griffiths	9	Griffiths	2		
T. Griffiths (Wales)	9	v					
		J. Parrott (Eng)	8			v	
		S. Davis (Eng)	9				
D. Mountjoy (Wales)	1	v		S. Davis	6		
v		Clark	5				
M. Clark (Eng)	9			v		Hendry	9
N. Foulds (Eng)	2						
v		Reynolds	8				
D. Reynolds (Eng)	9	v		Hendry	9		
		S. Hendry (Scot)	9				
Losers: £5,000		Losers: £10,000		Losers: £17,500		Loser: £30,000	
						Winner: £70,000	

High break: 142 – S. Hendry £5,000

Previous Years' Results

YEAR	WINNER	RUNNER-UP	SCORE
1988	(Everest) S. Davis (Eng)	J. Parrott (Eng)	9–5
1989	(Everest) J. White (Eng)	J. Parrott (Eng)	18–9

MERCANTILE CREDIT CLASSIC

Jimmy White, blessed with so much talent, should have needed to buy a much bigger trophy cabinet for his luxury home in the Surrey countryside after ten years on the pro circuit. However, it was only last season that he finally became a consistent and popular winner. Following his victory in the Coalite World Matchplay, White journeyed down to the Bournemouth International Centre on the South Coast and made it two wins in a row when he hammered Stephen Hendry 10–4 in the final of the Mercantile Credit Classic.

In fact, Hendry looked as though he was going to suffer what would have been an embarrassing 10–0 whitewash after the 'Whirlwind', compiling eleven breaks of more than 30, took a remarkable 9–0 first-session lead in just over two hours. The final was effectively finished as a contest but Hendry did win the first four frames in the evening before White captured the tenth frame with a break of 48 to pick up the £60,000 first prize.

White said: 'That's the first time I have won two tournaments on the bounce. Normally I celebrate after winning one event and promptly lose the next one, but that didn't happen after the World Matchplay. It's my first ranking tournament win for more than two years, and to beat Hendry in two successive finals is a great feeling.'

Of course, Hendry had seen his hopes of snooker's first Grand Slam disappear and it also ended his world-record-breaking run of thirty-six straight wins in ranking tournaments. He commented: 'I have never thought about records and I have always said the Grand Slam is an impossible dream but I didn't want to lose 10–0. I never like losing, but it's great to see Jimmy playing so well.'

In the semi-finals White had three breaks of more than 70 in beating Mike Hallett 6–4, while Hendry included runs of 76, 110, 65, 66 and 102 in a high-scoring 6–4 defeat of Neal Foulds in which Foulds gave as good as he got in an excellent encounter.

The Classic has always been known as the 'Tournament of Shocks' and 1991 again provided many surprises. Rod Lawler, a first-year professional from Liverpool, hammered John Virgo, Steve Newbury and Joe Johnson before going down 5–2 to Hallett in the last eight, while another rookie, Ken Doherty, the former world amateur champion from Dublin, was also a quarter-finalist before losing 5–3 to White. However, Doherty had a £5,000 bonus for the highest break of 126.

Previous Years' Results

YEAR	WINNER	RUNNER-UP	SCORE
1980	(Wilsons Classic) J. Spencer (Eng)	A. Higgins (NI)	4–3
1981	(Wilsons Classic) S. Davis (Eng)	Dennis Taylor (NI)	4–1
1982	(Lada) T. Griffiths (Wales)	S. Davis (Eng)	9–8
1983	(Lada) S. Davis (Eng)	W. Werbeniuk (Can)	9–5
1984	(Lada) S. Davis (Eng)	A. Meo (Eng)	9–8
1985	W. Thorne (Eng)	C. Thorburn (Can)	13–8
1986	J. White (Eng)	C. Thorburn (Can)	13–12
1987	S. Davis (Eng)	J. White (Eng)	13–12
1988	S. Davis (Eng)	J. Parrott (Eng)	13–11
1989	D. Mountjoy (Wales)	W. Jones (Wales)	13–11
1990	S. James (Eng)	W. King (Aust)	10–6

Mercantile Credit Classic Results

FOURTH ROUND		FIFTH ROUND		QUARTER-FINALS		SEMI-FINALS		FINAL	
J. Campbell (Aust)	0								
v		Johnson	3						
J. Johnson (Eng)	5			Lawler	2				
R. Lawler (Eng)	5	v							
v		Lawler	5						
S. Newbury (Wales)	2			v		Hallett	4		
A. Chappel (Wales)	3								
v		W. Jones	2						
W. Jones (Wales)	5	v		Hallett	5				
M. Hallett (Eng)	5								
v		Hallett	5						
B. West (Eng)	0					v		White	10
J. White (Eng)	5								
v		White	5						
J. Birch (Eng)	2	v		White	5				
A. Robidoux (Can)	3								
v		McManus	1						
A. McManus (Scot)	5			v		White	6		
K. Doherty (Rep Ire)	5								
v		Doherty	5						
J. Prince (NI)	3	v		Doherty	3				
J. Parrott (Eng)	1								
v		Charlton	2					v	
E. Charlton (Aust)	5								
S. Davis (Eng)	5								
v		S. Davis	1						
C. Wilson (Wales)	0	v		N. Foulds	5				
N. Foulds (Eng)	5								
v		N. Foulds	5						
I. Graham (Eng)	0			v		N. Foulds	4		
Dennis Taylor (NI)	4								
v		Gary Wilkinson	5						
Gary Wilkinson (Eng)	5	v		Gary Wilkinson	3				
D. Mountjoy (Wales)	3								
v		Wattana	2						
J. Wattana (Thai)	5					v		Hendry	4
M. Bennett (Wales)	3								
v		Chaperon	3						
R. Chaperon (Can)	5	v		Drago	4				
M. Clark (Eng)	2								
v		Drago	5						
A. Drago (Malta)	5			v		Hendry	6		
D. Roe (Eng)	4								
v		O'Kane	2						
D. O'Kane (NZ)	5	v		Hendry	5				
S. Hendry (Scot)	5								
v		Hendry	5						
D. Fowler (Eng)	0								
Losers: £2,625		Losers: £4,500		Losers: £9,000		Losers: £18,000		Loser: £36,000	
								Winner: £60,000	

High break: 126 – K. Doherty £5,000

MITA WORLD MASTERS

The Mita World Masters, with its Wimbledon-style format, was billed by promoter Barry Hearn as 'the most ambitious tournament in snooker history'. After fourteen days at the National Exhibition Centre in Birmingham, this brand-new project was hailed as an outstanding success. Sadly, the £1 million prize money and the high staging costs have meant that the tournament will not be held this season, though there are hopes that the World Masters could become a bi-annual competition. This global gathering included men's singles and doubles, women's singles and doubles, mixed doubles and an under-16 junior tournament, all being played at the same time on twelve tables under the same roof. In the end more than 200 competitors from forty-three countries, including many national amateur champions, took part and, by the end of the tournament, there had been 323 matches, sixty-two century breaks and a remarkable 2,230 frames of snooker. A tie-break was also introduced in which players, when the scores were level at a certain point, played a deciding frame using just one red on the side cushion level with the pink spot plus all the colours.

The men's singles, worth £700,000 in total prize money and sponsored by Black and Decker, was won by Jimmy White who overcome Tony Drago 10–6 to scoop £200,000. There had also been a 147 maxi-

mum. James Wattana, who went on to reach the semi-final after beating Stephen Hendry 6–4 in round 3, scored his maximum against Paul Dawkins. The break took just eight minutes, but unfortunately the cameras of BSkyB could not make it to the table in time.

The women's singles title and a cheque for £15,000 was won by world champion Karen Corr who beat Stacey Hillyard 6–2, but Stacey went home with a share of the women's doubles title after she teamed up with Allison Fisher to stop Ann-Marie Farren and Karen Corr 5–2 in the final.

Miss Fisher also teamed up with Steve Davis to take the mixed event with a 6–3 win over Caroline Walch and Jimmy White.

Hendry and Mike Hallett, the top seeds who had won the last world doubles event

Double act: Mike Hallett (top) and Stephen Hendry are pleased after winning the Mita World Masters Men's Doubles.

four years earlier, collected £25,000 each for winning the Black and Decker men's doubles with an 8–5 victory over surprise finalists Jim Wych and Brady Gollan from Canada.

Wych and Gollan beat John Parrott and Neal Foulds, the number 3 seeds, 7–1 in the semi-final and the Canadians produced an incredible spell of snooker. In four frames Parrott and Foulds managed just 22 points, while Gollan scored a break of 129 and Wych added a break of 111. That combined break of 240 was a world doubles record which beat the previous best of 217 by Davis and Tony Meo in 1986.

And Gollan and Wych also set another record when, in an earlier round, they beat Joe Johnson and Martin Clark 7–5 at 2.40am – snooker's second latest finish. When the winning shot went in, there were nine spectators including three cleaners!

The under-16 tournament proved one of

the most popular events, especially with spectators being able to wander around at will in the arena to see whatever match took their fancy. John Higgins, now a member of Ian Doyle's Cuemasters squad, won the £5,000 first prize by beating Mark Williams from Wales 6–1.

Blooming great: Stacey Hillyard (left) and Allison Fisher say it with flowers after taking the Women's Doubles title at the Mita World Masters.

World double: Karen Corr after winning the Mita World Masters title to go with her World Championship victory earlier in the season.

Mita World Masters – Black and Decker Men's Singles Results

THIRD ROUND

- S. Hendry (Scot) 4 v J. Wattana (Thai) 6
- A. Robidoux (Can) 5 v J. Johnson (Eng) 7
- A. Chappel (Wales) 6 v J. Prince (NI) 3
- N. Bond (Eng) 3 v P. Francisco (SA) 6
- S. Mazrocis (Eng) 2 v S. Longworth (Eng) 6
- K. Doherty (Rep Ire) 5 v J. Birch (Eng) 7
- B. Gollan (Can) 6 v N. Foulds (Eng) 4
- D. Fowler (Eng) 2 v J. White (Eng) 6
- J. Parrott (Eng) 2 v A. Drago (Malta) 6
- M. Henson (Ger) 3 v Gary Wilkinson (Eng) 6
- N. Dyson (Eng) 3 v T. Griffiths (Wales) 6
- W. Thorne (Eng) 6 v W. Jones (Wales) 3
- D. Morgan (Wales) 6 v Dennis Taylor (NI) 4
- M. Hallett (Eng) 6 v S. Francisco (SA) 2
- P. Davies (Wales) 2 v A. Meo (Eng) 6
- E. Henderson (Scot) 3 v S. Davis (Eng) 6

FOURTH ROUND

- Wattana 7 v Johnson 4
- Chappel 4 v P. Francisco 7
- Longworth 7 v Birch 4
- Gollan 0 v White 7
- Drago 7 v Gary Wilkinson 5
- Griffiths 8 v Thorne 7
- D. Morgan 8 v Hallett 7
- Meo 5 v S. Davis 7

QUARTER-FINALS

- Wattana 8 v P. Francisco 2
- Longworth 6 v White 8
- Drago 9 v Griffiths 8
- D. Morgan 8 v S. Davis 5

SEMI-FINALS

- Wattana 8 v White 10
- Drago 9 v D. Morgan 7

FINAL

- White 10 v Drago 6

Losers: £5,000
Losers: £8,000
Losers: £15,000
Losers: £30,000
Loser: £70,000
Winner: £200,000

High break: 147 – J. Wattana £6,000

Mita World Masters – Black and Decker Men's Doubles Results

QUARTER-FINALS: S. Hendry (Scot)/M. Hallett (Eng) bt C. Wilson (Wales)/A. Chappel (Wales) 6–4; K. Doherty (Rep Ire)/F. Chan (HK) bt D. Mountjoy (Wales)/W. Thorne (Eng) 6–3; J. Parrott (Eng)/N. Foulds (Eng) bt R. Lawler (Eng)/P. Davies (Wales) 6–1; J. Wych (Can)/B. Gollan (Can) bt A. Jones (Eng)/P. Ebdon (Eng) 6–3
Losers: £5,000 shared

SEMI-FINALS: Hendry/Hallett bt Doherty/Chan 7–4; Wych/Gollan bt Parrott/N. Foulds 7–1
Losers: £8,000 shared

FINAL: Hendry/Hallett bt Wych/Gollan 8–5
Losers: £20,000 shared
Winners: £50,000 shared

High break: 240 – J. Wych/B. Gollan £4,000 shared

Mita World Masters – Women's Singles Results

QUARTER-FINALS: S. Hillyard (Eng) bt L. Horsburgh (Scot) 5–4; A. Fisher (Eng) bt G. Aplin (Eng) 4–1; A. Farren (Eng) bt S. Dickson (Wales) 4–0; K. Corr (NI) bt T. Davidson (Eng) 4–2
Losers: £1,500

SEMI-FINALS: Hillyard bt A. Fisher 5–2; Corr bt Farren 5–3
Losers: £3,000

FINAL: Corr bt Hillyard 6–2
Loser: £5,000
Winner: £15,000

High break: 62 – A. Farren £2,000

Mita World Masters – Women's Doubles Results

QUARTER-FINALS: S. Hillyard (Eng)/A. Fisher (Eng) bt J. Banks (Eng)/G. Aplin (Eng) 3–0; L. Horsburgh (Scot)/S. Dickson (Wales) bt F. Lovis (Aust)/J. Kelly (Rep Ire) 3–0; M. Fisher (Eng)/T. Davidson (Eng) bt L. Field (NZ)/L. Lucas (Aust) 3–1; A. Farren (Eng)/K. Corr (NI) bt S. Smith (Eng)/J. Noon (Eng) 3–1
Losers: £1,000 shared

SEMI-FINALS: Hillyard/A. Fisher bt Horsburgh/Dickson 4–2; Farren/Corr bt M. Fisher/Davidson 5–3
Losers: £2,500 share

FINAL: Hillyard/A. Fisher bt Farren/Corr 5–2
Losers: £5,000 shared
Winners: £10,000 shared

High break: 123 – S. Hillyard/A. Fisher £1,000 shared

Mita World Masters – Under-16 Results

QUARTER-FINALS: J. Higgins (Scot) bt R. O'Sullivan (Eng) 5–4; J. Saunders (Eng) bt David Buskin (Eng) 4–2; M. Williams (Wales) bt M. O'Sullivan (Eng) 4–2; Q. Hann (Aust) bt Daniel Buskin (Eng) 5–3
Losers: £1,000

SEMI-FINALS: Higgins bt Saunders 6–5; Williams bt Hann 5–1
Losers: £2,000

FINAL: Higgins bt Williams 6–1
Loser: £3,000
Winner: £5,000

High break: 106 – R. O'Sullivan £1,000

Mita World Masters – Mixed Doubles Results

QUARTER-FINALS: S. Hendry (Scot)/S. Hillyard (Eng) bt D. Morgan (Wales)/K. Shaw (Eng) 4–0; J. White (Eng)/C. Walch (Eng) bt J. Wattana (Thai)/S. Smith (Eng) 5–3; M. Bennett (Wales)/S. Dickson (Wales) bt P. Ebdon (Eng)/J. Gillespie (Scot) 4–2; S. Davis (Eng)/A. Fisher (Eng) bt J. Johnson (Eng)/T. Davidson (Eng) 4–2
Losers: £1,500 shared

SEMI-FINALS: White/Walch bt Hendry/Hillyard 5–1; S. Davis/ A. Fisher bt M. Bennett/Dickson 5–2
Losers: £3,000 shared

FINAL: S. Davis/A. Fisher bt White/Walch 6–3
Losers: £5,000 shared
Winners: £15,000 shared

High break: 159 – S. Davis/A. Fisher £2,000 shared

BENSON AND HEDGES MASTERS

Stephen Hendry became the first player to win the Benson and Hedges Masters title three times in a row after completing a 'Houdini' escape in a magnificent final against Mike Hallett at the Wembley Conference Centre. The Scot's hat-trick dream had seemed in ruins as Hallett led 7–0 after the first session to leave Hendry with little chance of escaping a thrashing. Hallett, with breaks of 87, 80, 73 and 53, completely dominated the afternoon play and Hendry returned in front of a capacity Wembley crowd, knowing that the fans were not expecting miracles. However, a miracle was exactly what Stephen delivered.

Hendry, after winning the first two frames at night, saw Hallett go 8–2 ahead by winning the tenth 70–58. In most sporting dramas there is one major turning point and that moment arrived in the eleventh frame. Hendry was 61–1 in front, but Hallett fought back with a break of 48, needing just pink and black to take the match and the £100,000 first prize. The crowd held their breath as Hallett failed to get position on the pink and missed. Hendry potted it to make the score 8–3 and from then on there was an air of inevitability about a Hendry victory. Hallett's confidence sunk

fast and in the end Hendry lifted his fist in triumph after taking the seventeenth and deciding frame. It was one of the greatest comebacks in snooker history.

Hendry said: 'I just can't believe I won. It is the greatest comeback of my life and is one of my top three wins. Mike certainly had chances but he didn't take them – you can't have room for sympathy in a professional sport. At 7–0 down, all I was aiming to do was make the scoreline respectable.'

Worse was to follow for poor Hallett as he received a phone call saying that his house in Grimsby had been burgled and jewellery to the value of £5,000 had been stolen. He said: 'To hear that the house had been burgled on top of everything else made it the worst day of my life. Watching Hendry come back was like undergoing a public operation under the surgeon's knife. Anyone got a rope? Hendry didn't win it – I blew it and to lose like this is ridiculous.'

Jimmy White had hammered Hendry in their last two meetings in the finals of the Coalite World Matchplay and Mercantile Credit Classic but Hendry was completely on top as he crushed White 6–1 in the semi-final. Hallett had earned his final place when he recovered from 2–0 behind

Shattered: Mike Hallett after seeing leads of 7–0 and 8–2 disintegrate into a 9–8 defeat at the hands of Stephen Hendry in the final of the Benson and Hedges Masters at Wembley.

to overcome Terry Griffiths 6–3, including achieving a 125 clearance.

The Benson and Hedges Masters, snooker's most prestigious invitation tournament, was played out with London gripped in icy Arctic conditions but the action was just as hot as ever inside the luxurious Conference Centre.

In the quarter-finals, Hallett proved too good for Neal Foulds and won 5–1, Griffiths overwhelmed John Parrott 5–2 and Hendry included successive breaks of 131

Benson and Hedges Masters Results

FIRST ROUND		SECOND ROUND		QUARTER-FINALS		SEMI-FINALS		FINAL	
		S. Hendry (Scot)	5						
		v		Hendry	5				
		J. Virgo (Eng)	1						
A. Meo (Eng)	5	Meo	5	v		Hendry	6		
v		v		Meo	0				
Gary Wilkinson (Eng)	3	D. Reynolds (Eng)	2						
						v		Hendry	9
		D. Mountjoy (Wales)	4						
		v		James	4				
		S. James (Eng)	5			White	1		
				v					
		M. Clark (Eng)	1						
		v		White	5				
		J. White (Eng)	5					v	
		J. Parrott (Eng)	5						
		v		Parrott	2				
		W. Thorne (Eng)	3						
				v		Griffiths	3		
		Dennis Taylor (NI)	2						
		v		Griffiths	5				
		T. Griffiths (Wales)	5						
								Hallett	8
		M. Hallett (Eng)	5						
A. Robidoux (Can)	3	v		Hallett	5				
v		McManus	3			Hallett	6		
A. McManus (Scot)	5	N. Foulds (Eng)	5	v					
		v		Foulds	1				
		S. Davis (Eng)	4						
Losers: £6,000		Losers: £9,000		Losers: £15,000		Losers: £23,000		Loser: £50,000	
								Winner: £100,000	

High break: 135 – Dennis Taylor £10,000

Previous Years' Results

YEAR	WINNER	RUNNER-UP	SCORE
1975	J. Spencer (Eng)	R. Reardon (Wales)	9–8
1976	R. Reardon (Wales)	G. Miles (Eng)	7–3
1977	D. Mountjoy (Wales)	R. Reardon (Wales)	7–6
1978	A. Higgins (NI)	C. Thorburn (Can)	7–5
1979	P. Mans (SA)	A. Higgins (NI)	8–4
1980	T. Griffiths (Wales)	A. Higgins (NI)	9–5
1981	A. Higgins (NI)	T. Griffiths (Wales)	9–6
1982	S. Davis (Eng)	T. Griffiths (Wales)	9–5
1983	C. Thorburn (Can)	R. Reardon (Wales)	9–7
1984	J. White (Eng)	T. Griffiths (Wales)	9–5
1985	C. Thorburn (Can)	D. Mountjoy (Wales)	9–6
1986	C. Thorburn (Can)	J. White (Eng)	9–5
1987	Dennis Taylor (NI)	A. Higgins (NI)	9–8
1988	S. Davis (Eng)	M. Hallett (Eng)	9–0
1989	S. Hendry (Scot)	J. Parrott (Eng)	9–6
1990	S. Hendry (Scot)	J. Parrott (Eng)	9–4

and 114 as he completed one hundred centuries in his career during a 5–0 hammering of Tony Meo. White made it with four minutes to spare after getting caught in a traffic jam, but still managed to reach the last four by beating Steve James 5–4. Steve Davis was a 5–4 loser in the second round to Neal Foulds, while Alan McManus, the winner of the Benson and Hedges Satellite Tournament, went out 5–3 to Hallett after a first-round victory over Alain Robidoux. The high-break prize of £10,000 went to Dennis Taylor for a 135 against Griffiths in the first round but, unfortunately, the 1985 world champion still lost the match 5–2.

REGAL WELSH PROFESSIONAL CHAMPIONSHIP

Darren Morgan retained the last Regal Welsh Professional Championship with a comprehensive 9–3 final defeat of Mark Bennett at the Newport Centre in Gwent. Morgan said: 'I am pleased and delighted to be the last Welsh champion' – the tournament will go 'open' this season.

Defending champion Morgan had four half-century breaks in taking a 5–2 interval

Repeat success: Darren Morgan receives the Regal Welsh Championship trophy from Graham Blashill, the southern trading director of Imperial Tobacco, for the second year running.

lead and he began the evening with a 123 that eventually earned him the £1,500 high-break bonus. Bennett could manage only one frame at night as Morgan easily went home with the £11,000 winner's cheque.

Doug Mountjoy was absent because his daughter was getting married. The tournament will also be remembered for a rumpus involving the new interpretation of the 'miss' rule. In a quarter-final match with Wayne Jones, Cliff Wilson was called for two successive misses by referee Gus Lillygreen. Wilson argued about both decisions and walked out to find the tournament director, Simon Weaver. A heated discussion took place between Wilson, Lillygreen and Weaver before the referee returned and apologised, while Wilson conceded the frame and eventually lost 6–4.

Regal Welsh Championship Results

FIRST ROUND:	R. Reardon bt C. Roscoe 6–5 Loser: £1,000
QUARTER-FINALS:	D. Morgan bt Reardon 6–4; W. Jones bt C. Wilson 6–4; M. Bennett bt S. Newbury 6–4; A. Chappel bt T. Griffiths 6–3 Losers: £1,750
SEMI-FINALS:	Morgan bt Jones 9–8; Bennett bt Chappel 9–5 Losers: £3,750
FINAL:	Morgan bt Bennett 9–3 Loser: £7,000 Winner: £11,000

High break: 123 – D. Morgan £1,500

PEARL ASSURANCE BRITISH OPEN

There were doubters who, despite Stephen Hendry's deserved place at number 1 in the world rankings, were convinced that the young Scot did not have the necessary 'bottle' to stay the course for many years. However, he showed, following his brilliant comeback to win the Benson and Hedges Masters, that 'bottle' is a commodity he has in abundance as he won the Pearl Assurance British Open title in Derby.

After a none-too-convincing path to the final, Hendry came up against Cuemasters stablemate Gary Wilkinson and won 10–9 after a match that could have gone either way. Wilkinson, from Kirkby-in-Ashfield, was contesting the first major final of his career and was certainly in a buoyant mood after his 9–8 semi-final win over Jimmy White. Wilkinson's first title looked a distinct possibility as he led 6–3 at the end of the first session of the final.

When Hendry drew level at 6–6, the popular money was on his pulling away to claim the £75,000 first prize, but Wilkinson refused to buckle and opened a 8–6 lead. A fluke in frame 15, followed by a break of 118, brought the scores level at 8–8 and Wilkinson's fight looked to have finished as Hendry made it 9–8. Wilkinson, proving his character, knocked in a 91 to set up a last-frame decider, but when he missed a black Hendry soon delivered the killing blow to win 10–9.

Pearl Assurance British Open Results
(Redrawn at random from fourth round onwards)

FOURTH ROUND		FIFTH ROUND		QUARTER-FINALS		SEMI-FINALS		FINAL	
D. Mountjoy (Wales)	4								
v		Gary Wilkinson	5						
A. Meo (Eng)	5			S. Davis	5				
N. Foulds (Eng)	4	v							
v		Wattana	2			White	8		
R. Foldvari (Aust)	5			v					
D. Reynolds (Eng)	5								
v		Hallett	5						
W. King (Aust)	3	v		Hallett	3				
E. Charlton (Aust)	1								
v		Foldvari	2			v		Gary Wilkinson	9
C. Roscoe (Wales)	5								
T. Griffiths (Wales)	5								
v		Knowles	3						
R. Marshall (Eng)	3	v		Gary Wilkinson	5				
S. Davis (Eng)	5	A. Jones	5						
v				v		Gary Wilkinson	9		
M. Clark (Eng)	2								
A. Jones (Eng)	5								
v		Hendry	5						
K. Stevens (Can)	3	v		A. Jones	3				
J. White (Eng)	5	Meo	4					v	
v									
D. Fowler (Eng)	3								
S. Hendry (Scot)	5								
v		Robidoux	5						
F. Chan (HK)	0	v		White	5				
Gary Wilkinson (Eng)	5	Drago	0						
v				v		Hendry	9		
S. Francisco (SA)	2								
M. Hallett (Eng)	5								
v		Reynolds	1						
J. Johnson (Eng)	2	v		Robidoux	3				
Dennis Taylor (NI)	5	Dennis Taylor	5						
v						v		Hendry	10
B. Gollan (Can)	0								
P. Francisco (SA)	2								
v		White	5						
A. Robidoux (Can)	5	v		Hendry	5				
A. Cairns (Eng)	3	Griffiths	3						
v				v		S. Davis	7		
A. Drago (Malta)	5								
J. Wattana (Thai)	5								
v		S. Davis	5						
S. Murphy (Rep Ire)	2	v		Dennis Taylor	1				
A. Knowles (Eng)	5	Roscoe	3						
v									
M. Bennett (Wales)	1								
Losers: £4,000		Losers: £6,000		Losers: £11,000		Losers: £21,500		Loser: £44,000	
								Winner: 75,000	

High break: 139 – Gary Wilkinson £5,000

Previous Years' Results

YEAR	WINNER	RUNNER-UP	SCORE
1980	(British Gold Cup) A. Higgins (NI)	R. Reardon (Wales)	5–1
1981	(Yamaha) S. Davis (Eng)	David Taylor (Eng)	9–6
1982	(Yamaha) S. Davis (Eng)	T. Griffiths (Wales)	9–7
1983	(Yamaha) R. Reardon (Wales)	J. White (Eng)	9–6
1984	(Yamaha) Three-man play-off		
	D. Martin (Eng)	J. Dunning (Eng)	3–2
	S. Davis (Eng)	J. Dunning	4–1
	S. Davis	D. Martin	3–0
	Winner – Davis		
1985	(Dulux) S. Francisco (SA)	K. Stevens (Can)	12–9
1986	(Dulux) S. Davis (Eng)	W. Thorne (Eng)	12–7
1987	(Dulux) J. White (Eng)	N. Foulds (Eng)	13–9
1988	(MIM Britannia) S. Hendry (Scot)	M. Hallett (Eng)	13–2
1989	(Anglian Windows) A. Meo (Eng)	D. Reynolds (Eng)	13–6
1990	(Pearl) R. Chaperon (Can)	A. Higgins (NI)	10–8

Hendry said: 'At 6–3 down, I was fortunate that Gary didn't destroy me. Gary's fear was not of me but of winning his first ranking tournament.'

Wilkinson commented: 'I knew I'd blown it as soon as I missed that black in the last frame. If I'd stamped my authority on the game in the evening session, the trophy would have been mine.' He collected £44,000 plus £6,000 for the two high-break prizes – 139s scored before and during the televised stages.

Hendry had reached his final after an excellent 9–7 win over Steve Davis while Davis had recovered from 3–1 down to beat Mike Hallett 5–3 in the previous round. Welshman Colin Roscoe, ranked a lowly 48, reached the last sixteen with victories over John Parrott and Eddie Charlton before going down 5–3 to Davis. Bob Chaperon, the defending champion from Canada, didn't last long as he was beaten 5–4 in his opening match by Hong Kong's Franky Chan.

The British Open also set an unenviable record for the world's slowest nine-frame match as Robby Foldvari beat Neal Foulds 5–4 in 339 minutes.

TULIP EUROPEAN OPEN

The hectic ranking tournament season usually produces one major surprise winner and this year that 'accolade' went to Tony Jones, the world number 35 from Chesterfield, who won the Tulip European Open in the Dutch seaport of Rotterdam. A couple of years ago Jones was languishing in the middle of the rankings but knew his future was in jeopardy as he had failed to earn a single ranking point. Then he decided he would become more professional in his outlook on snooker and that dedication paid off when he beat Mark Johnston-Allen, another surprise package, 9–7 in the final to take the £35,000 first prize.

Johnston-Allen, the world number 59 from Bristol, scored a sensational 5–0 whitewash over Stephen Hendry in the fifth round and then accounted for Dene O'Kane and Cliff Thorburn on his way to the final. It was an excellent see-saw final and Jones came from 7–5 down to win

Tulip European Open Results

FOURTH ROUND		FIFTH ROUND		QUARTER-FINALS		SEMI-FINALS		FINAL	
D. Morgan (Wales)	1								
v		A. Jones	5						
A. Jones (Eng)	5			A. Jones	5				
S. James (Eng)	5	v							
v		James	3						
D. Campbell (Scot)	2			v		A. Jones	6		
Dennis Taylor (NI)	5								
v		Dennis Taylor	5						
N. Gilbert (Eng)	3	v		Dennis Taylor	3				
J. Wych (Can)	4								
v		C. Wilson	3					A. Jones	9
C. Wilson (Wales)	5					v			
D. Mountjoy (Wales)	5								
v		Mountjoy	5						
E. Charlton (Aust)	1	v		Mountjoy	2				
W. Thorne (Eng)	5								
v		Thorne	4	v		Gollan	2		
A. Knowles (Eng)	2								
J. McLaughlin (NI)	4			Gollan	5				
v		P. Francisco	2						
P. Francisco (SA)	5	v							
J. Wattana (Thai)	3								v
v		Gollan	5						
B. Gollan (Can)	5								
S. Davis (Eng)	5								
v		S. Davis	4	Thorburn	5				
Gary Wilkinson (Eng)	0	v							
A. Meo (Eng)	3	Thorburn	5						
v				v		Thorburn	4		
C. Thorburn (Can)	5								
N. Foulds (Eng)	5			N. Foulds	2				
v		N. Foulds	5						
C. Edwards (Eng)	4	v							
T. Griffiths (Wales)	1	Doherty	3			v		Johnston-Allen	7
v									
K. Doherty (Rep Ire)	5								
D. Reynolds (Eng)	5								
v		Reynolds	4	O'Kane	2				
J. Prince (NI)	3	v							
M. Clark (Eng)	1	O'Kane	5						
v				v		Johnston-Allen	6		
D. O'Kane (NZ)	5								
J. Virgo (Eng)	3			Johnston-Allen	5				
v		Johnston-Allen	5						
M. Johnston-Allen (Eng)	5	v							
S. Hendry (Scot)	5	Hendry	0						
v									
J. Johnson (Eng)	0								
Losers: £1,500		Losers: £4,500		Losers: £6,000		Losers: £12,000		Loser: £22,000	
								Winner: £35,000	

High break: 92 – M. Johnston-Allen £2,000

Previous Years' Results

YEAR	WINNER	RUNNER-UP	SCORE
1989	(ICI) J. Parrott (Eng)	T. Griffiths (Wales)	9–8
1990	J. Parrott (Eng)	S. Hendry (Scot)	10–6

four frames in a row to clinch victory. He said: 'In 1989 I packed up the late nights and the drinking and concentrated on snooker. It was either that or get a job.' The ultimate reward for Jones was a place in the top sixteen this season at number 15. For Johnston-Allen there was the consolation that he had inflicted on Hendry only the second whitewash of the world number 1's career and that he had finally won some ranking points after eighteen months in the doldrums.

As Hendry departed, Steve Davis was installed as the favourite, but he also went out in the round of the last sixteen – 5–4 at the hands of Thorburn. The game finished at 3.11am – the third latest finish in snooker history – and had lasted 324 minutes. It was also the third longest best-of-nine-frames match. By the time the semi-finals had arrived, there was no representative from the top sixteen and Jones beat Brady Gollan of Canada 6–2 on his way to a fantastic win.

NESCAFÉ EXTRA CHALLENGE

Joe Johnson, who had been out of the limelight since his 1986 World Championship success, was a deserving and worthy winner of the Nescafé Extra Challenge – a four-man round-robin invitation event in Bangkok, the capital of Thailand. The Challenge, featuring Johnson, Tony Drago, Alain Robidoux and the local sporting hero, James Wattana, was watched by millions of enthusiastic Thai TV viewers. In the end Johnson won all his three matches and fully merited going home with the £10,500 first prize.

Nescafé Extra Challenge Results

ROUND ROBIN: A. Robidoux (Can) bt A. Drago (Malta) 5–0; J. Johnson (Eng) bt J. Wattana (Thai) 5–1; Johnson bt Robidoux 5–3; Wattana bt Drago 5–1; Johnson bt Drago 5–3; Wattana bt Robidoux 5–3

LEAGUE TABLE:

PLAYER	PRIZE MONEY	P	W	L	F	A	PTS
1. J. Johnson	£10,500	3	3	0	15	7	6
2. J. Wattana	£5,250	3	2	1	11	9	4
3. A. Robidoux	£3,250	3	1	2	11	10	2
4. A. Drago	£2,100	3	0	3	4	15	0

High break: 142 – A. Drago

BENSON AND HEDGES IRISH MASTERS

It seemed hard to believe that almost a year had passed since Steve Davis had last won a title when he stepped up to take the Benson and Hedges Irish Masters trophy after a 9–5 victory over John Parrott at Goffs in County Kildare. Davis, who had been struggling to work out defects in his cueing action, had not won a title all season, but he put that to rights after he discovered that his problems 'were all due to a sloppy grip on the cue. I was fighting the cue which meant the cue and my hand were going in different directions.'

As the tournament favourites – Stephen Hendry and Jimmy White – fell by the wayside, Davis and Parrott fought out an intriguing first session of the final with Davis 4–0 ahead, happily settling for a 4–3 advantage at the end. At night Parrott levelled at 5–5, but then Davis pulled away to retain his Irish Masters title. It was the sixth time that Davis had won this traditional eve-of-World Championship event. He said: 'I had been playing well in practice but forgot I could produce it in a match.' Parrott commented: 'Anyone who has said Davis is gone should try and play him for a living. He is made of metal.'

In the semi-finals Parrott had beaten Dennis Taylor 6–2, while Davis came back from 3–0 down eventually to win 6–5 against White. It was an exciting match and was played out in front of yet another sell-out crowd.

WHO SAID THAT?

'I have never thought of retiring, even when I have been going through such a bad spell. I love this game too much.'

▲

– *Steve Davis after winning the Benson and Hedges Irish Masters, his first title for nearly a year.*

Anyone for tea?: John Parrott and wife Karen (left) and Steve and Judy Davis relax after the final of the Benson and Hedges Irish Masters. Davis beat Parrott 9–5 to win the title for the sixth time.

Irish snooker fans were cheered by the performance of Dublin's Ken Doherty who, after serving as a crowd-control steward two years earlier, returned this time as a player to beat Doug Mountjoy in the first round before losing 5–3 to Jimmy White.

Unfortunately, there was a controversial start to the tournament when Dean Reynolds, arriving late, lost 5–2 to Steve James and then admitted: 'I have got an alcohol problem that I must sort out. There is something really wrong and I don't know who to turn to.'

A major surprise came in the opening quarter-final when Dennis Taylor, a finalist last year, beat Hendry 5–2 with a winning shot on the pink that went down as 'the Fluke of the Year'.

Fan-tastic: Steve Davis is surrounded by his young fans after winning the Benson and Hedges Irish Masters.

Benson and Hedges Irish Masters Results

FIRST ROUND		QUARTER-FINALS		SEMI-FINALS		FINAL	
M. Hallett (Eng)	2	S. Hendry (Scot)	2	Dennis Taylor	2		
v		v					
Dennis Taylor (NI)	5	Dennis Taylor	5				
				v		Parrott	5
T. Griffiths (Wales)	0						
v		Bond	3	Parrott	6		
N. Bond (Eng)	5	v					
		J. Parrott (Eng)	5				
						v	
		J. White (Eng)	5				
D. Mountjoy (Wales)	4	v		White	5		
v		Doherty	3				
K. Doherty (Rep Ire)	5					S. Davis	9
				v			
D. Reynolds (Eng)	2						
v		James	3	S. Davis	6		
S. James (Eng)	5	v					
		S. Davis (Eng)	5				
Losers: £5,371.05		Losers: £8,056.58		Losers: £14,322.80		Loser: £21,484.20	
						Winner: £35,807.00	

High break: 97 – J. Parrott £3,580.70

Previous Years' Results

YEAR	WINNER	RUNNER-UP	SCORE
1978	J. Spencer (Eng)	D. Mountjoy (Wales)	5–3
1979	D. Mountjoy (Wales)	R. Reardon (Wales)	6–5
1980	T. Griffiths (Wales)	D. Mountjoy (Wales)	9–8
1981	T. Griffiths (Wales)	R. Reardon (Wales)	9–7
1982	T. Griffiths (Wales)	S. Davis (Eng)	9–5
1983	S. Davis (Eng)	R. Reardon (Wales)	9–2
1984	S. Davis (Eng)	T. Griffiths (Wales)	9–1
1985	J. White (Eng)	A. Higgins (NI)	9–5
1986	J. White (Eng)	W. Thorne (Eng)	9–5
1987	S. Davis (Eng)	W. Thorne (Eng)	9–1
1988	S. Davis (Eng)	N. Foulds (Eng)	9–4
1989	A. Higgins (NI)	S. Hendry (Scot)	9–8
1990	S. Davis (Eng)	Dennis Taylor (NI)	9–4

CONTINENTAL AIRLINES LONDON MASTERS

Steve Davis might have started the season in poor form but finished on a high note when he needed just fifty-five minutes to beat defending champion Stephen Hendry 4–0 in the final of the Continental Airlines London Masters at the Cafe Royal in London. Hendry, with seven titles under his belt and holding a record of seven straight wins against Davis, was the favourite to pick up the first prize. But after a dramatic first-frame win to Davis on the black, Hendry was always in trouble and managed just 3 more points in the next three frames.

Davis, looking happy and relaxed, compiled breaks of 50, 86, 35 and 74 and thoroughly deserved to take the £30,000 winner's cheque. Hendry had the consolation of winning £12,500 and a £3,500 bonus for the high break of 140. Afterwards Hendry said: 'I was beaten in the World Championship but I didn't sit around and mope – I got straight back to the practice table. But on the night Davis deserved to win.'

A touch of class: Lord Forte of Ripley with Steve Davis after Davis had won the Continental Airlines London Masters at the Cafe Royal in London.

It was Davis' second title of the season and only the third time Hendry had been whitewashed in his career.

Continental Airlines London Masters Results

FIRST ROUND:	S. Hendry (Scot) bt M. Clark (Eng) 4–1; J. Parrott (Eng) bt J. Wattana (Thai) 4–1; J. White (Eng) bt A. Fisher (Eng) 4–2; S. Davis (Eng) bt Gary Wilkinson 4–0 Losers: £3,500
SEMI-FINALS:	Hendry bt White 4–2; S. Davis bt Parrott 4–3 Losers: £7,500
FINAL:	S. Davis bt Hendry 4–0 Loser: £12,500 Winner: £30,000

High break: 140 – S. Hendry £3,500

TRUSTHOUSE FORTE MATCHROOM LEAGUE

Stephen Hendry might have lost his world crown but he still finished the season with a record-equalling total of eight titles and a record £694,056 in prize money. His final success came in the Trusthouse Forte Matchroom League as he took the £50,000 first prize for the first time. He had 'blown' his chances in the previous season when a series of below-par performances followed his World Championship triumph. This time there were a couple of hiccups before he safely pocketed the title with a 6–2 defeat of Doug Mountjoy in Stalybridge, Cheshire. There was just one defeat for Hendry – 5–3 at the hands of Willie Thorne – while Steve Davis, the champion for the four previous years, did not lose a match. Unluckily for Davis' points tally, six of his nine matches ended in draws.

As usual, there were some high-quality performances in this ten-man League, which featured forty-five matches around the UK and included two newcomers, James Wattana and Steve James. Jimmy White, who finished third, included successive total clearances of 131 and 135 in a 6–2 defeat of Dennis Taylor, while Wattana enjoyed consecutive breaks of 104 and 136 in a 4–4 draw with Davis. Wattana and Tony Meo were on the brink of maximum breaks, both failing on the yellow with the score on 120.

The high-break prize of 141 and a £5,000 bonus went to Steve Davis while, at the bottom of the table, Doug Mountjoy and Dennis Taylor were relegated, Taylor's 5–3 win over Tony Meo lasted 239 minutes with the final frame taking seventy-eight minutes – just four minutes short of the record for the longest frame in professional snooker. At the other end of the time scale White and James fought out the last match of the season in Brentwood, when the entire eight frames lasted just eighty-one minutes. There was also another landmark at this match with match recorder Keith Weston officiating at his 1,000th successive frame in a three-year spell with the League.

At the time of writing the League was scheduled to be increased to thirteen players with a total of seventy-eight matches. The five new players were world champion John Parrott, Gary Wilkinson, Mike Hallett, Tony Drago and the winner of the 1991 Forte Hotels Ladies' Championship which had yet to be played.

Trusthouse Forte Matchroom League Results

T. Meo 5, D. Mountjoy 3; S. Davis 7, Dennis Taylor 1; Meo 5, N. Foulds 3; S. James 6, Mountjoy 2; James 7, W. Thorne 1; J. White 4, Meo 4; S. Hendry 5, James 3; J. Wattana 5, White 3; Mountjoy 5, Foulds 3; Davis 4, James 4; Thorne 5, Taylor 3; White 4, Foulds 4; Wattana 4, Meo 4; Taylor 4, Foulds 4; Taylor 4, Mountjoy 4; White 5, Thorne 3; Foulds 7, James 1; White 6, Taylor 2; Thorne 4, Wattana 4; Hendry 7, White 1; Wattana 5, Mountjoy 3; Hendry 7, Taylor 1; Foulds 5, Wattana 3; Davis 4, Thorne 4; Foulds 5, Thorne 3; Davis 4, Wattana 4; Hendry 6, Meo 2; Davis 4, White 4; Davis 7, Mountjoy 1; Taylor 5, Meo 3; Davis 4, Foulds 4; Hendry 6, Foulds 2; Wattana 4, James 4; Davis 4, Hendry 4; Thorne 5, Hendry 3; James 6, Meo 2; White 7, Mountjoy 1; Hendry 6, Mountjoy 2; Thorne 5, Mountjoy 3; Davis 6, Meo 2; Wattana 6, Taylor 2; Thorne 5, Meo 3; Taylor 4, James 4; Hendry 5, Wattana 3; White 5, James 3.

Trusthouse Forte Matchroom League: Final Table

	P	W	D	L	F	A	Pts	Prize Money (£)
Stephen Hendry (Scot)	9	7	1	1	49	23	22	50,000
Steve Davis (Eng)	9	3	6	0	44	28	15	30,000
Jimmy White (Eng)	9	4	3	2	39	33	15	25,000
Willie Thorne (Eng)	9	4	2	3	35	37	14	20,000
James Wattana (Thai)	9	3	4	2	38	34	13	17,000
Steve James (Eng)	9	3	3	3	38	34	12	15,000
Neal Foulds (Eng)	9	3	3	3	37	35	12	13,000
Tony Meo (Eng)	9	2	2	5	30	42	8	11,000
Dennis Taylor (NI)	9	1	3	5	26	46	6	9,000
Doug Mountjoy (Wales)	9	1	1	7	24	48	4	5,000

High break: 141 – Steve Davis £5,000

EMBASSY WORLD CHAMPIONSHIP

As the final stages of the Embassy World Championship unfolded at the Crucible Theatre in Sheffield, there were few pundits who looked further than Stephen Hendry or Jimmy White to collect the £135,000 first prize at the end of this seventeen-day marathon. Liverpool's John Parrott proved them all completely wrong, and deservedly claimed the famous trophy for the first time with an 18–11 final defeat of White.

Parrott had been the most consistent player of the event and, after a 16–10 defeat of Steve Davis in the semi-final, he was confident enough to say: 'This year I have come here to win.' He gave notice of those intentions in the very opening sessions of the thirty-five-frame final when, in seventy-three breathtaking minutes, he compiled breaks of 97, 75, 88, 74 and 117 to take a 7–0 lead. 'That's the finest session by one player I have ever seen,' was the unanimous decision of most observers, including WPBSA chairman John Spencer and BBC TV's top commentator Ted Lowe. By the end of the day, White had recovered to 11–5, but that opening onslaught had created far too big a gap and Parrott pulled away to claim snooker's greatest prize.

Bubbling over: John Parrott and wife Karen celebrate with champagne after Parrott's victory in the Embassy World Championship final.

Embassy World Championship Results

FIRST ROUND		SECOND ROUND		QUARTER-FINALS		SEMI-FINALS		FINAL	
S. Hendry (Scot)	10								
v		Hendry	13						
W. King (Aust)	4			Hendry	11				
A. Robidoux (Can)	10								
v		Robidoux	8						
S. Newbury (Wales)	5					James	9		
				v					
S. James (Eng)	10								
v		James	13						
I. Graham (Eng)	3			James	13				
D. Reynolds (Eng)	10								
v		Reynolds	12					White	11
R. Marshall (Eng)	8					v			
D. Mountjoy (Wales)	2								
v		Gary Wilkinson	13						
Gary Wilkinson (Eng)	10			Gary Wilkinson	3				
M. Clark (Eng)	10								
v		Clark	9						
M. Bennett (Wales)	6					White	16		
				v					
N. Foulds (Eng)	10								
v		N. Foulds	12						
E. Charlton (Aust)	7			White	13				
J. White (Eng)	10								
v		White	13						
N. Dyson (Eng)	3							v	
J. Parrott (Eng)	10								
v		Parrott	13						
N. Gilbert (Eng)	6			Parrott	13				
J. Virgo (Eng)	8								
v		Knowles	1						
A. Knowles (Eng)	10					Parrott	16		
				v					
W. Thorne (Eng)	8								
v		McManus	12						
A. McManus (Scot)	10			Griffiths	10				
T. Griffiths (Wales)	10								
v		Griffiths	13						
B. Pinches (Eng)	3							Parrott	18
M. Hallett (Eng)	4					v			
v		A. Jones	8						
A. Jones (Eng)	10			Dennis Taylor	7				
Dennis Taylor (NI)	10								
v		Dennis Taylor	13						
J. Johnson (Eng)	6					S. Davis	10		
				v					
A. Meo (Eng)	10								
v		Meo	6						
C. Edwards (Eng)	7			S. Davis	13				
S. Davis (Eng)	10								
v		S. Davis	13						
K. Doherty (Rep Ire)	8								

Losers: £6,000

Losers: £11,000

Losers: £20,000

Losers: £42,000

Loser: £80,000
Winner: £135,000

High break: 140 – J. White £12,000

WHO SAID THAT?

'What I have done for John Parrott is give him the confidence to over-ride setbacks.'

▲

– *John Spencer, the WPBSA chairman, who helped Parrott in his preparation for his Embassy World Championship success.*

Two years earlier Parrott had been on the wrong end of an 18–3 world final defeat by Davis. That was all now forgotten as he celebrated with his friends and family, including his dad, Alan, who arrived at the venue minutes after he completed his victory. Alan had a heart attack three years earlier and no longer watches his son's matches, but nothing could keep him away on the night of John's greatest triumph.

Hendry, the favourite to retain the title, had departed at the quarter-final stage, when, leading 11–9, he succumbed to Steve James who, potting brilliantly, took four frames in a row for a memorable 13–11 win. But James could not maintain the momentum and White beat him 16–9 in the semi-final. Even so, James, who has now moved to number 7 in the world rankings, equalled a World Championship record against White when he compiled three centuries in four frames.

As always there were some memorable moments and memorable individual performances. The pick of the newcomers was Scotland's Alan McManus, who beat Willie Thorne 10–8 and then took Terry Griffiths all the way before losing 13–12 in the second round. Gay Wilkinson came agonisingly close to scoring a maximum in two separate matches. First, on a score of 120, he missed the easiest of yellows against Doug Mountjoy and then just failed to double the fifteenth red against White in the quarter-final.

In the end Sheffield belonged to Parrott. The likeable Liverpudlian had won four previous tournaments but, in many people's eyes, they didn't really count as they were earned away from the shores of the British Isles. Parrott, however, finally proved a winner in the biggest tournament of them all.

World Championship Roll of Honour 1927–90

YEAR	WINNER	RUNNER-UP	SCORE	VENUE
1927	J. Davis (Eng)	T. Dennis (Eng)	20–11	Camkin's Hall, Birmingham
1928	J. Davis (Eng)	F. Lawrence (Eng)	16–13	Camkin's Hall, Birmingham
1929	J. Davis (Eng)	T. Dennis (Eng)	19–14	Lounge Billiard Hall, Nottingham
1930	J. Davis (Eng)	T. Dennis (Eng)	25–12	Thurston's Hall, London
1931	J. Davis (Eng)	T. Dennis (Eng)	25–21	Lounge Billiard Hall, Nottingham
1932	J. Davis (Eng)	C. McConachy (NZ)	30–19	Thurston's Hall, London
1933	J. Davis (Eng)	W. Smith (Eng)	25–18	Joe Davis Billiards Centre, Chesterfield
1934	J. Davis (Eng)	T. Newman (Eng)	25–23	Lounge Billiard Hall, Nottingham
1935	J. Davis (Eng)	W. Smith (Eng)	25–20	Thurston's Hall, London
1936	J. Davis (Eng)	H. Lindrum (Aust)	34–27	Thurston's Hall, London
1937	J. Davis (Eng)	J. Lindrum (Aust)	32–29	Thurston's Hall, London
1938	J. Davis (Eng)	S. Smith (Eng)	37–24	Thurston's Hall, London
1939	J. Davis (Eng)	S. Smith (Eng)	43–30	Thurston's Hall, London
1940	J. Davis (Eng)	F. Davis (Eng)	37–36	Thurston's Hall, London
1941–45	No tournament held			
1946	J. Davis (Eng)	H. Lindrum (Aust)	78–67	Horticultural Hall, London
1947	W. Donaldson (Scot)	F. Davis (Eng)	82–63	Leicester Square Hall, London
1948	F. Davis (Eng)	W. Donaldson (Scot)	84–61	Leicester Square Hall, London
1949	F. Davis (Eng)	W. Donaldson (Scot)	80–65	Leicester Square Hall, London
1950	W. Donaldson (Scot)	F. Davis (Eng)	51–46	Tower Circus, Blackpool
1951	F. Davis (Eng)	W. Donaldson (Scot)	58–39	Tower Circus, Blackpool

BA&CC Tournament

YEAR	WINNER	RUNNER-UP	SCORE	VENUE
1952	H. Lindrum (Aust)	C. McConachy (NZ)	94–49	Houldsworth Hall, Manchester

World Matchplay Championship

YEAR	WINNER	RUNNER-UP	SCORE
1952	F. Davis (Eng)	W. Donaldson (Scot)	38–35
1953	F. Davis (Eng)	W. Donaldson (Scot)	37–34
1954	F. Davis (Eng)	W. Donaldson (Scot)	39–21
1955	F. Davis (Eng)	J. Pulman (Eng)	37–34
1956	F. Davis (Eng)	J. Pulman (Eng)	38–35
1957	J. Pulman (Eng)	J. Rea (NI)	39–34

Between 1958 and 1963 no matches took place. From 1964 the title was decided on a challenge basis which meant that there was often more than one event per year.

YEAR	WINNER	RUNNER-UP	SCORE	VENUE
1964	J. Pulman (Eng)	F. Davis (Eng)	19–16	Burroughes Hall, London
	J. Pulman (Eng)	R. Williams (Eng)	40–33	Burroughes Hall, London
1965	J. Pulman (Eng)	F. Davis (Eng)	37–36	Burroughes Hall, London
	J. Pulman (Eng)	R. Williams (Eng)	25–22	Match series in South Africa
	J. Pulman (Eng)	F. van Rensburg (SA)	39–12	South Africa
1966	J. Pulman (Eng)	F. Davis (Eng)	5–2	Match series at St George's Hall, Liverpool
1967	No tournament held			
1968	J. Pulman (Eng)	E. Charlton (Aust)	39–34	Co-operative Hall, Bolton
1969	Championship again organised on a knock-out basis (Players No. 6)			
	J. Spencer (Eng)	G. Owen (Wales)	37–24	Victoria Hall, London
1970	(Players No. 6)			
	R. Reardon (Wales)	J. Pulman (Eng)	37–33	Victoria Hall, London
1971	(actually held Nov 1970 as a round robin)			
	J. Spencer (Eng)	W. Simpson (Aust)	37–29	Sydney, Australia
1972	(reverted to knock-out basis)			
	A. Higgins (NI)	J. Spencer (Eng)	37–32	Selly Park British Legion, Birmingham
1973	(Park Drive)			
	R. Reardon (Wales)	E. Charlton (Aust)	38–32	City Exhibition Hall, Manchester
1974	(Park Drive)			
	R. Reardon (Wales)	G. Miles (Eng)	22–12	Belle Vue, Manchester
1975	R. Reardon (Wales)	E. Charlton (Aust)	31–30	Melbourne, Australia
1976	(Embassy until present day)			
	R. Reardon (Wales)	A. Higgins (NI)	27–16	Town Hall, Middlesbrough, and Wythenshawe Forum, Manchester
1977	J. Spencer (Eng)	C. Thorburn (Can)	25–12	Crucible Theatre, Sheffield
1978	R. Reardon (Wales)	P. Mans (SA)	25–18	Crucible Theatre, Sheffield
1979	T. Griffiths (Wales)	Dennis Taylor (NI)	24–16	Crucible Theatre, Sheffield
1980	C. Thorburn (Can)	A. Higgins (NI)	18–16	Crucible Theatre, Sheffield
1981	S. Davis (Eng)	D. Mountjoy (Wales)	18–12	Crucible Theatre, Sheffield
1982	A. Higgins (NI)	R. Reardon (Wales)	18–15	Crucible Theatre, Sheffield
1983	S. Davis (Eng)	C. Thorburn (Can)	18–6	Crucible Theatre, Sheffield
1984	S. Davis (Eng)	J. White (Eng)	18–16	Crucible Theatre, Sheffield
1985	Dennis Taylor (NI)	S. Davis (Eng)	18–17	Crucible Theatre, Sheffield
1986	J. Johnson (Eng)	S. Davis (Eng)	18–12	Crucible Theatre, Sheffield
1987	S. Davis (Eng)	J. Johnson (Eng)	18–14	Crucible Theatre, Sheffield
1988	S. Davis (Eng)	T. Griffiths (Wales)	18–11	Crucible Theatre, Sheffield
1989	S. Davis (Eng)	J. Parrott (Eng)	18–3	Crucible Theatre, Sheffield
1990	S. Hendry (Scot)	J. White (Eng)	18–12	Crucible Theatre, Sheffield

THIS SPORTING LIFE

Professional snooker is a tough, demanding business but there are still moments to relax and try different sporting activities. Here we captured on film some personalities as they took time off from the professional snooker circuit.

Owzat for style?: Allison Fisher, the four times ladies' world champion, prepares to bat for Matchroom during a testimonial match against Somerset.

All of a quiver: Welsh champion Darren Morgan takes an archery lesson.

Rallying point: Dennis Taylor took a new direction in his career when he joined the Cuemasters stable. Here he changes course again.

Bullseye: Jimmy White gets ready for a try at electronic darts.

Swinging along: Mike Hallett switches from a cue to a club on the golf course.

In the driving seat: Cuemasters chairman Ian Doyle tries his hand at moon-buggy racing.

On the ball: Tony Meo takes over in goal as he faces his two sons, Tony Jnr (left) and Sonny. Is there a passing resemblance between Tony Jnr and England soccer captain Gary Lineker?

THE SNOOKER AND BILLIARDS PICTURE POSTCARD ALBUM

by Roger Lee

The picture postcard was not invented: it evolved, and for obvious reasons could not have been around before the introduction of the penny post in 1840. Its use in England was not authorised until 1870, and was met at first by considerable opposition – the lack of privacy (the servants might read a postcard) being the most common cause for complaint.

Once postcards became established there was no holding back, and soon they were being produced in every civilised country in the world. Their terms of reference went from views of pleasure resorts and foreign places designed to impress the recipient, to sentimental, patriotic and even obscene cards. The authorities soon clamped down on the last type, but the rather 'vulgar' card can still be found in today's seaside souvenir shops.

Picture postcards had their heyday from 1895 through to the 1920s, delivering their 'Wish you were here' messages around the world. The craze for collecting them also seems to have begun in the 1890s, as even Queen Victoria requested a royal relative to form a collection on her behalf. Soon all 'respectable' households had examples on their drawing-room table, and the picture postcard album began to replace the photographic 'family album', which had been so dear to the previous generation.

However, with the popularising of the telephone in the second quarter of the twentieth century, postcards began to wane as a means of communicating the short message. They do, however, allow considerable insight into the social and domestic history of their time, which is not only preserved in the pictures themselves, but is also often underlined by what the sender has written.

If the sending of postcards has declined, the same cannot be said of collecting them. During the 1960s interest was rekindled, and by the 1970s the boom of the 1890s had returned, while today the appeal has grown dramatically. Now, on an international scale, postcard clubs and societies are thriving, and many of the major auction houses have regular sales, with prices reflecting the interest and scarcity of certain sought-after cards.

Sport has been an obvious subject for the picture postcard, with billiards, and later snooker, getting their fair share of attention. Both games were portrayed in many ways – from comical to romantic, portraiture to topography, military to political, and often by the pen of a leading cartoonist of the period: Lawson Wood, Tom Browne, George Davey, Lance Thackeray, Fred Buchanan, C. N. Payne and Louis Wayne to name but a few.

Starting with an illustration of an 'early' billiard match, here are just a few examples of how the game has been portrayed on postcards.

'Prehistoric Billiards', published in 1905, was the theme of this postcard. Although the match depicted was supposedly played some 2,000 years ago, it looks as though the man at the table is playing with John Spencer's old cue! This was a billiards match of '2,000,000 up for a pot of potted shrimps'. The prize money has improved since then!

From the ridiculous to the sublime. The Billiards Room of Queen Victoria's Osborne House on the Isle of Wight, showing the table and decorations designed by Prince Albert.

From an oil painting by Thomas Sheard (1866–1921) entitled 'Our Village Handicap'. The three characters, who were octogenarians, could be seen playing billiards nightly in a little village close to Oxford. Prints (24 × 18 inches) were being sold in 1902 for 1 guinea (£1.05).

Romantic cards were prevalent in the early 1900s, and these two linking the billiard term 'kiss' are typical.

'Billiards Made Easy' is a set of six postcards from originals by Tom Browne printed in 1905. This one is simply captioned: 'Not his own table'. True; but at least he has both feet behind the baulk line!

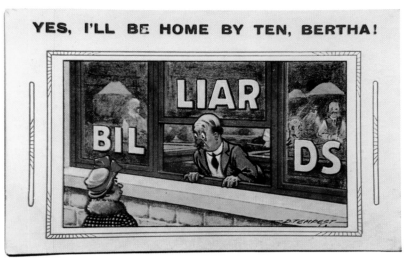

There is clever use of the word 'billiards' in this example – a good enough reason never to install sash windows.

This is obviously not a scene from one of the Temperance Billiard Halls which were widespread in the UK during the 1930s, 1940s and 1950s.

Children were encouraged at Temperance Billiard Halls, but without a box to stand on not much could be achieved by this young player of the early 1900s.

Walter Lindrum (1898–1960), endorsing a Thomas Padmore table in the early 1930s.

Joe Davis (1901–1978) who brought snooker to the public attention and was undefeated world champion for twenty years. An autograph on a card like this trebles its value to around £35.

Arthur Goundrill, a famous referee, who lost his forearm in the First World War, was no mean player himself, despite his disability. Along with many other players, Arthur raised great sums of money playing exhibitions for Second World War charities.

A classic seaside postcard of Joe Davis, ladies' champion Thelma Carpenter and New Zealand's Clark McConachy, taken on Bournemouth beach in 1932. Which of the two gentlemen was the fitness fanatic?

Billiards and snooker has tended to be a male preserve over the years, yet the fairer sex is well represented on postcards. This lady is all dressed up with nowhere to go but, judging by what she is wearing on her head, she obviously finds it cooler in the shade. The year is 1924.

Here are J. Roberts Jnr and E. Diggle at the turn of the century, on a card produced by H. Jasper Redfern, an entrepreneur of Sheffield. The match does not, however, appear to be at the Crucible Theatre!

ME AND MY DAD

by Steve Acteson

Morgan Morgan lends the phrase 'Give him some stick' a whole new meaning. A 6-foot, 18-stone former miner, Morgan has always believed in the old adage 'Spare the rod and spoil the child' as far as his son, rising snooker star Darren, is concerned. Not, it must be clearly spelt out, that Morgan Morgan is a bully, nor is he a harsh, unloving father – quite the opposite is true. As Darren puts it: 'Without him I would be nothing. I have unbelievable respect and love for my dad.'

But if he loses a match, Morgan Jnr knows his fiercest critic will be his father. Unable to take the flak, he provokes him deliberately by pretending he doesn't care that he has lost. Family love is the most intense of all, as are family arguments – and the arguments inherent in the Morgan household in the sleepy Welsh mining village of Cwmfelinfach are almost always centred on the snooker exploits of Darren.

That special moment: Darren Morgan, dad Morgan and mum Cynthia plus the Welsh Championship trophy in 1990.

They are as violent as a hand grenade exploding in a small space, but leave no debris. Harsh words are spoken on both sides and as quickly forgotten.

The players you see on television are not manufactured products. Some go it alone with family disapproval, as in the case of New Zealander Dene O'Kane, who used to sneak out at night to pursue his love of the game. In South Wales, however, snooker is pursued as passionately indoors as Rugby Union is outdoors. What is more, the denizens of the Valleys are not the sort of wimpish beings who believe that if an errant child receives a good whack it will damage his development irretrievably.

On the other hand it might be a bit embarrassing for Darren, should he one day win the World Championship and lose in round 1 of his next tournament. Picture the scene when he goes home, gives his critical father some lip and receives a clout across the shoulder from one of Morgan Morgan's walking sticks for his trouble. And that is far from a fanciful thought. These are not just walking sticks – they are talking sticks, and Darren has the message clearly imprinted upon more than just his memory.

At the age of sixteen and a half Darren was in love only with pool. His father had captained the local team in which he played and when the family went on holiday to Butlin's on Barry Island one summer Saturday, Darren was left to play for a League select team against Wales.

He recalls: 'The idea was to see if there was any new talent coming through and I did well enough to be offered a trial for Wales which I knew would please dad. I got to Barry the next day and after a couple of hours asked dad if he fancied a game of snooker. First poke I made a break of 60-odd and that was that. Dad banned me from pool straightaway, and when we got home he told the pool people I wasn't available after all.'

A new snooker club, the Red Triangle, had opened at Cross Keys near the Morgans' home, and Darren started going there three nights a week for hours of solitary practice, a game with his mates on Saturdays and a harder one with his father on Sundays after their regular 4-mile constitutional along by the railway line. The day before Darren's seventeenth birthday he made his first century, and the day after – having taken his birthday off – he made his second.

But by then his father's lifelong back problems were so bad that he had taken to his sticks: 'That really frustrated him. He was one of the best pool players in the Valleys and no mug at billiards or snooker either – his best snooker break was 97,' says Darren. 'But he was only in his forties when he had to stop work, and that was the worst thing for him. He loved work: he'd been thirteen years down the pits, thirteen as a postman and he's been a dustman. In fact he's on my birth certificate as a refuse collector.'

Two years on came a dilemma. Darren was earning only £30 a week as a glazier, 'which left precious little after I'd paid my board and lodging at home', and then he was made redundant. An offer came from a club in Newport to play there for £50 a week plus free table time and his amateur tournament expenses.

'Dad wasn't having any of that, though. He knew I didn't want to leave home and he had a word with a local businessman who owned the club,' remembers Darren. 'Although they couldn't entirely match the Newport offer, they offered me £25 a week and all the rest in turn for doing the tables and any other odd jobs. I jumped at it. I was getting my wages cash in hand but, trouble was, somebody shopped me to the dole office. We had to have a different deal

Bubbling with success: Darren Morgan and dad Morgan after Darren's win in the Pontin's Professional in 1989.

then. I signed off the dole and the idea was that if I could make enough from tournaments to earn a living, then they would pay my expenses. It cost dad thousands at first too. He drove me everywhere and paid what he could. The first year cost them both a packet, but when I was, oh, about nineteen and a half, I suddenly went potty on the amateur circuit, winning quite a few titles.

'The thing is, though, I've got a big mouth where my dad is concerned. I've got this nasty habit of winding him up, which is a bit daft really, considering his size. But I couldn't resist it anyway. Every time I lost he'd give me some terrible abuse, telling me I should give up and that I'd never get anywhere. I knew he never meant a word of it, but I still couldn't stop winding him up. Inside, if I lost, I was gutted. But I'd tell him it was only a game and didn't matter – and that would absolutely infuriate him.

'When I lost I'd go home and the house would be like hell. That was another reason for signing with Ian Doyle actually. Grateful as I was to the businessman, I knew he couldn't do as much for me as Ian, but I also thought it would take the pressure off at home. I couldn't have been more wrong there, though, because what it really meant was that when I lost I'd get it in the neck from Ian as well as my dad!'

Darren had also not reckoned with 'Dapper' Doyle's insistence upon impeccable standards of behaviour, whatever the table. One evening, at a black-tie dinner, Darren decided that his meal would be improved with the addition of tomato ketchup and called the waiter over to demand some. When he brought it, however, Darren wouldn't let him serve it from a silver bowl and instead grabbed the bottle and gave it a few hefty smacks to slosh it on to his plate. An appalled Doyle immediately slapped a £250 fine on Darren for his lack of etiquette, and when Morgan Morgan asked if that wasn't a bit hard on their lad, Doyle replied: 'Not really, Morgan. My first thought was to fine him £1,000 for his sauce.'

Darren adds: 'When I was younger my favourite place was the downstairs toilet. After I'd wound dad up enough he'd come chasing after me to give me a walloping and I'd squat on the floor in there with my hands over my head to protect myself. That was with his fists – he was fit then – but now he gives me a crack with one of his sticks – if he can catch me. Not that dad was ever vicious, mind. He was just trying to teach me a lesson. When I got older, I was too big to get down into that little space and dad wasn't able to run after me any more. So when I'd got him angry enough, I'd run out of the kitchen door. Trouble was, by then he'd resorted to chucking one of his sticks after me. I thought I'd be all right that way until he hit me on the back of the head a couple of times – it hurt, too.

'He still thumps me now if he can get hold of me. But it's not nasty, see. It's like kids play fighting really. We argue all the time and we both say some hurtful things, but five minutes later it's all forgotten and there is never any resentment. You get arguments like that in every family. His criticism can make me so mad, though. I remember how, when I was seventeen, I lost in the quarter-finals of the local League singles and he went on and on at me in the car every foot of the 4 miles home. By the time we'd got there I was so furious I whacked the porcelain biscuit barrel with my cue extension and smashed it to pieces. There were bits of biscuit, biscuit barrel and cue extension flying all over the house and I thought, "Oh God, he'll kill me now," and shot into the garden. He'd calmed down the time I came back in and so had I. I apologised for what I'd done and I've never done anything like it since.

'It didn't stop us arguing, though. In 1987 my cue snapped in half and I bought myself a new one, a maple Joe Davis cue it was. But after a month I still wasn't getting on with it and I came home one day and started moaning and groaning about it and suddenly he'd had enough. He grabbed the cue and took it into the garden and said: "I've had enough of you moaning. It's not the cue, it's you, and this is all this cue is good for – to grow runner beans up." And with that he speared it a foot into the ground. But I persevered with the cue and the funny thing was, three months later, I won the World Amateur Championship with it in Bangalore. Not bad for a runner-bean stick!

'When I was twenty I was playing in the Bargoed Open at the Emporium. I was playing all right and I got to the semi-finals, and dad had been quite good all day, which means he hadn't been cussing me upside down. I was 2–0 up against Paul Jones of Tredegar in the semi-finals, but I lost the next and then I heard dad start. He was standing on this little balcony saying things like: "He always does this. He just doesn't want to win." And when it went 2–2 he got even worse.

'Paul got in early in the next frame and dad was still going on, and then it occurred to me that if I could hear him then so could Paul and everyone else. So I asked Paul to stop while he was still in his break and walked up to dad and told him he'd got three alternatives. The first one was to stay there and shut up, the second was to go to the back of the room and say what he liked because none of us could hear him from there and the third was to use the exit door. He called me something I'd better not repeat and went. I won that match and the final and went home with the £600 in prize money. I thought he'd be all right by then, especially as I'd won, but instead he gave me the biggest rollicking of my life for depriving him of the chance of seeing me win the tournament.

'The thing is, though, the only reason he was ever like that was because he loves me so much and has always wanted so much for me to do well. Everything he's ever done was for my own good and if it hadn't been for dad I'd never have got through the front door as far as snooker is concerned. I owe everything to him. I've got unbelievable respect for my dad. I've always known he was hard, but the difference is that he's solid too. He's always straight and always speaks his mind, and he brought me up the same way. That's why we argue, but that's why we've also had incredible fun over the years. I'd be nothing if it wasn't for him.'

Morgan has blossomed in the last two years and begins the 1991/92 campaign at number 33 in the rankings. Most people agree it's only a matter of time before this talented left-hander makes his move into the world's top sixteen. For the past two years he has been the Welsh professional champion and last season, in this Regal-sponsored tournament, he overcame Mark Bennett 9–3 in a one-sided final to take the £11,000 first prize. And it's a title Morgan can never lose, as the tournament has become defunct with the WPBSA's decision to turn the event into an open-to-all ranking competition.

Considering the number of current pro-

fessionals and their relative youthfulness, father-and-son relationships are not as prevalent on the circuit as you might expect. John Parrott's father Alan is never seen. They agreed long ago that when Alan was at tournaments it placed too great a nervous strain on both of them. Martin Griffiths, however, has been a frequent visitor to the World and UK Championships as a quiet observer of his son Terry. And Geoff Foulds, whose own playing career never reached great heights, has lived another through his richly talented son Neal, and when Neal is losing Geoff goes from auditorium to hospitality room to press room to officials' room, ever on the move, trying to find that lucky seat from where he will witness his boy turning defeat into victory. Bill and Steve Davis are another

Proud dad: Alan Parrott was the happiest father in Sheffield the night son John lifted the Embassy World title.

Me and my dad and his dad: Three generations of the Foulds family – world number 6 Neal (right), Neal's son Darren and Neal's snooker-playing dad Geoff.

Nice one, son: Tommy White is certainly pleased as son Jimmy displays the Coalite World Matchplay trophy.

Family album: Dennis Taylor and his dad Tommy.

partnership forged in a holiday camp – snooker-wise that is. The Davis family was on holiday at St Mary's Bay, Kent, and as the miniature steam trains chuffed past nearby on the Romney, Hythe and Dymchurch light railway, inside the dim billiards hall twelve-year-old Davis Jnr was being taught the first tricks of a trade that were to make him a millionaire and world champion six times over.

Bill Davis and Geoff Foulds played and continue to play a direct role in the coaching development and fine-tuning of their offspring. But Bill still knows his place. Once, after seeing Steve miss a sitter, he muttered: 'Naughty boy. I'll have to stop his pocket money.' But after a moment's reflection he added: 'Better not say anything, though – he might stop mine.'

Tommy White would never dream of offering his brilliant son Jimmy any more than his best wishes. You sometimes suspect Tommy still doesn't believe that he sired such a genius. But the chirpy, endlessly cheerful father of one of the game's true superstars is not entirely unknown himself. In 1987, as Jimmy and Tommy were waiting in the VIP lounge at Heath-

One for the future: Steve Davis, the six times world champion, and Greg who arrived during the Embassy World Championship.

row for a flight to Toronto for the Labatt Masters, Tommy spotted Vera Lynn sitting across the room with her husband. 'There's good old Vera,' said Tommy. 'I know her, Jim. Tell you what, I'll just pop over and say hello.' The Whirlwind tried hard to stop him, thinking that dad was about to show himself up, but Tommy hadn't got half-way across the room before the Forces Sweetheart of the Second World War had jumped up and called out: 'Tommy, how wonderful to see you!' The astonished Jimmy hadn't realised that his father, a former carpenter, had supplemented the family fortunes to the tune of half a crown (12½p) an hour back in 1947 working as a stagehand at the Tooting Granada. 'I used to take Vera her Guinness every night – marvellous woman,' Tommy recalled.

Seeing double: Willie Thorne with his twin sons, Tristan (left) and Kieran.

RAY REARDON: GOODBYE TO A LEGEND?

by Alexander Clyde

When Steve Davis describes somebody as his role model, it is advisable to sit up, take notice and award the subject a prime position in the front row of snooker's Hall of Fame. Ray Reardon, the remarkable Welsh wizard who inspired the young Davis, dominated snooker through the 1970s in the same way that Davis bestrode the 1980s. Yet, sadly, Reardon was almost certainly waving a reluctant farewell to the tournament circuit in March 1991, at the comparatively early age of fifty-eight.

'I've been beaten by the system,' sighed one of Wales' most illustrious sporting sons after being eliminated in the second qualifying round of the Embassy World Championship at Preston.

Known affectionately as the Prince of Darkness because of his Count Dracula hairstyle and teeth to match, snooker's old prince had lost 10–5 to one of the game's new young princes – Ulsterman Jason Prince.

The system had defeated the man who had pocketed six world titles in nine years between 1970 and 1978 because, with the game going open, all the qualifying events for ranking tournaments have been rescheduled for the summer months – and that is when Reardon is fully committed by contract to coaching and exhibition work on the holiday-camp circuit.

'This decision has been forced on me because I still love snooker and I'm more active than ever,' added Reardon, whose only opportunity to continue as a competitive professional in the game he has graced for twenty-three years lies in seniors and invitation events.

It has been a rapid and somewhat cruel fall from grace for a man who contributed so much in laying the foundations for the current snooker boom. Barely four seasons earlier Reardon still held a place in the top sixteen of the rankings, and less than a decade ago he had appeared in his seventh Embassy World final, losing 18–15 to his old adversary Alex Higgins in 1982 at Sheffield's Crucible Theatre. The famous Reardon grin and shoulder-rattling laugh, so much a part of the TV snooker scene, disappeared from public view as he slithered down the rankings in the latter half of the 1980s. Problems with his eyesight, necessitating a pair of glasses, plus a divorce from the wife who had contributed so much to his success, sapped away much of the old Welsh dragon's fire and famous fighting spirit.

But Ray Reardon, MBE, is nothing if not resilient. Now happily settled with his second wife, Carol, in Devon, he has continued to stay busy with his flourishing coaching and exhibition work, particularly around the holiday camps. Anyone who knows of the hardships he overcame to make his mark in the game he has loved for over forty years will understand that Ray is made of pretty stern stuff – a man of real character and substance who has fully earned his place in the front row of snooker's Hall of Fame.

Unlike the modern champions with their narrow, almost blinkered view of the world – moving straight from school into the professional game without ever having to earn their living from a 'proper job' to give them perspective – Reardon is from the old school. Born in Tredegar in the heart of the Valleys in October 1932, he followed his father down the mines at fourteen. But, unlike most of the lads at the coal face,

Six times a champion: Ray Reardon holds aloft the World Championship trophy which he won for the sixth time in 1978.

young Reardon had a passion which would one day see him strike gold – playing snooker. At the time he never dreamed that he could earn his living and make his fame and fortune with a cue, but even then he always wore gloves down the mines to protect his hands.

The teenage Reardon soon established himself as an exceptional talent in the snooker-crazy Welsh Valleys and won his first title at seventeen. It was the *News of the World* amateur title and his prize was

an ash cue, presented to him by the legendary Joe Davis. That cue was to become his tried-and-trusted friend for the next thirty-five years and helped him gain all his world titles.

He won the Welsh amateur title six years running between 1950 and 1955; then, when the Tredegar pits closed in the mid-1950s, Reardon, by now married with a young family, moved to Stoke-on-Trent to continue life underground at the Florence Colliery. But after being buried alive for

A clearer perspective: Reardon worked both at the coal face and in the police force before finding fame and fortune in the snooker world.

three hours in a pit accident, he decided to look for a less hazardous way to earn a living and joined the police force! He became PC 184 on the beat in Stoke and soon showed his mettle by earning a commendation for bravery for disarming a potential shop breaker.

PC Reardon's amateur snooker continued to flourish and he won the coveted English amateur title for the first time in 1964, beating John Spencer in the final. Offers of sponsorship came in and, in 1967, Ray took the biggest gamble of his life by turning professional. It really was a gamble because, in those days, there was only a handful of pros touring the country on a limited exhibition circuit and the tournaments numbered precisely one – the World Championship.

The breakthrough came in 1970 when

Reardon captured his first world title at the age of thirty-seven and pocketed a cheque for £1,250 – a far cry from the millions on offer for today's prosperous young stars of the green baize. Ray beat John Pulman 37–33 in that 1970 world final at London's Victoria Hall and there wasn't a TV camera in sight. But the revolution had begun the previous year with the arrival of colour TV. The BBC had asked Ted Lowe to put together a snooker event to coincide with the introduction of colour. It was called *Pot Black* and Reardon was the first man to have his name engraved on the *Pot Black* trophy. The public liked what they saw. Colour TV and snooker clicked, and men like Reardon, Spencer and Fred Davis started to emerge as personalities via the powerful medium of television. Then a brash young Irishman called Alex Higgins burst on to the scene in 1972 by winning the world title at his first attempt at the age of twenty-two. Snooker was off and running as a growing sport.

Reardon was at his peak through the 1970s and dominated the ever-expanding professional snooker circuit with his combination of steely consistency and affable personality. He won the world title five times between 1973 and 1978, the second year that the event was staged at Sheffield's Crucible Theatre, now established as one of British sport's top venues. There were several firsts. Ray was the first snooker player to be featured on TV's *This is Your Life* and the first to be a guest on Roy Plomley's radio programme, *Desert Island Discs*. Reardon's career as a competitive professional may have declined during the 1980s but that is nothing to be ashamed of.

Clowning around: Snooker's 'grand old man' Ray Reardon dons a false beard to entertain the crowd.

Time catches up with all of us, yet he has maintained his dignity and, above all, his delightful sense of humour. He revelled in his affectionate nickname of Dracula, as can be seen from his choice of one of eight records to take with him on a desert island – Tony Hancock's 'The Blood Donor'!

It is no coincidence that Steve Davis, the man who dominated the game for the best part of a decade, modelled himself on the Welshman who dominated the previous decade. History will decide who was the greatest snooker player, but those who saw Ray Reardon at his peak in the 1970s will insist: 'He was the best of them all.'

It's a Funny Old Game

Chrysalis, the independent TV company which now produces snooker programmes for ITV, introduced many new ideas during their first season. Players were interviewed well away from the table and the casual approach certainly paid dividends. However, one of their innovations was the use of a computerised chalk line by which commentators could show viewers which way they thought a player would play a particular shot or how he would get out of a snooker. One commentator, who shall remain nameless, drew the line on the table and the eventual path of the ball followed that line perfectly . . . only to miss its intended target.

During the StormSeal UK Championship, Steve Davis went out to buy some socks from Marks and Spencer and was accosted by a friendly drunk.

'Where are you going?' the drunk asked.

'I'm going to Marks and Spencer,' replied Davis.

'Oh, that's a coincidence,' said the drunk. 'I've just nicked this from there' — and he promptly showed Davis a jumper still in its Marks and Spencer wrapper!

Alan Hughes, snooker's number 1 announcer, recalled a time when his great friend Willie Thorne was going to give up gambling. One of Willie's friends had a contact who was a psychiatrist who would give Willie a consultancy — free of charge. The psychiatrist turned up and an hour later emerged with Willie . . . and the psychiatrist was carrying the *Sporting Life*. They went straight to the nearest bookie's as it was all part of the treatment to show Willie that he didn't need to bet. Two hours later the pair came back and the psychiatrist was asked how he got on. He replied: 'I had a yankee bet and every one of them lost.'

Tony Drago (below) turned round to give a young 'fan' an autograph during the interval of his match with Jon Birch in the StormSeal UK in Preston — and was given a writ. Drago, apparently, owed money to a major bank but his debts were all cleared up when he won the £70,000 runners-up prize in the Mita World Masters in Birmingham.

One of the funniest sights of the year came in the 555 Asian Open in Guangzhou, China. A snooker table, weighing 2 tons, needed to be removed from the arena and, rather than dismantle the table, twenty-five people were press-ganged into service. Officials, the media and even John Booth, 555's international sponsorship manager, had to help, while instructions were bellowed out in English *and* Chinese. It was a miracle the table ever moved!

Last season, snooker's top referees were given a daily allowance of £25 to cover food and accommodation, but staying in hotels can be a costly business. Irish referee Len Ganley has got around the problem, however, by travelling around the UK circuit in a caravan (below). Len parks his caravan as near as possible to the venue and obviously cuts down his costs.

During the Coalite World Matchplay before Christmas, a Christmas party was arranged for the press and officials. Balding referee John Williams opened up his Christmas cracker to find . . . a toy hairbrush.

Tony Jones, from Chesterfield, decided to miss out on the New Year celebrations to prepare properly for his match in the Mercantile Credit Classic in Bournemouth. He recalled: 'On New Year's Eve I went to bed at 10pm in readiness for my match the next day. Unfortunately I wasn't playing until the day after and I could have celebrated after all!'

Jon Birch arrived in Bournemouth for the Mercantile Credit Classic with a bad shoulder. He said: 'I have been suffering from an inflamed shoulder and I made it a lot worse when I tried on a sweater I had received as a Christmas present from my girl-friend.'

Bedford's Mick Price played in the Mercantile Credit Classic . . . in carpet slippers. Price had trodden on a bottle while jumping over a wall at a local snooker club and badly damaged ligaments in his ankle. The ankle was so swollen that wearing shoes was out of the question and he obtained permission from the WPBSA to play in slippers. Unfortunately Mick 'slipped up' and lost 5–2 to Danny Fowler.

Juan Francisco Taylor Castaneda was one of the 'superstars' of the Mita World Masters when this Nicaraguan father of eight, who lives in Panama, arrived for the men's singles without a cue. Castaneda, who played only pool back home, thought he could pick up a cue just before his match. Fortunately Matchroom's sales director John Hines gave him a cue.

Castaneda lost 6–0 but, remarkably, knocked in a break of 50 in the final frame – not bad for a player who had never before played snooker on a full-sized table.

Middlesbrough's Jon Birch is famous for his colourful waistcoats but even he could not match Brazil's Rui Chapeu who played in an all-white suit plus a white flat cap during the Mita World Masters. Chapeu said: 'I only remove my hat when I lose.'

Motor vehicle repairers in Birmingham did a roaring trade during the Mita World Masters when six of the people involved – a journalist, a TV commentator and four players, including ladies' world champion Karen Corr and Liverpool's John Parrott (below with his damaged car) – had car crashes. Luckily no one was hurt, though Karen must have set some sort of record when she crashed her sponsored Ford Fiesta only seven hours after picking up the vehicle.

Steve Davis didn't give it a second thought when the phone rang at 2am at his Sheffield hotel and his wife Judy announced: 'The baby is on the way – don't panic.' He might be in the middle of the Embassy World Championship, but he had to get home. So he immediately caught a taxi, stayed with his wife until the baby, Greg Robert, was weighed in at 6lb 7oz and promptly returned to carry on the tournament. He recalled: 'When the wife said, "Don't panic," I promptly did.' It's nice to see that the icy-cool Davis, who has survived one thousand crises in his career, reacted just like any other father-to-be under pressure.

Not too many people in this world are invited to dine with the Prime Minister of Britain but Stephen Hendry, snooker's world number 1, has twice been offered that golden chance and said 'No' on both occasions. First, he turned down Margeret Thatcher because of 'work commitments' and then refused sports fan John Major because he already had a business engage-

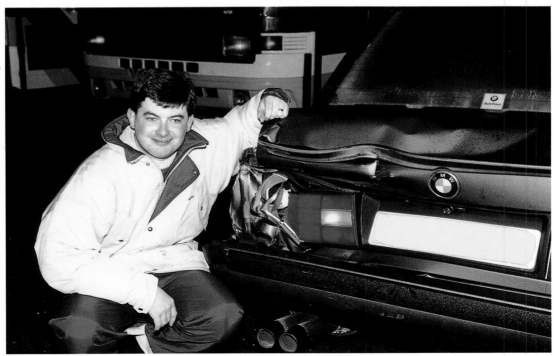

ment with sponsors Bostik. Hendry said: 'I just had no alternative. The last person I would want to upset is the Prime Minister – apart from my manager Ian Doyle.'

Ken Doherty, the young Irishman who enjoyed such a fine debut year on the circuit, has been using a cue he 'stole' from Jason's Snooker Centre in Dublin. Doherty said: 'I found this cue that I liked in the rack and borrowed it. I paid one of the young lads at the club £2 to keep quiet, although he wanted a fiver at first.' Jason's now know about Doherty's 'borrowed' cue and they are proud that he is still using the cue to such good effect.

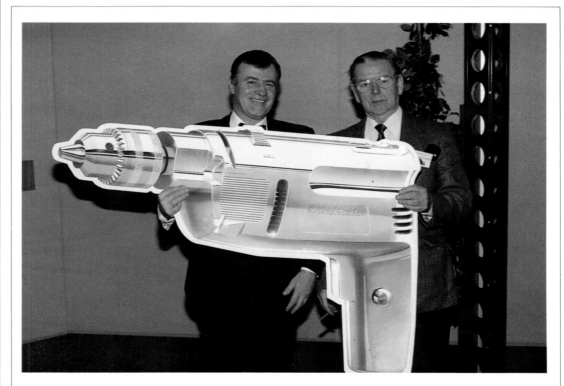

The Drill: Top coach Frank Callan (right) always tells his 'pupils' to concentrate on 'The Drill'. Doug Mountjoy and Frank are caught by our cameraman with a larger-than-life drill.

EDDIE CHARLTON: A GENUINE SPORTING ALL-ROUNDER

by Bob Holmes

Even without a cue in his hand or coal dust in his eyes, the young Eddie Charlton was probably not the sort of 'Olympian' of whom Baron Pierre de Coubertin would have approved. A typically cussed campaigner from Down Under, Charlton liked above all things to win – and the closest he came merely to 'taking part' was when he carried the torch at the Olympic Games in Melbourne in 1956. But after the heroes of that Olympiad have burned themselves out, the torch borne by 'Steady Eddie' is still ablaze. He has not actually conquered the worlds of snooker or billiards as the top titles have eluded him in both games, but he is still fighting very well and that, claimed the Olympic founder, is what it's all about.

The early days: Eddie Charlton (left) before the start of a match when he was only eighteen.

At sixty-two, Charlton is regarded as something of an all-rounder, being pretty good at pool as well as staying among the elite in both billiards and snooker. He is also rumoured to run a bit, be partial to health foods and, for an Aussie, to show a strange indifference to the amber nectar. Yet such things only hint at the rich seam of sporting achievement that this former miner from New South Wales generally keeps below the surface. In a glorious half-century on green baize and blue yonder, court and canvas, sod and turf, he has played no fewer than nine sports at near-representative level. Indeed, his trophy cabinet looks like something many clubs would envy – if they could keep up with the stock-taking.

Born in Swansea, New South Wales, in 1929, Charlton was from a coal-mining family in which mum was more sporting than dad, as a result of the constraints of the latter's job as a contract miner.

'Dad's work took him away a lot,' recalls Charlton, 'but my grandfather sort of stepped in and he owned a billiards club. For her part,' he continues, 'mum played "A" grade tennis and, when she reached fifty, turned to lawn bowls and started winning even more titles.' With such a pedigree, it was inevitable that Charlton was encouraged to play what he calls 'all the usual games' as a kid. When he adds that his granddad taught him to swim, row and fish, it sounds like the typical outdoor background of the all-Australian boy.

The weather was, of course, glorious, and young Eddie would have been the archetypal tanned and healthy colonial kid

Action man: Eddie Charlton (left) with his Swansea-based team-mates after winning the Australia Senior Surf Board Championship in 1950. Charlton's colleagues are (left to right) Colin MacMillan, Bill Behrends, Ben Behrends and Gordon MacMillan.

The all-rounder: Eddie Charlton (back row, third right) was also a soccer star in his youth and is pictured with the Blacksmiths team that won the Australian First Division title in 1953/54. Eddie used to play inside left.

but for the fact that he spent a good many hours indoors.

'My grandfather also got me to play billiards and snooker,' he says fondly, 'and throughout my life and among all the sports I've played, cue games were my biggest love.'

Not even an early sighting of Australian cricketing legend Don Bradman could sway him. Charlton became an accomplished cricketer, having been privileged to see 'the Don' pile up a double century at Sydney, but he had a much closer encounter with another Australian sporting legend of a different kind.

'During the war, Walter Lindrum played a series of sponsored billiards matches at major stores to raise money for the war effort,' he recalls, 'and my granddad wrote in suggesting I played against him. I was eleven years old.

'The first weekend I just watched in awe. In my opinion, Walter was quite simply the greatest player ever to play on a billiard table. He was a genius. Yet the second weekend I found myself playing him at snooker when I could barely see over the table. Not only that, but I ended up "beating" him on the black!

'He mucked about for a while and then let me win before 2,500 people. That was my first sponsorship engagement and was really something to crow about to my mates at school. I suppose my career just flowed from there.'

However, the time Charlton could allocate to the table was curtailed by his other commitments and a burgeoning interest in swimming, football, cricket, tennis, roller-skating and Rugby League took some fitting in! Not all of these more strenuous pursuits met with granddad's approval. 'He was not very keen on the body-contact sports,' says Charlton, 'as he felt I could damage my hands for billiards.' But after taking a trampling or two and a few cuffs around the ear in Rugby League from bigger boys, Charlton decided to risk even

Splash of colour: Eddie Charlton turned artist to produce this painting which he donated to the Barnardos Children's Homes charity for auction at a fund-raising dinner.

further wrath from granddad by taking steps to look after himself. 'I said to my dad: "I want to learn boxing so these bigger guys won't get away with it." He agreed and I soon put a stop to the aggro. I ended up boxing for ten years, but it nearly broke my granddad's heart.'

Already the keenest competitor around and captain of the school team at most sports, Charlton found that his ability to put his best foot forward and lead from the front led him to four major titles as a formidable middleweight – and yet another close encounter with an all-Australian hero.

'The late and great Dave Sands was probably the best boxer Australia ever produced,' he says with obvious pride. 'He came over to the UK and beat Randolph Turpin and I had the honour of boxing a four-round exhibition with him as part of a fund-raising exercise for our surf club.'

Charlton was a member of the club that won both the Australian junior and senior surfboard championships, but by now he was into soccer in a big way and had also taken up athletics. Homework? 'I didn't concentrate as much as I should,' he chuckles.

Leaving school just before the Second World War ended, Charlton could hardly have found a more unfriendly working environment for his healthy, outdoor lifestyle – he went down the local pit. If that sound like a penance for neglecting his books, he will have none of it. On the contrary, there is pride in his voice as he explains: 'My father and his father were coal miners and my younger brother Jimmy followed three years after me. My father got us the jobs.'

Nor did he allow the hard graft, dust and conditions to cramp his style. He says:

'I carried on playing all my sports and we were lucky that Swansea was the first mechanised mine in the New South Wales coalfield. Conditions were actually pretty good as the coalface was watered and dust and gas were always both under control. Actually, my dad was responsible for safety standards and the miners were always very safety-conscious. Both he and my granddad lived well into their eighties and I don't think I stayed down there long enough to have done too much damage.'

When it came to being brought up with a balanced diet and healthy habits, Charlton's mum did not stop at making young Eddie eat his spinach. 'She made sure my two brothers and sister all had a variety of foods and plenty of exercise without being fanatical,' he remembers.

'Sport was my life,' he says in the next breath, 'even though I stayed at the mine

Working out the angles: Eddie Charlton looks for the best shot to play.

for twenty-two years, fifteen of them underground.' If cue sports were favourites, soccer assumed a leading role too, Charlton playing for twenty-seven years as an old-fashioned inside forward. 'The last ten were in the First Division,' he reminds you, so you are left with the feeling that not only did he play in those teams that make up the summer pools coupon, but he may even have denied you a dividend – with a last-minute goal, of course.

Married at twenty-two to Gloria, who was nineteen, Charlton soon had a young family of three to support – another reason for him to stay in the steady employ of the Wallarah Mining Company. The other reason was that, for all his diverse talents, the only sports at which he was good enough to make it to the very top were billiards and snooker. And nobody in their right mind would have turned pro Down Under in those days, would they?

There was only a handful of professionals left as snooker sank almost into oblivion in the late 1950s. But Charlton got the break he was not even dreaming about when one of 'the Few' toured Australia in 1960. As Australian amateur champion, it was natural that Charlton should take on the visitor, but what really clinched his involvement in the road show and persuaded him to take a leave of absence from the mine was his ability to set up and dismantle the tables.

However, it was his ability to build breaks and dismantle opponents that impressed Fred Davis, and the visiting Englishman told Charlton that he would be crazy to return to the mine. 'Fred offered to organise a three-month tour of the UK for me if I turned pro,' recalls Charlton, 'and after some thought and a few wins over him, I took his advice. Besides Fred and myself, there was only John Pulman and Rex Williams, but after I played "Pully" for the World Championship (when it was held on a challenge basis) over six days and seventy-three frames at Bolton's Co-

operative Hall, things really took off. John Spencer, Ray Reardon and Gary Owen, the amateur champion, all came along, decided to turn pro and the World Professional Championship proper took place the following year. My own game improved and I decided to stop some of the other sports. I made a lot of friends over here very quickly and Jack Karnehm and his wife were particularly kind to me, allowing me to stay with them in North London. Jack also fixed up practice facilities and I even played under the watchful gaze of Joe Davis. I immediately took to coming over and it was not that much of a culture shock – I had done a bit of touring in Australia. I also made a bit of money and never had any doubts that I had done the right thing. After over one hundred visits, I think I can safely say I was right.'

In 1973 Charlton came close to being the first overseas player to win the world crown, dispatching Perrie Mans, Graham Miles and the young Alex Higgins, who had just burst on the scene, having won the title the previous year. In the final, at Manchester's Exhibition Hall, Charlton met Ray Reardon at his best, and although the Aussie went into a 7–0 lead he eventually lost 38–32.

However, Charlton had kept the promise made after losing to Pulman – 'Now I know what's ahead of me, I know what lines to practise on when I get back to Australia,' he had said. He kept on them well enough to stay ranked in the top four until 1981.

Involved in organising at an early stage, Charlton had a hand in taking the World Championship to his native Australia in 1970 but could not get past his compatriot Warren Simpson, who beat him 27–22 in the semi-final. He did beat Reardon 31–30 before 2,500 fans in Melbourne to win the World Matchplay title in 1976 – and his wins over the doyen of the 1970s were the most satisfying of his career. 'He was a helluva player, you know.'

Although most of Charlton's major clashes occurred in the UK – to which, he claimed, 'I ought to have a season ticket' – he began to pot his way around the globe, travelling to places as far apart as Holland and Papua New Guinea, South Africa and Singapore. Not all this, however, met with his wife's approval. 'Gloria wanted me to stay at home more,' he says, 'and I wrestled with the problem for a couple of years before we agreed to go our separate ways. We parted amicably, but I just could not stop what I was doing.'

Charlton eventually married Robyn, his secretary, and the couple have two sons, Andrew and Peter who was born last February. Andrew was four years old the day his dad brought off one of his best wins of recent times – a 5–1 drubbing of John Parrott in the fourth round of the 1991 Mercantile Credit Classic.

'Robyn is a great supporter of my playing career,' he says, and it is a great comfort to Charlton that his wife, who is seventeen years his junior, is a firm believer in the philosophy: 'We do not stop playing because we are old; we grow old because we stop playing.' No one knows the sage who said this, but if it was a member of the green-baize fraternity, Charlton would be the prime suspect. He may not have the words tattooed on his chest or etched on his business card, but their essential message is unmistakable every time he juts that defiant jaw of his over the table.

Snooker may be a young man's game but Steady Eddie intends to stay young to play it. He certainly has no intention of either growing old or stopping. 'If I got the feeling I could not win matches, I'd stop,' he says. 'But I still think I can beat anybody on my day.' And you know he believes it.

What a wind-up: Barry Hearn (left) delivers a 'K-O' to Jim Wych (centre) after being set up by Canadian Wych and his doubles partner Brady Gollan at the Mita World Masters. Wych made out that he had broken his arm while on a publicity shoot at an ice-skating stadium.

Little and large: England's Les Dodd, the biggest competitor in the Mita World Masters, and eleven-year-old David Gray, the smallest entrant.

All white: Brazil's Rui Chapeu has a natty line in snooker wear during the Mita World Masters. Chapeu actually played in his white flat cap.

BUT STILL FUN

Ball boys: World champion Stephen Hendry and world number 3 Jimmy White watch England soccer star David Platt in action.

Fleecy lining?: Steve Davis is pictured during a visit to Spring Valley Mills, the Yorkshire home of Hainsworth which makes Toptable billiard cloth.

Where did you get that hat?: ITV tipster John McCririck looks as though he should be covering skiing rather than snooker.

Floor show: Stephen Hendry seems lost for words as a girl cabaret performer gets a new view of life during a night out organised by Bostik, the Cuemasters team sponsor.

SNOOKER WINNERS

Stephen Hendry, predictably, collected the Player of the Year Award for 1990 at the WPBSA's Annual Awards Lunch at the Cafe Royal in London.

Snooker journalists carry the voting power and Hendry, who was then world champion and world number 1, was a unanimous choice, while his stablemate Nigel Bond was voted Newcomer of the Year after reaching the final of the Rothmans Grand Prix.

The Services to Snooker trophy was taken by John Spencer who won the world title three times and is currently chairman of the WPBSA.

The lunch was held in association with Emirates Airlines, the official carriers for the Dubai Duty Free Classic.

Top man:
Player of the Year
Stephen Hendry.

The joker: John Spencer with his special headgear after collecting his Services to Snooker trophy.

Star talent: Newcomer of the Year Nigel Bond.

WHO SAID THAT?

'I could have been serving on a nuclear submarine or aircraft carrier in the Gulf.'

– *New professional Jon Birch who revealed that he had signed on to join the Royal Navy but knocked in a break of more than 100 when he started playing snooker. He never joined the Navy.*

'It's just great to be playing snooker again.'

– *Cliff Thorburn during the Mercantile Credit Classic. He had twice cheated death when he suffered a burst appendix and then a blood clot in his lung.*

'My mum's last words to me were: "Stop messing about and put your mind to it."'

– *Tony Jones who dedicated his Tulip European Open victory to his mother, Gladys, who had died three months earlier.*

'I watched the way twelve-year-olds played at the Mita World Masters and told myself: "That's how to do it from now on."'

– *Terry Griffiths.*

'The Mita World Masters was a tournament of tears, tantrums and tie-breaks and was a fantastic success.'

– *Promoter Barry Hearn.*

'I fear no one but myself and that's the worst person to fear.'

– *Tony Meo.*

'I have travelled all the way to China and reached the final. I have come 10 miles to Preston and got beaten.'

– *Dennis Taylor (below) after losing 9–6 to Alan McManus in the third round of the StormSeal UK Championship.*

'Stephen Hendry is absolute perfection. I have always felt that Steve Davis is the best ever, but I have to say that Stephen is even better. I can now die happy.'

– *Top coach Frank Callan after watching Stephen Hendry beat Steve Davis 16–15 in the final of the StormSeal UK Championship.*

THE MAN BEHIND THE MIC: JOHN PULMAN – A CHAMPION AND A GENTLEMAN

by Terry Smith

John Pulman, ITV's number 1 commentator, might never have taken an interest in billiards and snooker if his father, Ernest, had not decided to sell his bakery and confectionery business. That was way back in 1929 when John was just six years old and living with his family in Teignmouth, Devon.

'My dad decided to move to Plymouth and buy a billiards club,' said John. 'I started playing when I was nine – as soon as I was old enough to see over the table.'

Landing place: John Pulman at the Hotel Normandy in the French seaside resort of Deauville. John was commentating on the Fiat Snooker/Pool Challenge.

He quickly became quite proficient at billiards – then *the* table game – and made his first century break when he was only twelve and a half. By then the professionals of the day had made their way down to the West Country and played at Ernest's new club in Exeter.

'I used to "field" the balls for the pros during their exhibitions,' recalled Pulman, 'and one of them, Tom Newman, said to me: "Keep it up – I might be playing you one day." Sadly, that was not to be as Tom died of a tragic illness in 1943. Newman, a genuine Cockney, won the world billiards title on six occasions.

In 1938 John, now fifteen, entered the British Boys Snooker Championship and travelled down to London where he was due to appear at the famous Burroughes & Watts Hall in Soho Square. He got there safely – but without his cue!

'I came up by train and we had to make an unscheduled change at Basingstoke. I left my cue on the train and by the time I realised what I had done, it was too late,' explained John. 'When I arrived at the championship, they took me into a room where there were dozens of cues and told me to take my pick. I chose a cue for the event and I have had the same one all my life.'

The metal plate on the butt bore the name of Sidney Smith, a renowned professional of the day who is credited with the first total clearance, a 133 in 1937. John laughed as he remembered: 'When I turned professional, I filed Sidney's name off the

Golden moment: John Pulman, twenty-two, after winning the English Amateur Championship in 1946.

cue because I couldn't go to exhibitions using another professional's cue.'

Then came the war and John joined the Army . . . for three months. He said: 'I had varicose veins and instead of putting me in the Pay Corps, or something like that, they decided I was more use to the war effort making Spitfire wings in Exeter.'

The war over, he started to make headway in the snooker world, and a victory that he still rates as 'the finest of my career' occurred in 1946. He recalled: 'I had won the Devon area in the English Amateur Championship and I had to come to London for the finals. It was the first time I had entered the event and I was lucky enough to take the title.' For the record, John beat Albert Brown in the final and they both promptly turned professional.

John's first 'booking' was in Jersey where he was to perform five exhibitions at the Mechanics Institute for 50 guineas (£52.50) – a fortune in the 1940s when most people earned only about £5 a week. John added: 'I had a week's holiday, paid for my board and lodging and still came home with quite a bit of money in my pocket.'

The year John joined the paid ranks was that in which the incomparable Joe Davis decided to stop playing in the World Championship. Joe had won the title every year it had been held since the first tournament in 1927. Now John is in no doubt who is the greatest player of all time. 'It is definitely Joe Davis,' he said with a degree of reverence. 'Joe was the complete professional sportsman. He was a great all-round player, he had complete control of the cue ball, and don't forget that he was one of the world's greatest billiards players. There was also his tremendous business acumen, and when he went into a room there was this aura about him. Even if people didn't know who he was, they knew that Joe Davis was someone special. I would make Joe Davis my number 1, Steve Davis my number 2 and Stephen Hendry number 3 with Fred Davis, Joe's brother, at number 4. I never played Joe in the World Championship, but I did play him in other events and beat him a couple of times, though he was giving me one black start.

'Steve Davis is the best player in the modern era, but I believe Hendry has the ability to become the greatest player the game has ever seen – better even than Joe Davis. But to get to that position, Hendry must work hard. He practises a lot now, but he must be prepared to put in six to eight hours a day. However, he's only twenty-two and what he has achieved in such a short space of time is incredible.'

John remembered one amusing incident that occurred when he was playing Fred Davis in a match at the Leicester Square Hall in London: 'I had made a mess of a shot and decided that I would leave the room to go to the manager's office. The manager at the time was Ted Lowe and there was a buzzer in the room to let us

So elegant: John Pulman in action.

know when we had to return. I had no sooner arrived in the office than the buzzer sounded. I couldn't believe it, because I had left what seemed to me a lot of points on the table for Fred to pick up. When I returned I was snookered right behind the brown and the crowd was having a good laugh. I didn't know what was happening, but when I asked Fred later, he said: "I didn't make too many and then decided to snooker you. I said to the crowd: 'If you thought John was in a bad mood when he went out, fasten your seat belts for when he comes back in!'"'

John finally achieved the ultimate goal of any professional when he won the world title in 1957 by beating Jack Rea 39–34, but he said: 'I still rate the amateur title the best of my career.' Snooker, by now, was beginning to go into decline, though John held the title all the way through until 1969 when he was beaten in the first round by John Spencer. He commented: 'The world title was held on a challenge basis and I defended it successfully a

number of times.'

Pulman reached the final in 1970 but was beaten by Ray Reardon as the Welshman collected the first of his six titles with a 37–33 victory. There were to be no more world titles; however, John did reach the semi-finals in 1977 – the first year that the event was held at the now-famous Crucible Theatre in Sheffield. John went down 18–16 to John Spencer, the eventual winner.

What was the greatest match in which Pulman competed? He said: 'That had to be at the Burroughes Hall in London in 1965 when I was challenged for the world title by Fred Davis and won 37–36 after winning the final two frames. It was a fantastic match and lasted six days with twelve frames a day and thirteen on the final day.'

And the greatest match he witnessed? Pulman recalled: 'It was 1946 – the first world final after the war – at the Horticultural Hall in London between Joe Davis and Horace Lindrum. Joe won 78–67 and he decided to "retire" from the World Championship after that tournament. There were some wonderful crowds and it was a tremendous occasion. Joe had two century breaks of 133 and 136 – both setting championship records.'

In 1981 Pulman's illustrious career approached its end when he was seriously injured after being hit by a bus after leaving a club in Lewisham. His left leg was smashed in five places and he spent six months in hospital. He never played professional snooker again.

'I was thinking of retiring anyway,' he said. 'I was getting bored with practice and I had lost motivation. But I still needed money to live and it was while I was in hospital that I was offered a contract to commentate on snooker for ITV. I had been lucky enough to do some commentating in Scotland for STV and that led to other work for the BBC and ITV. I signed up and I have been with ITV ever since.'

John has many fans – just as Ted Lowe has over on the BBC. Of course, they are the best of friends, having known each other in almost a lifetime of snooker. While some players-turned-commentators can

The maestro in action: Joe Davis lines up a shot watched intently by John Pulman.

John Pulman, known for enjoying the odd glass of whisky, made his fellow ITV commentators laugh at one tournament when he said: 'I had kippers for breakfast today but I have kept away from them all week. They make me thirsty and that could be fatal for me.'

bore their viewers with too much technical jargon, Pulman, like Lowe, treats the audience as though they are old friends.

John has a voice that is ideal for snooker and some of his comments are pure class. Take, for instance, the 1980 World Championship final, which was interrupted by live coverage of the siege at the Iranian Embassy in London. When they returned to the snooker, his first words were: 'And welcome back to the World Championship. It's a case of from one Embassy to another.'

There is a lifetime of good memories for John, but there has been one regret – he has never scored a maximum 147 break. He said: 'I once scored 146 against Rex Williams and I compiled 54 total clearances. It would have been nice to make a 147.'

But while John is a lifelong snooker addict and has watched the best for many, many years, he loves nothing better than returning to his native West Country from his home in Northampton to go fishing. He has his own boat and likes to spend summer days out on the ocean catching bass or big conger. In fact, one day last year, he hauled in a personal best conger eel of 67lb.

Sit next to John in the hospitality room at a tournament and you will soon be regaled with magnificent stories of yesteryear. A glass of Bell's is sure to be nearby and an hour with John Pulman leads you to believe that, despite all the pessimism, everything is right in the snooker world today. He is quite a character!

Fishy tales: John Pulman (right) and top international referee John Street show off their catch after a day at sea.

JOHN SMYTH: FROM COCKFOSTERS TO THE CRUCIBLE

by Bob Holmes

John Smyth's first glimpse of the green baize was a surreptitious and very Irish experience. He was four at the time and fond of peering through the swing doors of a billiard hall just off O'Connell Street in Dublin. 'The trouble was,' recalls John, 'my father thought everyone who went in there was a villain and forbade me from going near the place. That wasn't easy as we lived next door.'

Although dad deterred him from taking up snooker until he was sixteen, Smyth retained his fascination for the game throughout a less-than-blissful childhood, and once he did wield a cue it was with telling effect. 'I could pot a few,' he remembers with the modesty of a natural. But it was on an altogether different sort of emerald surface that he first tried to pursue a sporting career.

'I had always loved horses and decided I wanted to be a jockey,' he recalls. 'So I got a job as stableboy for Paddy Prendergast. I enjoyed it but soon found there was no future in it for me. You'd get paid on Friday and travel with the horses on Saturday, invariably coming back skint. I tried it over the jumps a few times but didn't take to hitting the ground – it's very hard from that height.'

It was after frequently coming down to earth with a bump that he decided to cross the Irish Sea and, being a versatile sort, try his luck in England. A mere 8 stone in weight when he arrived, he had been a milkman, a telegraph boy and a greyhound handler, so he did not bat an eyelid when the best this land of opportunity could offer him was a job as a kitchen porter.

In charge: John Smyth gets ready to officiate at the Benson and Hedges Masters at Wembley in 1987.

'I had become frustrated in Ireland,' he says. His mother had died when he was seven and he never got on with his dad. The eldest of four children, he had been raised by his grandparents but could find no one in the family who approved of either turf or table.

'We were not a sporting family and I never played soccer, rugger or Gaelic football like other kids,' he says. 'As for snooker, I started late and had no one to coach me. We'd only just about heard of Joe Davis and never dreamed you could make a living at it.'

After a difficult period, during which he had a spell back home when he became run down – 'The diet didn't suit me and neither did rationing,' he explains – things began to pick up. John, who had met his future wife at a roller-skating rink in Dublin, persuaded her to join him in London and they were married in 1952. By then he had joined London Transport as a station man, and he renewed his acquaintance with his cue at their Club Institute.

'My greatest claim to fame as a player was winning the London Transport Snooker Championship six times in a row,' he recalls with justifiable pride. 'And one year I did the double, getting the billiards title as well. But I was nothing brilliant – I should think my best break at snooker was about 72 and only 40-odd at billiards. I was practising four nights a week at the

Going underground: John Smyth on his way to work as a London Transport tube train driver.

time at the Mildmay – a CIU Club – where I was in the team and the standard was quite good there. I can remember Mark Wildman winning the title one year. It was at this club that I was approached by Frank Little to have a go at refereeing – there was a real shortage of refs around the London area in the early fifties. Naturally, as a player, I was a bit reluctant, but I quite enjoyed it. Little did I know what it would lead to.'

From the moment he first donned the white cotton gloves, it took John twenty-eight years to become snooker's first professional referee in 1978. All that time he had worked on the London Underground – graduating to guard and motor man before becoming a fully-fledged driver.

'I worked on the Piccadilly Line, going from Cockfosters to Uxbridge and, later, to Heathrow. It was quite a responsibility, having 1,000 or more people in your train,' he says.

Snooker was the perfect antidote, even though he had had enough of the red, the yellow and the green with the signals in London's tunnels on each shift. Indeed, it was a relief to go from the rattling subterranean environment to the sepulchral hush of snooker although, John claims, 'both roles demanded discipline and were, to some extent, routine and repetitious.'

He began to make a name as a referee in the early seventies, when the big clashes invariably involved the likes of Alex Higgins, Ray Reardon, John Pulman and John Spencer. It is not surprising that they made an impression on him – but John can even recall the shots!

Talk to him now and he'll tell you that 'Pulman was very unlucky to miss a brown into the side pocket in the sixth', while 'Alex potted an incredible blue against Spenny when he looked out of it'. But it was John's mild manners, calm authority and sense of humour even more than his encyclopaedic memory that impressed officials in those days.

'The atmosphere was different when I began refereeing,' he says. 'It was more reverential. For instance, if a spectator lit a cigarette in the front row during a game, he could find himself smoking it outside. The old timers were much more stern than we try to be today and such a person was Frank Little who thought nothing of having somebody frogmarched out of the arena if a match was struck.

'Frank watched me when I was learning the trade at places like Herbert Holt's club in Windmill Street. The match room was the inner sanctum – a sort of holier-than-holy place where you could hear a pin drop on the carpet and feel the eyes of whoever was judging your performance pierce the back of your head. I once dropped a ball and just wanted the floor to swallow me.

'You get watched today but you don't know who it is, whereas Frank, who was the doyen of refs in those days, used to scare the living daylights out of you. He had no qualms about giving you a rucking during a match. But it wasn't just officials whom I had a healthy respect for – Rex Williams used to frighten me, too. I used to dread refereeing Rex as he was always so immaculately dressed. He frightened the life out of me and I told him so. We would have a good laugh about it. But the next time I saw that camel-hair coat, those stiff cuffs and that starched shirt, I would still feel a bit intimidated.

'My first really big occasion was an exhibition between Alex and John Spencer at Haringey – very handy for me when I was living at Highbury – but even then I never, in my wildest dreams, ever looked upon refereeing as a possible career. You don't when all you get is a couple of sandwiches, a cup of tea and a handshake! I used to do many a match without expenses and never really thought about it – I was just honoured to have been chosen. But I was grateful for my tube pass. You could say that my own game was also going down the

Star trio: Referees John Smyth (bottom left), Alan Chamberlain (top left) and John Williams.

tube as I was reffing more and playing less. Later expenses and modest fees came in, but it took a long time. Once when I asked for a fiver to do a match in Sidcup, I was told in no uncertain terms: "You're too dear."'

However, John lost his wife in 1972 and the camaraderie of the burgeoning circuit appealed to the avuncular Irishman more and more. 'Ducking and diving under London at 40mph can be a lonely old life,' he recalls. 'I even used to refer to the rats as "my old mates", so I was over the moon when I decided to turn professional.'

Smyth was the forerunner of the current gang of pro refs and has been a fixture on the scene ever since. Asked what the charac-

Sign here, please: Canadian Alain Robidoux signs the official scoresheet for John Smyth.

teristics of a good ref are, he pauses for thought before saying: 'Dedication, professionalism, remaining calm but stamping your authority on things in a quiet way. You can have a bit of frivolity but you must not let it get out of hand. And, of course, we refs are our own harshest critics.'

John was not harsh enough, however, for Ray Reardon at the UK Open in 1982. 'I think he should have his eyes tested,' declared Dracula after a famous 'touching ball' incident. After some understandable reluctance, John took his advice and became the only ref with glasses. 'When Ray saw me in them for the first time after that,' he remembers, 'he did a double take.'

John has officiated at every World Championship since 1974, except when the contest was held in Australia, and has been involved in every other type of event from ranking tournaments to Courage exhibition nights with Steve Davis. Of course, he was a stalwart at the Benson and Hedges Masters – he officiated at the first Masters tournament in 1975 at the West Centre Hotel in London and was an ever-present until his last appearance in 1987. John recalls: 'I refereed the final between Dennis Taylor and Alex Higgins and it was a tremendous match with Taylor coming back to beat Higgins 9–8. I have some wonderful memories of the Benson and Hedges Masters as it is truly one of the most prestigious events on the circuit.'

Seldom happier than when driving his Nissan Bluebird from tournament to tournament, listening to his favourite Country and Western music, snooker's first professional referee can reflect on having made the right decision when the game went big. 'It's a great crack,' he says. 'And I love the people.' Villains indeed!

KAREN CORR: A BUBBLING WORLD CHAMPION

by Gaye Jones

Karen Corr, the 1990 world champion and Mita World Masters title holder, has enjoyed the best year of her life during her reign as the Queen of Ladies' Snooker.

From Karen's first morning as the twenty-one-year-old Trusthouse Forte world champion, when she had to abandon her breakfast to talk to the media waiting on the doorstep of London's Waldorf Hotel, she hasn't stopped. Her effervescence was almost tangible as she raced from one engagement to the next, mixing League matches and billiards events with ladies' ranking tournaments, pool exhibi-

tions and promotional engagements. She never lost her vitality and enthusiasm as she bubbled and giggled her way through everything, endearing herself to all who met her.

Karen's rise to supremacy has brought a breath of fresh air to the ladies' game which was dominated throughout the 1980s by Allison Fisher, with Stacey Hillyard and 1987 world champion Ann-Marie Farren as the three closest rivals. At the age of fourteen, she met Mark Wildman and Des Heald at Mark's Peterborough club and learned the rudiments of billiards and

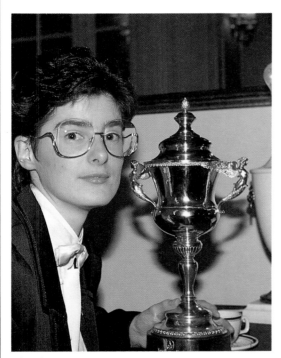

The champ (1): Karen Corr with the Trusthouse Forte Ladies' World Championship trophy.

The champ (2): Karen Corr with her Mita World Masters trophy.

In the money: The top four girls (left to right), Stacey Hillyard, Karen Corr, Ann-Marie Farren and Allison Fisher at the launch of the Ladies' World Championship in London.

snooker. When she had come through the 'novice' stage, Wildman started practising with her regularly and much of the maturity in her game today is due to his help and instruction. He commented: 'Karen's very keen to learn and I'm delighted to say that when she won the world title and the Mita World Masters, she became even more eager to discover new skills in both games. She didn't think that, having made it to the top, she knew everything.

'Karen has a distinct advantage over her contemporaries in that she has an extensive knowledge of the nap of the cloth and the use of side, both of which are intrinsic in the game of billiards, and she is developing the subtlety of touch that billiards requires and which will help enormously in her snooker. She will make centuries at billiards within the next twelve months as she develops into a useful billiards player and a mature snooker player. In my opinion she's the best all-rounder in the ladies' game.'

Like all the top players, Karen receives an enormous amount of support from her family who, seeing her talent, built a snooker room on to the back of their home to give her the opportunity to develop her potential to the full. Their efforts have been rewarded by a cabinet full of trophies.

She said: 'I started playing at the Pyramid Club in Bourne and without that I wouldn't have achieved anything near what I've done. Dad enjoyed snooker and he watched it on the television with my brother, Brian. I was a bit of a tomboy at thirteen and I was prepared to get into anything. Dad and Brian weren't too keen on me playing at first, but I won one of the local competitions and they just followed me and supported me all the way.

'I'm playing out of the Boston Snooker Centre now. I get free table time, they drive me around and the members have been really good to me. The move gave me a fresh start to snooker which was what I needed, because I'd been working in a club and things didn't work out. Spending a lot of time there working, I was too tired to play and I lost a bit of interest in snooker. But I was given renewed interest when I

Mark of success: Karen Corr with Mark Wildman who has done so much to help her playing career.

went to Boston, and manager Keith Pawley and his wife Hazel have really encouraged me. All I do now is play snooker and billiards and I enjoy it.'

Karen's snooker hero is Jimmy White and she said: 'I've always admired him. I had his pictures on my wall until last year but dad wanted to decorate the room and they all came down. I like Jimmy for his flair and the way he plays, just like Alex Higgins. The Hurricane brought something into the game that nobody else did and he set up a totally new era.'

In the early days Karen's leaning towards Jimmy White's style of play was apparent in her own game. A prolific potter and capable of tremendous cue-ball control and power, Karen won matches by potting people off the table, in much the same way as Stacey Hillyard did years ago. What was missing in both cases was a safety game. The about-turn in the standard of ladies' snooker was partly due to both these players learning about safety and introducing tactical awareness into their matchplay.

Having won the game's two major titles and having picked up £28,000 in the space of three months last season, Karen's ambition was to 'remain consistent in my tournaments, get a few good results and go to number 1. It would be absolutely fantastic to do everything in one year. I hope I'll also get some exhibition work and a few tours and the opportunity to visit a few other countries.'

Her move to the number 1 position in ladies' snooker is going to be a hard struggle as she will have to contend with Stacey Hillyard, who wrested the number 1 spot from Allison Fisher in 1990. Allison, toppled from the pinnacle she had held throughout the 1980s, is aiming to return to the top. Last February she demonstrated her intentions with two emphatic wins over Stacey and Karen, the first time she had beaten the latter in four meetings, including the World Championship.

Allison said: 'I think Karen's done very well, especially to take the World Masters as well as the World Championship. That's some achievement. There must have been some pressure on her and it's going to continue, because she's up there with the two biggest titles in the game. Now she's got to try to keep her head down, but it's difficult, and I feel that it's taken some of the pressure off me. Now I've got everything to aim for.'

When Barry Hearn offered Karen a management contract with his Matchroom organisation it was the culmination of a fantastic year. She said: 'To win the World Championship was a dream and then to have Barry sign me up was the icing on the cake. It was my ambition to be signed with one of the top two – either Cuemasters or Matchroom. They can do more for me than anybody in the game because they've got all the top players. It's really nice to be involved with the Matchroom team with such brilliant players as Steve Davis and Terry Griffiths.'

Karen's Matchroom contract has in-

Me and my boss: Karen Corr with her manager Barry Hearn.

volved her in a large number of personal appearances throughout Britain for World Championship sponsors Forte Hotels as well as in several overseas engagements, plus publicity and promotional appearances for Matchroom tables and products.

Karen Corr and Allison Fisher are in the forefront of ladies' snooker because of their Matchroom connections and, along with Stacey Hillyard, Ann-Marie Farren and Georgina Aplin, they joined the professional ranks for the current season. That was the culmination of many years of struggling and campaigning for recognition for the women's game within the snooker world.

There are many critics and sceptics who will monitor the progress of the game's new lady professionals and their results will undoubtedly be under the microscope much more than those of their rookie contemporaries. It takes most new professionals a couple of seasons to acclimatise themselves to the rarefied atmosphere of the professional tournament circuit and very few male players have ever made a major showing in their first season. It will be interesting to see if the girls are given the same time-span or whether those who have always pooh-poohed the idea of professional women players will condemn them from the outset.

Karen viewed her entry into professional snooker with a maturity that belied her twenty-one years and she said: 'I think initially for myself it's not a case of proving anything really. I just want to gain experience, and if I can get a couple of good results on the way it'll be great.

'I think it's really giving encouragement to other lady players or even young girls who are just starting in the game – they're the ones who are going to be our future. I believe that at the end of the day if a woman is going to win the World Professional Championship, it'll be some ten-year-old who's out there now who will come through. In the years to come it will be accepted that the ladies can play snooker as well as the men, whereas it's still a learning process at the moment. It's really good that we're going to become a part of playing against the men. People have said there's no reason why we can't play as well as the men, which is right, given the time and the opportunities. Now we've been given every opportunity to go out and prove ourselves.'

The life of a ladies' world champion is not all glitz and glamour, as I discovered when I spent an evening with Karen travelling to a pool exhibition. 'I rang the social club and told them that I'm a snooker player really and that they should get a proper pool player, but they insisted they wanted me!' she laughed.

We arrived at the tiny Lincolnshire village and found the social club – alias hockey/cricket pavilion – and about thirty people waiting for her. To the irritation of the club manager, the local pool team had vetoed the evening because the table wouldn't be free!

Having lost the first three frames, the opening one being to an accomplished lady pool player, Karen got the hang of the tiny table and things looked up. But the trick shots were a disaster because of the different reactions and size of the pool table, with the exception of the one which requires a willing (and small in the case of pool) volunteer to lie on the table, chalk in mouth, with the black ball balanced carefully on the chalk while Karen pots the black into the corner pocket.

'That was a relief,' she told me. 'I tried that one somewhere else and I couldn't get it right and in the end I clobbered the bloke in the mouth – twice! By then I was laughing so much that I asked him if he wanted to have a go. So he did and he got his own back, because he clobbered me in the mouth, and the audience were in fits. But then he managed to do the trick – at least one of us got it right! He got a rapturous round of applause. I said to him: "Good stuff, keep it going."'

Take aim: Karen Corr tries a tricky shot during an exhibition at a pool club.

Laughter is one of the keys to Karen's success and she loves to communicate with the audience at exhibitions. But the laughter is balanced by a sensible and responsible approach to her life in snooker.

She said: 'I have continued to play in my local Leagues since I won the titles. People say: "Why do you chase around for your local League?" but it's nice to go back to your roots. Without playing in Leagues originally, I wouldn't have got what I have out of the game, and it's nice to put a little bit back. I enjoy it; it sharpens you up. I play more billiards than snooker in the League. I like it because it gives you two days off from playing snooker but you're still cueing a ball, you're still learning a lot about the game through billiards.'

As far as her position in the ladies' game is concerned, Karen feels that 'there's not a lot of difference between the top four in standard at the moment. We all know we're capable of beating each other. Allison has not slipped back in her standard – it's just that the other ladies have got better because she set such a high standard over the last four or five years. She was a phenomenal player; she still is. She set that standard for the rest of us to follow and we followed it and we've reached her.'

Allison sees her slip from pole position as a temporary hiccup. Signing for Matchroom and then the first major sponsorship deal for a lady player – all these things put pressure on her. She said: 'I was doing more things outside snooker, photographic and promotional stuff, and although I was doing enough hours at practice, my mind wasn't on it 100 per cent.

'Over the years I've had a lot of success and there's no reason why it can't continue. Obviously you become more wary of players because the standard's improving and you know you're not unbeatable. My game hasn't deteriorated – everyone else's has come up, but I'm hoping that mine's improved as well. I've altered a few things in my cue action and I feel that I'm improving, but it's a case of how we go on, really, how everyone else improves and how much improvement they've got left in them. I'm hitting the ball well and when you get consistent breaks you know you're playing well.

'I've enjoyed the professional circuit with its longer matches and nice conditions. Obviously you can't expect to jump in and do well straight away. I've looked at it in that respect and put no pressure on myself but just tried to do my best.'

Finally, back to Karen, who looks to the future of the ladies' game and says: 'There's a big job to be done to recruit players. There's more money in our game, there's more publicity and there should be a lot more players. But it's a big job.

'My own future? Well, I want to get everything I can out of the game before I settle down!' It's hard to envisage Karen ever 'settling down'. Her whirlwind lifestyle and panache and her infectious character have breathed new life into ladies' snooker. Long may it continue.

How to Become a Professional Referee

by John Street

Many youngsters dream of becoming world snooker champion like Stephen Hendry or Steve Davis but know they haven't the ability to get to the very top. There are also lots of people who want to be involved in the world of snooker but are aware that their talent is limited on the table. That's why there is a growing number of snooker enthusiasts turning to refereeing, hoping one day to step out at the Crucible Theatre in charge of an Embassy World Championship match.

Big break: Referee Martin Webb did not receive his broken arm while officiating at a top snooker match but on the football field. Fellow referee John Williams does not appear to be offering much sympathy.

However, the path to the top is a long one. So let's take the hypothetical example of a person who just plays snooker for fun and will never improve at the game but sits 'glued' to the TV whenever snooker is on. Suddenly, he – or she; there is no discrimination against ladies – decides to become a professional referee. So how does he go about it?

The first step is to obtain an up-to-date copy of the rules, costing £1.30, from the local referees' association or from the Billiards & Snooker Control Council (B&SCC) at 92 Kirkstall Road, Leeds LS3 1LT. He must then study these rules and, if he feels it necessary, obtain clarification on certain aspects of the rules from an official examiner. He could also try to arrange some coaching from that referee. The rules can be very complex and talking to someone will help him to understand them a lot more quickly than just reading them.

When he is confident of his knowledge of the rules and their interpretation, he should then contact his local referees' examiner for an examination to be arranged. If he does not know of an examiner in his area, he can write to the B&SCC for further details. The examination will be an oral one, in a private room using a billiard table to set up various situations. He will be expected to use the terminology in the rule book – 'top cushion', 'in-hand', 'non-striker', etc. – although allowances may be made for some errors. These will be corrected by the examiner while other information will also be given to the candidate during the examination.

If the candidate is successful, he will be

informed immediately and the appropriate form will be completed and forwarded to the B&SCC together with the required fee. The current rate to become a Class 3 referee is £5.11 annual subscription plus one-off payments of £1 for the certificate and £2 for the examiner. Examinations usually last up to one and a half hours.

After two years a Class 3 referee can apply for upgrading to Class 2. Once again an examination, costing £2, will be arranged and part of the test will be for the candidate to referee a match to the satisfaction of the examiner, who will then check that the person is fully acquainted with the latest rules and amendments. Again a fee must be paid and the certificate will be returned to the B&SCC for upgrading. A Class 2 referee is considered to be a competent referee capable of officiating at *all* types of matches.

After five years as a Class 2 referee, promotion to Class 1 can be sought, but first a referee must be nominated by a national or county association and then satisfy an area assessment panel. Class 1 referees will prove their capabilities by officiating at the highest-grade matches in their area. These Class 1 officials form a select panel of specialists of exceptional merit and from within their ranks are chosen the official examiners. The fee for this is £5, though the annual sub. of £5.11 remains the same.

All referees are encouraged to join the local referees' association. At frequent meetings the latest rule changes are explained, problems are ironed out, match referees are appointed and valuable and vital information is made available. Referees joining these local associations will be expected to wear the accepted dress (blazer, badges, tie, gloves, etc.) and to conform to a referees' Code of Practice whenever they are officiating.

There is an Association of Billiards and Snooker Referees whose secretary, Arthur Raison, will be only too pleased to offer

Superstar ref?: No, John Street, one of snooker's top officials, was just having a bit of fun with a false number plate. John, of course, did not take the vehicle out on a public road.

any advice to budding referees. Mr Raison can be reached at 14 Maypole Grove, Warstock, Birmingham B14 41P.

The candidate is now a Class 1 referee, but he should bear in mind that he is at least seven years older than when he started. However, he is still just as keen and can't wait to referee on television. Provided that he is under fifty-five, he can now apply to join the Professional Referees' Association. From them he will receive an application form on which he will have to give details of all his qualifications. This form will then be placed before the PRA committee.

If accepted, he will be invited to become an associate member for a period of two years, during which time he will be asked to referee at qualifying-round matches at

No sex discrimination: Top international referee John Williams meets Holland's Linda Diedyk who one day hopes to become a Class 1 referee.

world professional ranking tournaments. He has to be prepared to referee for at least fourteen days a year in the first two years, and while he is carrying out his duties his performance will be monitored by an assessor appointed by the WPBSA. The assessor's job is to see just how good he is and, if necessary, advise and help him to improve his standard.

He will be paid a fee for this work, but should not run away with the idea that refereeing is easy. The hours are long and on some days he could be on his feet for ten hours. He has to give total concentration to the job, but if he is one of those people who cannot concentrate for long periods at a time, then the advice is to forget the ambition to become a professional referee.

After this two-year probation period, he will, hopefully, have proved to be above average and will be accepted as a full member of the PRA. His name will then be forwarded to the WPBSA who select all referees for the final stages of all tournaments, held at various venues. The candidate will then start refereeing for some of the top players in the game. However, he will still be under the close eye of the WPBSA assessors. If he can pass this final test with flying colours, he will be invited to make his debut at a televised stage of a tournament.

He has finally achieved his ambition to become a top referee. It will have taken something like ten years to reach this stage, and the last step is to referee the final of the World Championship. That's the dream of every ambitious referee. Good luck to you all.

BILLIARDS: THE GREAT SPORTING SURVIVOR

by Mark Wildman

Professional billiards, looked upon by many as a 'Cinderella sport' alongside snooker, has, despite the doubters, a thriving and competitive circuit. Billiards does not receive the vast amounts of prize money that go into the snooker coffers but the sport, at the time of writing, was far from being on its last legs.

The World Championship, after an absence of two years, was retained by Mike Russell in the Indian capital of Delhi. There was £20,000 in prize money and Russell collected £5,000 for his 1,352–957 victory over Robby Foldvari of Australia.

The 1990/91 season began with forty-nine billiards members of the WPBSA. The largest tournament entry was thirty-five for the Strachan UK Championship, which was held at the Radion Plaza Club in Sheffield. This could prove, in years to come, to be the permanent home of professional billiards.

The Kenilworth Sports Club was the venue for the qualifying matches of the Barbican British Open and the World Matchplay Championship. Four players qualified for each of the finals, with Moscow a tantalising venue for the Matchplay and London's Barbican Centre, which was celebrating Mozart's bicentenary year with a billiards connection, the elitist stage for the British Open. Both events offered diversions in the form of sister tournaments with carom, so popular on the European

Magic Mike: Mike Russell receives his Strachan UK Championship trophy from Brian Pegler, the sales director of Strachan.

mainland, at the Barbican and snooker and pyramids in Moscow.

Mike Russell became, at twenty, the youngest world champion in history in 1989, but he suffered a severe jolt in the qualifiers for the British Open when he lost 4–1 to India's Geet Sethi. However, Russell came through safely in the World Matchplay and four players – Russell, Robby Foldvari, Ian Williamson and Sethi – made their way to Moscow.

The Muscovites came in vast numbers to watch and quickly picked up an understanding of billiards. More than 15,000 attended the championship and saw an excellent final. Russell, with three centuries, took a 6–1 lead before Sethi got going with three centuries of his own to level at 6–6. However, Russell pipped him at the post 7–6. An average crowd for a session in Moscow was in excess of 2,000, proving that bil-

liards has a tremendous future in this part of the world. At times there are fewer than 100 spectators watching professional billiards in the UK.

Norman Dagley, sixty-one and a former world champion, won the £3,000 first prize in the Barbican British Open which was staged in the conservatory on the ninth floor of the Barbican Centre. In the first semi-final, Peter Gilchrist, a fast natural player, went down 4–1 to Ian Williamson while Dagley came through an excellent semi-final by a 4–3 margin over Sethi. Dagley, a regular winner in previous years, had been without a title for more than a year, though this must have had something to do with a particular nasty illness he had suffered but from which, thankfully, he has now recovered. In the final Williamson led 5–3 but Dagley, the Peter Pan of billiards, won four frames in a row to take the title 7–5.

Kick-off: Mike Russell (left) and Robby Foldvari 'string' for break in the semi-final of the World Matchplay in Moscow. Russell went on to take the title.

Norman's conquest: Evergreen Norman Dagley receives his British Open trophy from 'Wolfgang Amadeus Mozart'. The British Open was held at the Barbican Centre in London as part of the festivities to mark the bicentenary of the death of the composer, who was a keen billiards player.

The Strachan UK was played over two-hour sessions and could offer bigger breaks than the 150-up style adopted for the World Matchplay and British Open. Sethi recorded breaks of 580 and 690, while Russell, ever mindful of Sethi's shadow, compiled a personal match record of 606. Inevitably these two young men, who now stand in comparison with pre-war legends, met each other in a classic encounter which was played out in front of a full house. Russell, at one stage nearly 500 points behind, came back to win 1,839–1,538.

Running parallel at this tournament was the Strachan UK Carom Championship, which attracted twenty-four entries. The scoring system of 1 point per cannon, with an extra point for each cushion contacted by the cue ball, produced an interesting event with India's Michael Ferreira beating David Edwards 100–81 in the final. On average, games took about forty minutes and provided an interesting distraction for the spectators.

The 1990/91 season has seen a step forward in the progress of professional billiards. Ranking tournaments carried prize money of more than £50,000 and opportunities were better than ever for all players to experience international travel and competition. The colossal market of the USSR has been tapped with a very positive response and TV coverage has been harnessed in the USSR, India and indeed throughout Europe. To carry this historical game into new areas, billiards enthusiasts everywhere should see tangible signs of expansion in the near future.

Billiards also initiated a history-making meeting in Bristol which could see one or more forms of cue sports incorporated in the Olympics in years to come. Representatives from the entire world of billiards sports met at the Bristol headquarters of the WPBSA. The associations were: the Billiards Congress of America, the Union Mondiale de Billard, the Confédération Européenne de Billard (Carom), the Billiards World Association (Professional Carom), the World Pool Billiard Association, the International Billiards and Snooker Federation, the Billiards and Snooker Control Council and, of course, the WPBSA.

Every time the International Olympic Committee has been approached, they advised that it would be better if cue sports had a world representative body. That body – the World Confederation of Billiard Sports – has now been formed with three delegates from snooker, carom and pool. Meetings are being held and hopefully one day – and perhaps sooner rather than later – one or more cue sports could be included in the Olympics.

World Matchplay Results

SECOND ROUND: M. Russell (Eng) bt M. Wildman (Eng) 4–0; E. Charlton (Aust) bt J. Karnehm (Eng) 4–0; M. Ferreira (Ind) bt H. Nimmo (Scot) 4–3; R. Foldvari (Aust) bt P. Gilchrist (Eng) 4–1; I. Williamson (Eng) bt H. Griffiths (Wales) 4–0; C. Everton (Wales) w/o R. Edmonds (Eng); R. Close (Eng) bt J. Murphy (Eng) 4–3; G. Sethi (Ind) bt N. Dagley (Eng) 4–1
Losers: £125

QUARTER-FINALS: Russell bt Charlton 4–1; Foldvari bt Ferreira 4–1; Williamson bt Everton 4–3; Sethi bt Close 4–2
Losers: £500

SEMI-FINALS: Russell bt Foldvari 4–2; Sethi bt Williamson 4–0
Losers: £1,000

FINAL: Russell bt Sethi 7–6
Loser: £2,000
Winner: £3,000

Barbican British Open Results

SECOND ROUND: P. Gilchrist (Eng) bt M. Wildman (Eng) 4–2; M. Ferreira (Ind) bt D. Edwards (Wales) 4–1; E. Charlton (Aust) bt E. Hughes (Rep Ire) 4–3; I. Williamson (Eng) bt C. Everton (Wales) 4–1; N. Dagley (Eng) bt R. Foldvari (Aust) 4–3; R. Edmonds (Eng) bt J. Karnehm (Eng) 4–1; R. Close (Eng) bt G. Thompson (Eng) 4–0; G. Sethi (Ind) bt M. Russell (Eng) 4–1
Losers: £125

QUARTER-FINALS: Gilchrist bt Ferreira 4–1; Williamson bt Charlton 4–1; Dagley bt Edmonds 4–1; Sethi bt Close 4–0
Losers: £500

SEMI-FINALS: Williamson bt Gilchrist 4–1; Dagley bt Sethi 4–3
Losers: £1,000

FINAL: Dagley bt Williamson 7–5
Loser: £2,000
Winner: £3,000

Strachan UK Results

SECOND ROUND: M. Russell (Eng) bt J. Karnehm (Eng) 869–472; R. Foldvari (Aust) bt M. Ferreira (Ind) 638–346; R. Close (Eng) bt F. Davis (Eng) 626–421; P. Gilchrist (Eng) bt M. Kothari (Ind) 927–319; I. Williamson (Eng) bt H. Nimmo (Scot) 638–277; J. Murphy (Eng) bt R. Edmonds (Eng) 713–541; G. Sethi (Ind) bt P. Cavney (Eng) 1,142–401; D. Edwards (Wales) bt N. Dagley (Eng) 595–547
Losers: £150

QUARTER-FINALS: Russell bt Foldvari 806–389; Gilchrist bt Close 728–505; Williamson bt Murphy 622–303; Sethi bt Edwards 1,065–406
Losers: £500

SEMI-FINALS: Russell bt Gilchrist 2,058–1,054; Sethi bt Williamson 2,065–811
Losers: £1,000

FINAL: Russell bt Sethi 1,839–1,538

Mysore Lamps World Championship Results

SECOND ROUND: M. Russell (Eng) bt D. Edwards (Eng) 2,003–846; C. Everton (Wales) w/o E. Charlton (Aust); H. Nimmo (Scot) bt M. Ferreira (Ind) 1,463–742; P. Gilchrist (Eng) bt J. Murphy (Eng) 1,704–976; I. Williamson (Eng) bt M. Wildman (Eng) 1,136–582; R. Foldvari (Aust) bt R. Edmonds (Eng) 1,263–687; G. Sethi (Ind) bt B. Close (Eng) 1,231–1,213; N. Dagley (Eng) bt D. Heald (Eng) 1,572–726
Losers: £725

QUARTER-FINALS: Russell bt Everton 1,693–723; Gilchrist bt Nimmo 1,423–1,127; Foldvari bt Williamson 850–757; Sethi bt Dagley 1,389–1,194
Losers: £1,000

SEMI-FINALS: Russell bt Gilchrist 1,907–1,024; Foldvari bt Sethi 941–899
Losers: £1,250

FINAL: Russell bt Foldvari 1,352–957
Loser: £2,500
Winner: £5,000

A LOOK AT THE AMATEURS

IBSF WORLD CHAMPIONSHIP

Stephen O'Connor proved that snooker is becoming a young man's game when, at the age of eighteen years and forty days, he was crowned the youngest world amateur champion in history. Dubliner O'Connor finally overcame Steve Lemmens of Belgium 11–8 after a superb final of the IBSF World Championship in the Sri Lankan capital of Colombo. O'Connor's name now goes into the record books and beats the previous best of eighteen years and one hundred and ninety-one days set by Jimmy White in 1980. O'Connor is the second player from the Republic of Ireland to win the title – the first being Ken Doherty, a fellow Dubliner, in 1989.

In the final, O'Connor led 6–2 but was pegged back to 7–5 by the end of day 1. The excellent play continued on the second day, with Lemmens knocking in an excellent break of 136 in the fourteenth frame, but O'Connor pulled away for his deserved success. Lemmens, however, proved conclusively that European snooker has made tremendous strides in recent years, scoring a 5–3 victory over Stefan Mazrocis, the European champion and the number 1 seed from England, in the last sixteen. He knocked in a World Championship record break of 141 in the second frame. Lemmens said: 'That's the best break I have ever made in tournament or practice.'

Both O'Connor and Lemmens turned professional this season.

There were twenty century breaks throughout the tournament, and another

Getting younger: Dublin's Stephen O'Connor who, at eighteen years and forty days, became the youngest winner of the IBSF World Amateur Championship in Sri Lanka.

European, Norwegian Bjorn L'Orange, reached the semi-final before losing 8–7 to O'Connor.

BCE ENGLISH AMATEUR CHAMPIONSHIP

Steve Judd, the Northern Area champion from Nottingham, won the BCE English Amateur Championship with a 13–10 final defeat of Ilford's fifteen-year-old Ronnie O'Sullivan at the Northern Snooker Centre in Leeds. O'Sullivan, the Southern Area representative, went into the final hoping to become the youngest ever winner of the title – a record that still remains with Jimmy White who was sixteen when he took the crown in 1979. But O'Sullivan has still gone into the snooker record books for a magnificent 147 he compiled during the Southern Area quarter-finals at the Royale Hampshire Snooker Lodge in Aldershot. He became, at fifteen years and ninety-seven days, the youngest player to score a 147 under approved tournament conditions.

However, he was unable to achieve a record double and Judd, who once quit the game for fifteen months because of 'cueitis', thoroughly deserved his triumph before he joined the professional circuit. Judd said: 'I packed up because I could not follow through with my shot and I got a job in a frozen meat depot. But then a friend suggested we play a game and the "cueitis" had gone.'

Signing on: Ronnie O'Sullivan joins Barry Hearn's Matchroom organisation. Ronnie became the youngest player to score a 147 maximum under tournament conditions and also finished runner-up to Steve Judd in the BCE English Amateur Championship. He later took the IBSF World Junior title.

IBSF WORLD JUNIOR CHAMPIONSHIP

Ronnie O'Sullivan, at fifteen, became the youngest winner of the IBSF World Junior title when he beat Belgium's Patrick Delsemme 11–4 in the final in Bangalore, India.

It was a season to remember for O'Sullivan as he had earlier become the youngest player to score a 147 in tournament play during the English Amateur Championship, and then he was signed by Barry Hearn's Matchroom organisation.

O'Sullivan was in total control of the final throughout and knocked in a brilliant best break of 131 that included fifteen reds, eleven blacks, two blues, one pink and a green and then all the colours except the black.

The black was difficult but success would have given O'Sullivan, from Ilford, Essex, a championship best break, beating the 135 made by Peter Ebdon in Brisbane in 1990.

Manager Hearn said: 'I am convinced that Ronnie could go on to become the youngest world professional champion of all time.'

BENSON AND HEDGES CHALLENGE

Johnny Kemp, from Falkirk, picked up the top prize of £2,000 when he won the Benson and Hedges Challenge with an 8–3 win over Glasgow's Jim McNellan at the Edmiston Club in Glasgow. It was a tense battle but Kemp took the first three frames without apparent difficulty and stretched the lead to 5–1 after McNellan left a blue over the middle pocket. Kemp moved 7–1 ahead and though McNellan took the next two frames it was Kemp who came away to take the eleventh frame for an 8–3 win.

Scottish star: Johnny Kemp receives his Benson and Hedges Challenge trophy from Bill Faloon, the Benson and Hedges Divisional Sales Manager.

BENSON AND HEDGES WELSH SENIOR CHAMPIONSHIP

Dominic Dale, a nineteen-year-old from Pencader, captured the inaugural Benson and Hedges Welsh Senior Championship title with an 8–5 victory over Barry's David Bell in a fine final at the National Sports Centre in Cardiff. Dale picked up a £1,000 first prize and a bonus of a £750 air ticket to represent Wales in this year's IBSF World Championship in Bangkok, Thailand. Bell won the first frame, though Dale held a 4–2 advantage at the end of the first session. After ten frames the scores were level at 5–5 but then Dale pulled away to win his first amateur title.

Welsh Champ: Dominic Dale receives his Benson and Hedges Welsh Senior Championship trophy from John Griffin, the Benson and Hedges Divisional Sales Manager.

Amateur Results 1990/91

SNOOKER

IBSF World Championship (Sri Lanka)
Stephen O'Connor (Rep Ire) 11
Steve Lemmens (Bel) 8

BCE English Championship
Steve Judd (Nottingham) 13
Ronnie O'Sullivan (Ilford) 10

IBSF World Junior Championship
Ronnie O'Sullivan (England) 11
Patrick Delsemme (Belgium) 4

British Isles Under-19
Andy Hicks (Devon) 4
Bradley Jones (Surrey) 3

British Isles Under-16
Mark Williams (Wales) 4
John Higgins (Scotland) 0

BCE Grand Masters
George Wood (Tyne & Wear) 4
Terry Parsons (Mid Glamorgan) 3

UK Pairs
Tony Marsh and Nicky Marsh (Devon) 3
Gary Baldrey and Lee Richardson
(Northants) 1

Inter-Counties
North West 5
Yorkshire 4

Inter-Counties Under-19
North West 5
Derbyshire 4

Pontin's Home International
Seniors: England
Juniors: Scotland
Ladies: England

Pot Black/Pontin's Under-19
Mark Pugh (Birkenhead) 4
Steve Lemmens (Bel) 3

Pot Back/Pontin's Under-15
Jamie Burnett (Hamilton) 3
Matthew Stevens (Carmarthen) 1

Benson and Hedges Challenge
Johnny Kemp (Falkirk) 8
Jim McNellan (Glasgow) 3

Benson and Hedges Welsh Championship
Dominic Dale (Pencader) 8
David Bell (Cardiff) 5

BILLIARDS

*IBSF World Championship
(Bangalore, India)*
Manoj Kothari (India) 2,890
Ashok Shandilya (India) 2,422

English Championship
Martin Goodwill (Lyneham) 2,357
Steve Crosland (Burley-in-Wharfedale) 1,380

British Isles Under-19
David Causier (Middlesbrough) 320
Lee Lagan (Middlesbrough) 285

British Isles Under-16
Michael Westthorp (Middlesbrough) 364
Peter Sheehan (Cheshire) 185

Inter-Counties
Cleveland 830
Merseyside 791

RULES OF THE GAME OF SNOOKER *

Authorized by
THE BILLIARDS AND SNOOKER CONTROL COUNCIL

THE BILLIARDS ASSOCIATION
Established 1885

THE BILLIARDS CONTROL CLUB
Established 1908

AMALGAMATED 1919

Chairman: Stan Brooke
Secretary and Chief Executive: David Ford

SECTION 1. EQUIPMENT

1. Table (Imperial)
1M. Table (Metric)
2. Balls
3. Cue
4. Ancillary

SECTION 2. DEFINITIONS

1. Frame
2. Game
3. Match
4. Balls
5. Striker
6. Stroke
7. In-hand
8. In play
9. On
10. Nominated
11. Pot
12. Break
13. Forced off
14. Foul
15. Snookered
16. Angled
17. Occupied
18. Push-stroke
19. Jump Shot
20. Miss

SECTION 3. THE GAME

1. Description
2. Position of Balls
3. Mode of play
4. Play from in-hand
5. Simultaneous hit
6. Spotting colours
7. Touching balls
8. Edge of pocket
9. Free ball
10. Foul
11. Penalties
12. Movement of ball
13. Stalemate
14. Four handed

SECTION 4. THE PLAYERS

1. Time wasting
2. Unfair conduct
3. Penalty
4. Non-striker
5. Four-handed

SECTION 5. THE OFFICIALS

1. Referee
2. Marker

SECTION 1. EQUIPMENT

1. The Standard Table – Imperial

Dimensions

(a) the playing area within the cushion faces shall measure 11ft 8½ins × 5ft 10ins with a tolerance on both dimensions of ±½in.

Height

(b) the height of the table from the floor to the top of the cushion rail shall be 2ft 9½ins to 2ft 10½ins.

Pocket Openings

(c) (i) There shall be pockets at the corners (two at the Spot end known as the top pockets and two at the Baulk end known as the bottom pockets) and at the middle of the longer sides.

(ii) the pocket openings shall conform to the templates authorized by the Billiards and Snooker Control Council.

Baulk-line and Baulk

(d) a straight line drawn 29ins from the face of the bottom cushion and parallel to it is called the Baulk-line and the intervening space termed the Baulk.

The 'D'

(e) the 'D' is a semi-circle described in Baulk with its centre at the middle of the Baulk-line and with a radius of 11½ins.

Spots

(f) four spots marked on the centre longitudinal line of the table.

(i) the Spot: 12¾ins from the point perpendicular below the face of the top cushion.

(ii) the Centre Spot: Midway between the centre pockets and equidistant from the faces of the top and bottom cushions.

(iii) the Pyramid Spot: Midway between the centre spot and the face of the top cushion.

(iv) the Middle of the Baulk-line.

1M. The Standard Table – Metric

Dimensions

(a) the playing area within the cushion faces shall measure 3500 mm × 1750 mm with a tolerance on both dimensions of ±3 mm.

Height

(b) the height of the table from the floor to the top of the cushion rail shall be from 850 mm to 875 mm.

Pocket Openings

(c) (i) There shall be pockets at the corners (two at the Spot end known as the top pockets and two at the

Baulk end known as the bottom pockets) and at the middle of the longer sides.

(ii) the pocket openings shall conform to the templates authorized by the Billiards and Snooker Control Council.

Baulk-line and Baulk

(d) a straight line drawn 700 mm ($\frac{1}{5}$th the length of the playing area) from the face of the bottom cushion and parallel to it is called the Baulk-line and the intervening space termed the Baulk.

The 'D'

(e) the 'D' is a semi-circle described in Baulk with its centre at the middle of the Baulk-line and with a radius of 292 mm ($\frac{1}{6}$th the width of the Playing area).

Spots

(f) four spots marked on the centre longitudinal line of the table.
(i) the Spot: 320 mm ($\frac{1}{11}$th the length of the playing area) from the point perpendicular below the face of the top cushion.
(ii) the Centre Spot: Midway between the centre pockets and equidistant from the faces of the top and bottom cushions.
(iii) the Pyramid Spot: Midway between the centre spot and the face of the top cushion.
(iv) the Middle of the Baulk-line.

2. Balls

9(a) the balls shall have a diameter of 52.5 mm ($2\frac{1}{16}$ins) with a tolerance of $+00.5$ mm -0.08 mm.

(b) they shall be of equal weight within a tolerance of 3 gms per Snooker set.

NOTE: A BALL OR SET OF BALLS MAY BE CHANGED WITH THE CONSENT OF THE PLAYERS OR ON A DECISION OF THE REFEREE.

3. Cue

The cue shall be not less than 910 mm (3ft) in length and shall show no substantial departure from the traditional and generally accepted shape and form.

4. Ancillary

'Rests' may be used to provide a bridge for the cue.

NOTE: IT IS THE PLAYERS RESPONSIBILITY TO BOTH PLACE THE REST ON AND REMOVE IT FROM THE TABLE.

SECTION 2. DEFINITIONS

1. Frame

a frame is completed when
(a) conceded, or
(b) the black is finally potted or fouled.

2. Game

a game is an agreed number of frames.

3. Match

a match is an agreed number of games.

4. Balls

(a) the white ball is the cue-ball.
(b) the 15 reds, and
(c) the 6 colours, are object balls.

5. Striker

The person about to play or in play is the striker and remains so until completion of the stroke or break (Sec. 2 Rules 6 & 12).

6. Stroke

(a) a stroke is made when the striker strikes the cue-ball with the tip of the cue.
(b) for the stroke to be a 'Fair Stroke' the following conditions must be met:
(i) At the moment of striking, all balls must be at rest, and where necessary, colours correctly spotted.
(ii) The cue ball must be struck and not pushed.
(iii) The cue ball must not be struck more than once in the same stroke.
(iv) At the moment of striking, at least one of the strikers feet must be touching the floor.
(v) The striker must not touch any ball other than the cue ball as in section (a) above.
(c) a stroke is not completed until all balls have come to rest and the referee has decided the striker has left the table.

7. In-hand

(a) the cue-ball is in-hand when it has entered a pocket or has been forced off the table.
(b) it remains in-hand until played fairly from in-hand or a foul is committed whilst the ball is on the table.

8. Ball in Play

(a) the cue-ball is in play when not in-hand.
(b) object balls are in play when spotted and remain so until pocketed or forced off the table.

NOTE: USING THE CUE TO POSITION THE CUE-BALL
IF THE REFEREE CONSIDERS THE PLAYER IS NOT ATTEMPTING TO PLAY A STROKE, EVEN THOUGH THE TIP OF THE CUE TOUCHES THE CUE-BALL, THE BALL IS NOT IN PLAY.

9. Ball on

Any ball which may be lawfully hit by the first impact of the cue-ball is said to be *on*.

10. Nominated ball

A nominated ball is the object ball which the striker declares, or indicates to the satisfaction of the referee, he undertakes to hit with the first impact of the cue-ball.

NOTE: IF REQUESTED BY THE REFEREE THE STRIKER MUST DECLARE WHICH BALL HE IS ON.

11. Pot

(a) a pot is when an object ball, after contact with another ball, and without any contravention of these rules, enters a pocket.
(b) if a colour, it shall be spotted before the next stroke is made, until finally potted under Sec. 3 Rule 3.
(c) if a stroke is made, with a ball or balls not correctly spotted, and a foul is not awarded, the ball or balls
(i) if on the table will be considered to be correctly spotted.
(ii) if not on the table will be spotted when discovered.

NOTE:
(I) IT IS THE STRIKERS RESPONSIBILITY TO ENSURE THAT ALL BALLS ARE CORRECTLY SPOTTED BEFORE STRIKING.
(II) SUBJECT TO SEC. 3 RULES 8 AND 12, REDS ARE NEVER REPLACED ON THE TABLE DESPITE THE FACT THAT A PLAYER MAY BENEFIT FROM A FOUL.

12. Break
(a) if a ball is potted, the same player plays the next stroke.
(b) a break is a number of pots in succession made in any one turn.

13. Forced off the table
(a) a ball is forced off the table if it comes to rest other than on the bed of the table or in a pocket.
(b) if a colour it shall be spotted as per Sec. 3 Rule 6 before the next stroke is make.

14. Foul
A foul is any act in contravention of these rules.

15. Snookered
(a) the cue-ball is snookered when a direct stroke in a straight line to any part of every ball *on* is obstructed by a ball or balls not *on*.

NOTE: IF THERE IS ANY ONE BALL THAT IS NOT SO OB-STRUCTED, THE CUE-BALL IS NOT SNOOKERED.

(b) if in-hand, the cue-ball is snookered only if obstructed from all positions on or within the lines of the 'D'.
(c) if the cue ball is obstructed by more than one ball, the one nearest to the cue-ball is the effective snookering ball.

16. Angled
(a) the cue-ball is angled when a direct stroke in a straight line to any part of every ball *on* is obstructed by a corner of the cushion.

NOTE: IF THERE IS ANY ONE BALL THAT IS NOT SO OB-STRUCTED, THE CUE-BALL IS NOT ANGLED.

if angled after a foul,
(b) the referee will state angled ball, and
(c) it may be played from in-hand at the strikers discretion.

17. Occupied
A spot is said to be occupied if a ball cannot be placed on it without it touching another ball.

18. Push Stroke
A push stroke is a foul and is made when the tip of the cue remains in contact with the cue-ball,
(a) when the cue-ball makes contact with the object ball, or
(b) after the cue-ball has commenced its forward motion. PROVIDED that where the cue-ball and an object ball are almost touching, it shall be deemed a fair stroke if the cue-ball hits the finest possible edge of the object ball.

19. Jump Shot
A jump shot is when the cue-ball jumps over any ball except when it first strikes a ball *on* and then jumps over another ball.

NOTE: IF THE CUE-BALL FINISHES ON THE FAR SIDE OF A BALL *ON*, EVEN THOUGH TOUCHING IT IN THE PROCESS, IT IS CONSIDERED TO HAVE JUMPED OVER.

NOTE: AFTER STRIKING THE BALL *ON* FAIRLY IF THE CUE-BALL SHOULD THEN JUMP OVER THAT BALL AFTER HITTING A CUSHION, IT SHALL BE DEEMED TO BE A FAIR STROKE.

20. Miss
A miss is when the referee considers the striker has not endeavoured to hit the ball *on*.

3. THE GAME

1. Description
The game of Snooker is played on an English Billiard Table and may be played by two or more persons, either as sides or independently.

Points are awarded for scoring strokes and forfeits from an opponents fouls.

The winner is the player or side making the highest score or to whom the game is awarded under Sec. 4 Rule 2.

Each player uses the same WHITE cue-ball and there are twenty-one object balls – fifteen reds each valued 1 and six colours: yellow valued 2, green 3, brown 4, blue 5, pink 6 and black 7.

Scoring strokes are made by potting reds and colours alternately until all reds are off the table and then the colours in the ascending order of their value i.e. – yellow through to black.

2. Position of Balls
At the commencement of each frame the object balls are positioned as follows: BLACK on the SPOT; PINK on the PYRAMID SPOT; BLUE on the CENTRE SPOT; BROWN on the MIDDLE of the BAULK-line; GREEN on the LEFT-HAND and YELLOW on the RIGHT-HAND corner of the 'D'.

The reds in the form of a triangle, the ball at the apex standing as near to the pink as possible, without touching it, the base being parallel with and nearest to the top cushion.

NOTE: THE POSITIONS FOR THE OBJECT BALLS ARE COMMONLY REFERRED TO BY THE COLOUR, E.G. BLACK SPOT, PINK SPOT, ETC.

3. Mode of Play
(a) the players shall determine the order of play which (subject to Sec. 3 Rule 10) must remain unaltered throughout the *frame*.

NOTE: THE PLAYER TO STRIKE FIRST AT EACH FRAME SHALL ALTERNATE DURING A GAME.

(b) the first player shall play from *in hand* and the frame starts with the first stroke.
(c) the cue ball
(i) must first hit a ball *on*, and
(ii) must not enter a pocket.
(d) a ball not *on* must not enter a pocket.
(e) (i) for the first stroke of each turn, until all are off the table, red is the ball *on*.
(ii) the value of each red, or ball nominated as red, potted in the same stroke is scored.
(f) if a red is potted, the next ball *on* is a colour, which if potted is scored. The colour is then re-spotted.
(g) (i) until all reds are off the table the break is continued by potting reds and colours alternately.
(ii) the colours then become *on* in the ascending order of their value (Sec. 3 Rule 1) and when potted remain off the table (except as provided for in paragraph (j)).
(h) if the striker fails to score the next player plays from where the cue-ball comes to rest.
(j) when only the Black is left the first score or foul ends the frame, unless the scores are equal, in which case:

(i) the Black is spotted.

(ii) the players draw lots for choice of playing.

(iii) the next player plays from *in hand* and

(iv) the next score or foul ends the frame.

NOTE: AGGREGATE SCORES

IN GAMES OR MATCHES WHERE AGGREGATE SCORES ARE RELEVANT IT IS ONLY WHEN THE SCORES ARE EQUAL AS A RESULT OF THE LAST FRAME THAT THE ABOVE APPLIES.

(k) The striker shall to the best of his ability endeavour to hit the ball *on*. If the referee considers the rule infringed he shall call foul and miss.

NOTE: BALL *ON* IMPOSSIBLE TO BE HIT

IN THIS SITUATION IT HAS TO BE CONSIDERED THAT THE STRIKER *IS* ATTEMPTING TO HIT THE BALL *ON*.

4. To play from in-hand

To play from in-hand the cue-ball must be struck from a position on or within the lines of the 'D'.

NOTE: THE REFEREE WILL ANSWER IF ASKED IF THE BALL IS PROPERLY PLACED.

5. Hitting two balls simultaneously

Two balls, other than two reds or a *free ball* and the ball *on*, must not be hit simultaneously by the cue-ball.

6. Spotting colours

(a) if a colour has to be spotted, and its own spot is *occupied*, it shall be placed on the highest value spot available.

(b) if there is more than one colour, and their own spots are *occupied*, the highest value ball takes precedence.

(c) if all spots are *occupied*, the colour shall be placed as near as possible to its own spot between that spot and the nearest part of the top cushion.

(d) if, in the case of the Black and the Pink, the space between its own spot and the nearest part of the top cushion is *occupied*, the colour shall be placed as near as possible to its own spot on the centre line of the table below that spot.

7. Touching Ball

(a) if the cue-ball is touching another ball which is, or can be, *on*, the referee shall state TOUCHING BALL.

(b) the striker must play away from it or it is a *push stroke*.

(c) no penalty is incurred for thus playing away if:

(i) the ball is not *on*

(ii) the ball is *on* and the striker *nominates* such a ball, or

(iii) the ball is *on* and the striker *nominates*, and first hits, another ball.

NOTE: MOVEMENT OF TOUCHING BALL

IF THE REFEREE CONSIDERS THAT A TOUCHING BALL HAS MOVED THROUGH AN AGENCY OTHER THAN THE PLAYER, IT IS NOT A FOUL.

8. Ball on edge of pocket

(a) if a ball falls into a pocket without being hit by another ball it shall be replaced.

(b) (i) if it would have been hit by any ball involved in a stroke, all balls will be replaced and the stroke re-played.

(ii) if a foul is committed the player incurs the penalty prescribed and all balls will be replaced – subject to Rule 10(c)(ii).

(c) if the ball balances momentarily on the edge and falls in, it must not be replaced.

9. Free ball

(a) after a foul, if the cue-ball is *snookered*, the referee shall state FREE BALL.

(b) if the non-offending player takes the next stroke he may nominate any ball as *on*.

(c) for this stroke, such ball shall (subject to para (e) (i)) be regarded as, and acquire the value of, the ball *on*.

(d) if is a foul, should the cue-ball

(i) fail to first hit, or

(ii) except when only pink and black remain on the table, be *snookered* by, the *free ball*.

(e) if the *free ball* is potted it

(i) is spotted, and

(ii) the value of the ball *on* is scored.

(f) if the ball *on* is potted it is scored.

(g) if both the *free ball* and the ball *on* are potted only the value of the ball *on* is scored (subject to Sec. 3 Rule 3(e)(ii)).

10. Fouls

(a) if a foul is committed:

(i) the referee shall immediately state FOUL and on completion of the stroke announce the penalty.

(ii) unless awarded by the referee or claimed by the non-striker, before the next stroke is made, it is condoned.

(iii) any ball not correctly spotted shall remain where positioned, except that if off the table it shall be correctly spotted.

(iv) all points scored before the foul is awarded or claimed are allowed.

(v) the next stroke is made from where the cue-ball comes to rest.

(b) should more than one foul be committed in the same stroke the highest value penalty shall be incurred.

(c) the player who committed the foul:

(i) incurs the penalty prescribed (which is added to the opponent's score), and

(ii) has to play again if requested by the next player. Once such a request has been made it cannot be withdrawn.

(iii) if a breach of Section 3.3(k) occurs, the offending player has to play again from the original position, if requested by the next player.

11. Penalties

The following are fouls and incur a penalty of four points or the higher one prescribed.

(a) value of the ball *on*:

by striking

(i) when the balls ar not at rest (Sec. 2 Rule 6).

(ii) the cue-ball more than once (2–6).

(iii) with both feet off the floor (2–6).

(iv) out of turn (3–3).

(v) improperly from *in-hand* (3–4).

by causing

(iv) the cue-ball to miss all object balls (3–3).

(vii) the cue-ball to enter a pocket (3–3).

(viii) a *snooker* with *free ball* (3–9)

(ix) a *jump shot* (2–19).

(b) value of the ball *on* or ball concerned:

by causing

(i) a ball not *on* to enter a pocket (3–3).

(ii) the cue-ball to first hit a ball not *on* (3–3).

(iii) a *push stroke* (2–18).
(iv) by striking with a ball not correctly spotted (2–11).
(v) by touching a ball with other than the tip of the cue (2–6).
(vi) by forcing a ball off the table (2–13).
(c) value of the ball *on* or higher value of the two balls by causing the cue-ball to hit simultaneously two balls other than two reds or a *free ball* and the ball *on* (3–5).
(d) a penalty of seven points is incurred if:
   the striker
   (i) after potting a red commits a foul before *nominating* a colour,
   (ii) uses a ball off the table for any purpose,
   (iii) plays at reds in successive strokes, or
   (iv) uses as the cue-ball any ball other than white.

12. Ball moved by other than striker

If a ball, stationary or moving, is disturbed other than by the striker it shall be re-positioned by the referee.

NOTE: THIS COVERS THE CASE IN WHICH ANOTHER AGENCY CAUSES THE STRIKER TO TOUCH A BALL. NO PLAYER SHALL BE RESPONSIBLE FOR ANY DISTURBANCE OF THE BALLS BY THE REFEREE.

13. Stalemate

If the referee considers a position of stalemate is being approached, he should warn the players that if the situation is not altered in a short period of time he will declare the frame null and void. The frame should be re-started with the same order of play.

14. Four-handed snooker

(a) in a four-handed game each side shall open alternate frames, the order of play shall be determined at the commencement of each frame, and must be maintained throughout that frame.
(b) players may change order of play at the beginning of each frame.
(c) if a foul is committed and a request made to play again, the player who committed the foul plays again, and the original order of play is maintained.
(d) when a frame ends in a tie Snooker Rule 3(j) applies. The pair who play the first stroke have the choice of which player plays that stroke. The order of play must then be maintained as in the frame.
(e) Partners may confer during a game but not whilst one is the striker and the striker is at the table or after the first stroke of his break.

SECTION 4. THE PLAYERS

1. Time wasting

If the referee considers that a player is taking an abnormal amount of time over a stroke, he should be warned that he is liable to be disqualified.

2. Unfair conduct

For refusing to continue a frame or for conduct which, in the opinion of the referee is wilfully or persistently unfair a player shall lose the game. He is liable to be disqualified from competitions held under the control of The Billiards and Snooker Council and its Affiliated Associations.

3. Penalty

If a game is awarded to a player under this section the offender shall:
(i) lose the game, and
(ii) forfeit all points scored, and the non-offender shall receive the value of the balls still on the table (each red counting eight points).

NOTE: PROVIDED THAT WHERE AGGREGATE POINTS SCORES APPLY, THE OFFENDER SHALL ALSO FORFEIT 147 POINTS FOR EACH UNPLAYED FRAME, TO THE NUMBER REQUIRED TO COMPLETE THE GAME.

4. Non-striker

The non-striker shall, when the striker is playing, avoid standing or moving in the line of sight; he should sit or stand at a fair distance from the table.

5. Absence

In case of his absence from the room he may appoint a substitute to watch his interests, and claim a foul if necessary.

SECTION 5. THE OFFICIALS

1. The Referee

(a) the referee shall
   (i) be the sole judge of fair and unfair play, and responsible for the proper conduct of the game under these Rules.
   (ii) intervene if he sees any contravention.
   (iii) if a player is colour blind, tell him the colour of a ball if requested.
   (iv) clean a ball on a player's request.
(b) he shall not
   (i) answer any question not authorized in the Rules.
   (ii) give any indication that a player is about to make a foul stroke.
   (iii) give any advice or opinion on points affecting play.
(c) if he has failed to notice any incident he may take the evidence of the spectators best placed for observation to assist his decision.

NOTE: THE REFEREE WILL NOT ANSWER A QUESTION REGARDING THE DIFFERENCE IN SCORES.

2. The Marker

The marker shall keep the score on the marking board and assist the referee in carrying out his duties.

NOTE: IF REQUESTED BY THE STRIKER, THE REFEREE OR MARKER MAY MOVE AND HOLD IN POSITION ANY LIGHT SHADE WHICH INTERFERES WITH THE ACTION OF THE STRIKER.

Rules of the
Game of English Billiards*

Authorised by
THE BILLIARDS AND SNOOKER CONTROL COUNCIL

THE BILLIARDS ASSOCIATION
Established 1885

THE BILLIARDS CONTROL CLUB
Established 1908

AMALGAMATED 1919

Chairman: Stan Brooke
Secretary and Chief Executive: David Ford

* Copyright © Billiards and Snooker Control Council

SECTION 1. EQUIPMENT

1. The Standard Table – Imperial

Dimensions

(a) the playing area within the cushion faces shall measure 11ft 8½ins × 5ft 10ins with a tolerance on both dimensions of ±½ in.

Height

(b) the height of the table from the floor to the top of the cushion rail shall be from 2ft 9½ins to 2ft 10½ins.

Pocket Openings

(c) (i) There shall be pockets at the corners (two at the Spot end known as the top pockets and two at the Baulk end known as the bottom pockets) and at the middle of the longer sides.

(ii) the pocket openings shall conform to the templates authorized by the Billiards and Snooker Control Council.

Baulk-line and Baulk

(d) a straight line drawn 29ins from the face of the bottom cushion and parallel to it is called the Baulk-line and the intervening space termed the Baulk.

The 'D'

(e) the 'D' is a semi-circle described in Baulk with its centre at the middle of the Baulk-line and with a radius of 11½ins.

Spots

(f) four spots marked on the centre longitudinal line of the table.

(i) the Spot: 12¾ins from the point perpendicular below the face of the top cushion.

(ii) the Centre Spot: Midway between the centre pockets and equidistant from the faces of the top and bottom cushions.

(iii) the Pyramid Spot: Midway between the centre spot and the face of the top cushion.

(iv) the Middle of the Baulk-line.

1M. The Standard Table – Metric

Dimensions

(a) the playing area within the cushion faces shall measure

3500 mm × 1750 mm with a tolerance on both dimensions of ±3 mm.

Height

(b) the height of the table from the floor to the top of the cushion rail shall be from 850 mm to 875 mm.

Pocket Openings

(c) (i) There shall be pockets at the corners (two at the Spot end known as the top pockets and two at the Baulk end known as the bottom pockets) and at the middle of the longer sides.

(ii) the pocket openings shall confirm to the templates authorized by the Billiards and Snooker Control Council.

Baulk-line and Baulk

(d) a straight line drawn 700 mm (⅕th the length of the playing area) from the face of the bottom cushion and parallel to it is called the Baulk-line and the intervening space termed the Baulk.

The 'D'

(e) the 'D' is a semi-circle described in Baulk with its centre at the middle of the Baulk-line and with a radius of 292 mm (⅙th the width of the Playing area).

Spots

(f) four spots marked on the centre longitudinal line of the table.

(i) the Spot: 320 mm (1/11th the length of the playing area) from the point perpendicular below the face of the top cushion.

(ii) the Centre Spot: Midway between the centre pockets and equidistant from the faces of the top and bottom cushions.

(iii) the Pyramid Spot: Midway between the centre spot and the face of the top cushion.

(iv) the Middle of the Baulk-line.

2. Balls

(a) the balls shall have a diameter of 52.5 mm ($2\frac{1}{16}$ins) with a tolerance of +00.5 mm −0.08 mm.

(b) they shall be equal weight within a tolerance of 0.05 gms per Billiard set.

NOTE: A BALL OR SET OF BALLS MAY BE CHANGED WITH THE CONSENT OF THE PLAYERS OR ON A DECISION OF THE REFEREE.

3. Cue

The cue shall be not less than 910 mm (3ft) in length and shall show no substantial departure from the traditional and generally accepted shape and form.

4. Ancillary

'Rests' may be used to provide a bridge for the cue.

NOTE: IT IS THE PLAYERS RESPONSIBILITY TO BOTH PLACE THE REST ON AND REMOVE IT FROM THE TABLE.

SECTION 2. DEFINITIONS

1. Game

A game is completed

(a) at the expiry of a specified period of play, or

(b) when the number of points agreed on is first scored.

2. Match

A match is an agreed number of games.

3. Balls

(a) the cue ball is the ball of the striker.

(b) the other balls are object balls.

4. String

To string is to play together from the Baulk-line to the top cushion with the object of leaving the player's ball as near as possible to the bottom cushion.

5. Striker

The person about to play or in play is the striker and remains so until completion of the stroke or break.

6. Stroke

(a) a stroke is made when the striker strikes the cue-ball with the tip of the cue.

(b) for the stroke to be a 'Fair Stroke' the following conditions must be met:

(i) At the moment of striking, all balls must be at rest, and where necessary, object balls correctly spotted.

(ii) The cue ball must be struck and not pushed.

(iii) The cue ball must not be struck more than once in the same stroke.

(iv) At the moment of striking, at least one of the strikers feet must be touching the floor.

(v) The striker must not touch any ball other than the cue ball as in section (a) above.

(vi) A ball or balls must not be 'forced off the table'.

(c) a stroke is not completed until all balls have come to rest and the referee has decided the striker has left the table.

7. In-hand

(a) A player's ball is in-hand when it is off the table, and

(b) It remains in-hand until played fairly from in-hand or a foul is committed whilst the ball is on the table.

(c) When the non-striker's ball is in-hand it remains so until his turn to play or is spotted as in Sec. 3 Rule 7.

8. Ball in Play

(a) A player's ball is in play when not in-hand.

(b) The red is in play when spotted and remains so until potted or forced off the table.

NOTE: USING THE CUE TO POSITION THE CUE-BALL
IF THE REFEREE CONSIDERS THE PLAYER IS NOT ATTEMPTING TO PLAY A STROKE, EVEN THOUGH THE TIP OF THE CUE TOUCHES THE BALL, THE BALL IS NOT IN PLAY.

9. Hazard

a hazard is

(a) A pot, or

(b) An in-off.

NOTE: A POT IS OFTEN REFERRED TO AS A WINNING HAZARD AND AN IN-OFF AS A LOSING HAZARD.

10. Pot

A pot is when an object ball, after contact with another ball, and without any contravention of these rules, enters a pocket.

11. In-Off

An in-off is when the cue-ball, after contact with an object ball, and without any contravention of these rules, enters a pocket.

12. Cannon

A cannon is when the cue-ball hits both the object balls, without any contravention of these rules.

13. Miss

A miss is when the cue-ball fails to hit any other ball.

14. Break

A break is a succession of scoring strokes made in any one turn.

15. Forced off the table

A ball is forced off the table if it comes to rest other than on the bed of the table or in a pocket.

16. Foul

A foul is any act in contravention of these rules.

17. Occupied

A spot is said to be occupied if a ball cannot be placed on it without it touching another ball.

18. Push Stroke

A push stroke is a foul and is made when the tip of the cue remains in contact with the cue-ball.

(a) when the cue-ball makes contact with the object ball, or

(b) after the cue-ball has commenced its forward motion. PROVIDED that where the cue-ball and an object ball are almost touching, it shall be deemed a fair stroke if the cue-ball hits the finest possible edge of the object ball.

19. Jump Shot

A jump shot is when the cue-ball jumps over any ball except when it first strikes the ball on and then jumps over another ball.

NOTE: IF THE CUE-BALL FINISHES ON THE FAR SIDE OF THE OBJECT BALL, EVEN THOUGH TOUCHING IT IN THE PROCESS, IT IS CONSIDERED TO HAVE JUMPED OVER.

SECTION 3. THE GAME

1. Description

The game of English Billiards is played by two or more persons, either as sides or independently. Three balls are used, 'plain' white, 'spot' white and red.

It is a game of *pots*, *in-offs*, *cannons* and positional play. Points are awarded for scoring strokes and forfeits from an opponents fouls.

The winner is the player, or side, who has scored most points at the expiry of an agreed period, first scores an agreed number or points or to whom the game is awarded under Sec. 4 Rule 2.

2. Commencement of Game

(a) The choice of ball and order of play, unless mutually agreed upon, shall be decided by *stringing*, the winner having the option, and shall remain unaltered throughout the game.

(b) At the commencement of the game the red is placed on the spot, the first player plays from *in-hand* and the game starts with the first *stroke*.

3. Order of Play

The players play alternately unless a score is made, in which case the *striker* continues the *break* playing from where his ball rests, or, after an *in-off* or as in Sec. 3 Rule 11, from *in-hand*.

4. Spotting the Red Ball

(a) If the red is *potted* or *forced off* the table it is placed on the spot. If the spot is *occupied* it is placed on the pyramid spot. If that spot is also *occupied* it is placed on the centre spot.

(b) If the red is potted twice in succession in one break from the spot or from the pyramid spot, not in conjunction with another score, it is placed on the centre spot. If this spot is *occupied* it is placed on the pyramid spot or if both these spots are *occupied* on the spot. If again potted it shall be placed on the spot.

NOTE: IF DURING A STROKE THE RED COMES TO REST ON THE SPOT, IT IS NOT CONSIDERED TO BE SPOTTED. IT IS THE STRIKER'S RESPONSIBILITY TO ENSURE THAT ALL BALLS ARE CORRECTLY SPOTTED BEFORE STRIKING.

5. Details of Scoring

Points are awarded as follows:

(a) for a *cannon*, *pot* white and *in-off* white, two.

(b) for a *pot* and *in-off* red, three.

(c) if more than one *hazard* or a combination of *hazards* and a *cannon* are made in the same *stroke* all are scored.

(d) when an *in-off* is combined with a *cannon* it shall score two or three according to whether the white or red was first hit.

(e) should both be hit simultaneously the *in-off* shall count two.

6. To Play from In-hand

The cue-ball

(a) must be struck from a position on or within the lines of the 'D'.

NOTE: THE REFEREE WILL ANSWER, IF ASKED IF THE BALL IS PROPERLY PLACED.

(b) must hit a ball or cushion out of baulk before hitting a ball in baulk.

(c) may be placed against a cushion in baulk to hit a ball out of baulk.

NOTE: IF THE STRIKER IS IN-HAND THE REFEREE WILL ANSWER, IF ASKED, IF A BALL IS IN OR OUT OF BAULK.

7. Limitation of Hazards

Consecutive *hazards*, not in conjunction with a *cannon*, are limited to fifteen.

If more than one *hazard* is made in the same *stroke* it shall count for one for the purpose of this rule but all points shall be scored.

After ten *hazards*, or on request, the referee shall inform the *striker*.

Should the non-striker's ball be off the table as a result of the non-striker's last stroke, it shall be spotted after the fifteenth *hazard* on the middle spot of the 'D', or if *occupied* on the right-hand corner of the 'D'.

NOTE: SHOULD THE REFEREE FAIL TO INFORM THE STRIKER AFTER TEN HAZARDS THE STRIKER IS ENTITLED TO PLAY A FURTHER FIVE HAZARDS AFTER HE IS INFORMED.

8. Limitation of Cannons

Consecutive *cannons*, not in conjunction with a *hazard*, are limited to seventy-five.

After seventy *cannons*, or on request, the referee shall inform the *striker*.

NOTE: SHOULD THE REFEREE FAIL TO INFORM THE STRIKER AFTER SEVENTY CANNONS THE STRIKER IS ENTITLED TO PLAY A FURTHER FIVE CANNONS AFTER HE IS INFORMED.

9. Ball on edge of pocket

(a) if a ball falls into a pocket without being hit by another ball it shall be replaced.

(b) (i) if it would have been hit by any ball involved in a *stroke*, all balls will be replaced and the *stroke* replayed.
(ii) if a foul is committed the player incurs the penalty prescribed.

(c) if the ball balances momentarily on the edge and falls in, it must not be replaced.

10. Ball moved by other than striker

If a ball, stationary or moving, is disturbed other than by the *striker* it shall be repositioned by the referee.

NOTE: THIS COVERS THE CASE IN WHICH ANOTHER AGENCY CAUSES THE STRIKER TO TOUCH A BALL. NO PLAYER SHALL BE RESPONSIBLE FOR ANY DISTURBANCE OF THE BALLS BY THE REFEREE.

11. Balls Touching

When the *striker's* ball remains touching another ball, red shall be placed on the spot, the non-striker's ball, if on the table, shall be placed on the centre spot, and the striker shall play from *in hand*.

12. Miss

(a) For a *miss* the striker incurs a penalty of two points.

(b) a *miss* is a foul except when the striker is *in hand* and there is no ball out of baulk.

13. Fouls

(a) if a foul is committed:
(i) the referee shall immediately state foul.
(ii) unless awarded by the referee or claimed by the non-striker, before the next stroke is made, it is condoned.
(iii) any ball not correctly spotted shall remain where positioned, except that if off the table it shall be correctly spotted.
(iv) all points scored before the foul is awarded or claimed are allowed.

(b) the player committing the foul incurs a penalty of two points, which are added to his opponent's score.

(c) the next player has the option of playing
(i) from where the balls are at rest (the red if off the table having been spotted), or
(ii) from *in-hand*, the red and white being spotted on the spot and centre spot respectively.

(d) the following acts are fouls:
by striking
(i) when the balls are not at rest (Sec. 2 Rule 6).
(ii) the *cue-ball* more than once (2–6).
(iii) with both feet off the floor (2–6).
(iv) out of turn (3–3).
(v) improperly from *in-hand* (3–6).
(vi) with a ball not correctly spotted.
(vii) a ball other than the *cue-ball* (2–6).
by making
(viii) a *jump shot* (2–19).
(ix) a *push stroke* (2–18).
(x) more than fifteen *hazards* (3–7).
(xi) more than seventy-five *cannons* (3–8).
(xii) by touching a ball with other than the tip of the cue (2–6).
(xiii) by forcing a ball off the table (2–6).
(xiv) by using a ball off the table for any purpose.

SECTION 4. THE PLAYERS

1. Time wasting

If the referee considers that a player is taking an abnormal amount of time over a stroke, he should be warned that he is liable to be disqualified.

2. Unfair conduct

For refusing to continue a frame or for conduct which, in the opinion of the referee, is wilfully or persistently unfair a player shall lose the game. He is liable to be disqualified from competitions held under the control of The Billiards and Snooker Council and its Affiliated Associations.

3. Penalty

If a game is awarded to a player under this section the offender shall:
(i) lose the game, and
(ii) if the game was to be decided on a number of agreed points he shall forfeit all points scored and the non-offender shall receive the agreed number of points, or
(iii) if the game be decided at the expiry of a specified period of play and forms part of a team match the whole match shall be forfeited.

4. Non-striker

The non-striker shall, when the striker is playing, avoid standing or moving in the line of sight; he should sit or stand at a fair distance from the table.

5. Absence

In the case of his absence from the room he may appoint a substitute to watch his interests, and claim a foul if necessary.

SECTION 5. THE OFFICIALS

1. The Referee

(a) the referee shall
(i) be the sole judge of fair and unfair play, and responsible for the proper conduct of the game under these Rules.
(ii) intervene if he sees any contravention.
(iii) if a player is colour blind, tell him the colour of a ball if requested.
(iv) clean the ball on a player's request.

(b) he shall not
(i) answer any question not authorized in the Rules.
(ii) give any indication that a player is about to make a foul stroke.
(iii) give any advice or opinion on points affecting play.

(c) if he has failed to notice any incident he may take the evidence of the spectators best placed for observation to assist his decision.

NOTE: THE REFEREE WILL NOT ANSWER A QUESTION REGARDING THE DIFFERENCE IN SCORES.

2. The Marker

The marker shall keep the score on the marking board and assist the referee in carrying out his duties.

NOTE: IF REQUESTED BY THE STRIKER, THE REFEREE OR MARKER MAY MOVE AND HOLD IN POSITION ANY LIGHT SHADE WHICH INTERFERES WITH THE ACTION OF THE STRIKER.